P...

AND ~~POWER~~

TWO CENTURIES OF
AMERICAN FOREIGN RELATIONS

Policy and Power *is one in a group of new books dealing with American history. The purpose of these topical histories is to present in brief compass the author's interpretation of the subject. Aïda DiPace Donald is consulting editor. The other books in this series are:*

The Reins of Power: A Constitutional History of the United States *by Bernard Schwartz*

The Sinews of American Capitalism: An Economic History *by Clark C. Spence*

From Plantation to Ghetto *by August Meier and Elliott M. Rudwick*

POLICY
AND POWER

TWO CENTURIES OF
AMERICAN FOREIGN RELATIONS

by

Ruhl Bartlett

American Century Series
HILL AND WANG · NEW YORK

To
L. M. B.

FOREWORD

IT IS A CHALLENGING and somewhat hazardous enterprise to undertake in brief form an account of American foreign relations. The task involves not only the selection of the items of foreign policy deemed most significant, but also the selection of data considered indispensable for an accurate analysis of particular items. This difficulty increases as it is applied to the last half-century, when American foreign relations have merged into world politics and the impact of world affairs on American life and institutions has been on an ever increasing scale. The United States is confronted with the necessity in its own national interest of using its great power and influence toward the creation of a more just, orderly, and peaceful world, and at the same time with the equal necessity of refraining from abusing its power abroad and from impairing its own free institutions in the exercise of power. It is one of the ironies of the present situation that as American foreign policies become more far flung and more interwoven with economic and military considerations, and, therefore, more complex and difficult to reduce to simple, clear, and brief analyses, the requirements of a responsible American citizenship make such analyses more imperative and increase the need for their examination in historical perspective. The unacceptable alternative is to delegate the great decisions of foreign policy to a central bureaucracy, and thus to permit the gradual erosion of American democratic society. But the perplexities of a problem do not provide an excuse for its neglect.

It is a truism regarding the study of human affairs that the past, present, and future merge in the thinking of any individual. His beliefs about the past, about human experience, will largely determine his estimate of events and trends of the fleeting present, and this estimate will not be separate from his vision of the future. It seems obvious, therefore, that accurate knowledge about the past is essential for any rational view of what constitutes the "good society," and for any hope of progress toward that goal. Since every situation in the world today has somehow emerged from its antecedents, no world problem can be understood except in the context of its origin and development. If history throws no light on the pathway of the future, the human race is doomed indeed to walk in darkness.

It would be presumptuous in the extreme to suppose that the present volume includes all the essential and useful knowledge about American foreign relations. Its purposes are no more ambitious than to make a beginning, to provide a background of American experience in dealing with its foreign affairs, and hopefully to stimulate further investigation.

R.B.

Somerville, Massachusetts
May, 1963

CONTENTS

MAPS

POLICY
AND POWER

TWO CENTURIES OF
AMERICAN FOREIGN RELATIONS

I

THREE CENTURIES OF WAR AND DIPLOMACY

FOR ALMOST three centuries prior to the American Revolutionary War the New World was one of the principal stakes of European diplomacy. During the first of these centuries Spain and Portugal maintained a virtual monopoly of colonial enterprise in the Western Hemisphere, but after the beginning of the seventeenth century, France and England became the major colonizers of North America and eventually clashed in a struggle for empire that lasted over a century and a half, leaving Britain triumphant and her American colonies secure from either French or Spanish encroachment. Of all the colonies in the Western Hemisphere, the British Colonies alone enjoyed freedom of local self-government and, possibly for that reason, developed a nationalism of their own. They were the first colonies to rebel, but their independence was achieved with European assistance and their national boundaries were largely the product of the European contest for empire during the preceding three centuries.

DISCOVERY AND PARTITION OF NEW LANDS

In the list of European scientists and explorers whose efforts, prior to those of Columbus, led to the discovery of America, the

1

place of primacy easily belongs to Prince Henry the Navigator, third son of John I of Portugal. Inspired by a zest for learning, a hatred for the Moors, and a vision of empire that embraced the treasures of India, Prince Henry established himself on the "Sacred Promontory" of Portugal and sent his mariners into the Atlantic. In the course of about forty-five years, 1415–1460, they rediscovered the Azores, the Madeira and Cape Verde Islands, and sailed down the African coast as far as Sierra Leone. Exploration southward was continued after the death of Prince Henry, and gradually Portuguese traders and explorers found their way past the Equator until, in 1488, Bartholomeu Diaz rounded the Cape of Good Hope.

Confident that she controlled the shortest route to India, Portugal missed the golden opportunity of westward exploration in rejecting the services of Columbus which the Spanish sovereigns had the luck or foresight to embrace. When Columbus returned from his first voyage, believing he had reached India, possibly in Portuguese territory, hostility between Spain and Portugal might well have resulted. The two nations realized, however, the disadvantages of conflict between themselves and on June 7, 1494, signed the Treaty of Tordesillas. Under this treaty a boundary line was to be drawn in the "ocean sea" from the Arctic to the Antarctic poles, straight north and south, and 370 leagues west of the Cape Verde Islands. All lands discovered, or to be discovered, east of the line were to be Portuguese and all lands west of the line were to be Spanish. The distance westward from the Cape Verde Islands was to be measured in degrees, or in a manner agreed upon, and a joint expedition was to sail within ten months to establish and mark the line. The expedition never sailed, and the two countries never reached an agreement regarding the particular island of the Cape Verde group from which the distance was to be measured or the number of leagues in a degree. Nor did the treaty specify whether the line was to extend around the world dividing the respective spheres of the rival sovereigns in the antipodes.

The latter problem became acute as soon as Portuguese explorers, sailing east around the Cape of Good Hope, and the Spanish, sailing west through the Strait of Magellan or around Cape Horn, reached the Moluccas and came into conflict for the

America. But their maritime and colonial interests were far flung, and the lure of other enterprises led them to neglect their American opportunities. New Netherland passed into English hands in 1664 without resistance or regret on the part of the dissatisfied Dutch colonists. This narrowed the contest to England and France whose implacable rivalry acquired world scope and endured for a hundred and fifty years.

In America the advantage of strategic location seemed to favor the French. They had established themselves on the St. Lawrence and had reached westward to embrace the Great Lakes and eventually the entire length of the Mississippi River, and thus held both main doors and the spacious center of the virgin continent. Their colonial administration was centralized, and their relations with the Indians were friendly. In contrast, the British Colonies, independent of each other and quasi-autonomous within the Empire, were scattered along the Atlantic Coast and were confronted, in their westward advance, by the imposing Appalachian barrier.

Among the American people there has been a pleasant national tradition, fostered by the glowing patriotism of the post-revolutionary historians, that the English colonists would have triumphed over the French even if England had given them no assistance. This indeed was the contemporary French view, and might well have been the result if France had remained aloof. For the English were superior in numbers and wealth, equal at least in ambition and enterprise, and were favored with far greater resources. The French colonial impulse had been weak, capital scarce, and the rigid social structure of the homeland had been transferred to Canada where nearly half the French settlers lived on ecclesiastical *seigneuries*. French colonists occupied strategic positions, but the English possessed the sinews of Empire. France, however, did not remain aloof. The colonists were not left to their own devices.

After three relatively minor "intercolonial wars," spaced between 1689 and 1754, the two contestants reached the point of serious conflict. The Comte de la Galissonière, the alert and able Governor of New France from 1747 to 1749, had awakened the French to the dangers inherent in British claims and colonial advance. By the British contention that Nova Scotia, "with its an-

cient boundaries," included all the lands bordering on the Bay of
Fundy, France was deprived of a winter route to Quebec by way
of the St. John River. British claims to the area south of Lake
Ontario and west of the Allegheny River, together with expansion westward from the Carolinas and Georgia, endangered, so
France thought, her entire American domain. France believed,
therefore, that the British should be contained in Nova Scotia
within the area east of the isthmus and south of the Penobscot
River, thus placing the coast of the Bay of Fundy within French
territory. In the west, the British should be confined to the area
south of Lake Champlain and east of the Allegheny watershed,
leaving all the Great Lakes, the Allegheny and the Ohio valleys,
and the entire Mississippi basin within New France. Forts and
military posts should be established at strategic points to safeguard
this containment. Although La Galissonière admitted, in a famous
memorandum to his government, that the French possessions in
the Caribbean might produce more wealth to the realm and be
more easily defended than Canada and Louisiana, he urged that
the motives of "honor, glory, and religion" impelled the French
to hold their continental possessions. But the French ministry had
even more potent reasons for defending New France. If it were
lost, New Spain and the fertile Spanish and French Caribbean
islands would be exposed to British acquisition. Enriched and
strengthened by the commerce from these areas, Britain could
become a greater menace to France. To the French, New France
was a counterpoise in the *European* balance of power.

Yet neither nation desired to precipitate a general war, and
both were willing, in 1749, to establish a joint Anglo-French commission to seek accommodation for their many conflicts, including
colonial boundaries. Discussion in this commission was lengthy,
repetitious, and in the end, futile. Even with the perspective of
two centuries, it is difficult to determine which nation was the
more intransigent, aggressive, and responsible for the great war
that followed. On the whole, however, Great Britain had the better
historical and legal position for her boundary claims in Nova
Scotia and on the northwestern frontier. She could plead, too, before the court of time, that she made the more conciliatory proposals. She offered to restrict her westward colonial advance to a

line drawn southward from Cuyahoga Bay, on Lake Erie, to 37 degrees north latitude, with the understanding that France would not advance east of the Maumee and the Wabash rivers, the intervening area being left open to the peaceful trade of both parties. Lakes Champlain, Ontario, and Erie were similarly to be open to access and to commerce of both sides, and the Nova Scotia boundaries were to be drawn with a buffer territory between the two lines. In rejecting these overtures, or some reasonable modification of them, the French ministry bungled their only opportunity to delay, at least, the loss of New France.

There is a note, nevertheless, of the classical tragic drama, of inexorable fate, in this contest for empire. If France had been willing to let "Americans fight Americans," there is no good reason to doubt the gradual advance of the British colonists to the limits of their colonial charters. This was what France feared and was unwilling to permit. But once she sent French soldiers to sustain her colonial levies, it was inevitable that British colonists would call upon the mother country for similar assistance and that Britain would not refuse the call. And what was the sea power of either nation for if not to prevent enemy supplies and recruits from reaching the areas of conflict? Thus the flames of war that began in Nova Scotia and in the Ohio Valley spread to the high seas, soon crossed the "lines of amity," and reached Minorca, then Europe, and beyond. Seizing the opportunity afforded by the Anglo-French colonial conflict, Frederick of Prussia quickly involved those two powers in his own schemes of conquest, and brought on the Seven Years' War. In this spreading conflagration France lost not only the principal part of her empire but also her proud position in Europe, and from the war's unquenched embers arose the new American Republic.

THE TREATY OF PARIS AND AMERICAN BOUNDARIES

During the four years following 1754, French arms in America were everywhere victorious. But 1759 and 1760 were years of astounding British victories. William Pitt (Lord Chatham) was the brilliant architect of British victory, the Earl of Bute the weak negotiator of the peace. Pitt's decline in power and the rise of

Bute symbolize the conflict over policy within the British government and explain the muddled character of Great Britain's diplomacy at this pinnacle of her power. Pitt had a clear policy
whatever its merits might be. He would extend the Empire as far
as he could, return nothing to France that would be to her advantage, and so ruin her power that she would not attempt another
war. The peace advocates in the British ministry were willing to
accept the French overtures of 1761, or some minor modifications
of them, that would have left France in possession of Louisiana,
and with rights in the Newfoundland fisheries. Some of them
wanted Guadeloupe restored to France and others, depending on
their interests, wanted Canada restored but Guadeloupe retained. The ministry was split wide open on peace terms and
pamphleteers carried the issues to the public.

The debate over Guadeloupe and Canada had begun almost as
soon as those areas had been conquered from the French. "Some,"
said William Pitt in the House of Commons, "are for keeping
Canada; some Guadeloupe; who will tell me which I shall be
hanged for not keeping?" In the view of one faction, the presence
of the French on the American frontiers would keep the English
colonists in constant need of British protection, as the existing
war so clearly demonstrated, and would insure colonial loyalty.
The opposite view was cogently presented by Benjamin Franklin,
then in England, who suggested that the presence of an enemy
of Britain on the American frontiers would be a source of aid to
the colonists if they should become disaffected. He argued that
the removal of the French would encourage westward migration,
diffuse the population, and divert it from manufacturing. As for
the fear of American independence, Franklin stressed the spirit of
particularism among the Colonies, a spirit so strong that it had
prevented them from uniting against France when the French and
Indians were "burning their villages and murdering their people."
He maintained that this spirit would also be strong enough to
avert unity against Britain, "without the most grievous tyranny
and oppression."

As a result partly of Pitt's firmness and partly of the divisions
within the British ministry, the negotiations of 1761 were broken
off and Spain entered the war on the side of France under the

Third Bourbon Family Compact. But the campaigns that followed were disastrous for France and Spain alike. Spain's feebleness was a French liability. Britain swept the Spanish fleet in the Caribbean from the sea and captured Puerto Rico and Cuba, and from France, Martinique, St. Lucia, Grenada, and St. Vincent. In the Pacific, Britain captured Manila. The French Foreign Minister, the Duc de Choiseul, realized that the time for peace was overdue, and fortune smiled upon France in the person of Lord Bute. The situation was extraordinary, for Bute feared that popular demand and Parliamentary pressure would restore Pitt to power unless peace could be made quickly. He renewed negotiations with the anxiety of a suppliant. Both ministers were driven by necessity, personal and political in one case, military and national in the other. In this atmosphere of hurry and confusion the Treaty of Paris was concluded.

France ceded to Great Britain all her territories on the American continent east of a line drawn through the middle of the Mississippi River from its source to the Iberville, thence by a similar line through that river and through lakes Maurepas and Pontchartrain to the sea. The navigation of the Mississippi, in its length, was to be equally free to the subjects of both powers, and their vessels could not be "stopped, visited, or subjected to the payment of any duty." Britain agreed that the inhabitants of the ceded area should have freedom of the Roman Catholic religion, "as far as the laws of Britain" permitted. Britain received from France the Island of Cape Breton, all other islands in the Gulf and River of St. Lawrence, Grenada and the Grenadines in the Caribbean, and all the "neutral islands" except St. Lucia. France was granted the "liberty of fishing and drying fish" on parts of the coast of Newfoundland, as under the Treaty of Utrecht, limited fishing rights in the Gulf of St. Lawrence, and the islands of St. Pierre and Miquelon as fishing stations which she would not be allowed to fortify or garrison. Britain restored to her Guadeloupe, Martinique, Marie Galante, Désirade, and St. Lucia. Spain ceded Florida to Britain and recovered Puerto Rico, Cuba, and Manila. She recognized the right of British subjects to reside and to carry on logging operations on the Spanish coasts and territories in the Bay of Honduras, and in "other places of the territory of Spain in that part of the world." In a separate treaty France ceded to Spain New Orleans and all her vast territorial possessions westward from the Mississippi.

It is not very profitable to speculate on the suppositions of history. When one supposition is advanced, it is immediately necessary to provide it with a context of probabilities. Truth is replaced by fancy. It may be true, however, as the historian Francis Parkman has suggested, that the history of New France was dwarfed to an episode by the "faults of constitution and the bigotry and folly of rulers." In this view the failure of French diplomacy and foreign policy were less basic and important than the inability of France to discard the anachronistic character of her thought and institutions. But it is Pitt's probable policies that offer opportunity for the most arresting reflections. What would have been the future of the United States if Lord Bute had shared La Galissonière's convictions that Louisiana was a unit which could not be separated without planting the seeds of future controversy, and had demanded the whole of Louisiana? What would have been the result if Bute had retained the French sugar islands, deprived France of all American fishing rights, refused to return French trading stations in India or to restore Goree, the center of the French slave trade, and had, as Pitt desired, ruined France as a colonial and maritime power instead of leaving her crippled and humiliated but eager to strike at Great Britain again whenever the opportunity arose? If that is too large an order, speculation could be restricted to the historical effect of Britain's decision to restore Cuba and the Philippines to Spain.

Confined to realities, however, the war had far-reaching results. It left Britain triumphant over France in North America and determined, as far as one great event could, the speech, institutions, and culture that would dominate the civilization of the United States. It left Great Britain with preponderant sea power and with the mightiest colonial area in the world. Well might the Earl of Granville say: "This has been the most glorious war and the most triumphant peace that England ever knew."

II

THE DIPLOMACY OF INDEPENDENCE

THE AMERICAN REVOLUTIONARY WAR gradually expanded into a larger conflict which included not only Great Britain but also France, Spain, and the Netherlands, and through the Armed Neutrality League involved Russia and other European states. France regarded the war as a continuation of its struggle against Britain for the purpose of regaining French prestige and influence in Europe and redressing the European balance of power. It encouraged the Colonies to rebel, gave them "secret" aid, and urged its ally, Spain, to follow its example. Spain pursued a devious course, but finally entered the war against Britain in the hope of recovering Gibraltar and Florida, and possibly of securing other British territory. The Netherlands became involved in the war as the result of conflict with Britain over maritime rights.

The United States made a military alliance with France and tried to make similar alliances elsewhere in Europe in order to diffuse British strength as widely as possible. Except with France, its alliance diplomacy was unsuccessful. Britain's involvement with its European enemies was a major factor in its decision to agree to the independence of the United States and to make a peace settlement favorable to it.

THE AMERICAN DECISION FOR INDEPENDENCE

When the First Continental Congress met in Philadelphia in September, 1774, most of its members were not thinking in terms of colonial independence. A few of them were primarily concerned with the adoption of strong measures for the redress of grievances, and a few were devoted mainly to reconciliation with Great Britain, but most of them were seeking some middle way through which both of these objectives could be substantially achieved. They were divided, however, on ways and means for reaching their goal. One member, Joseph Galloway of Pennsylvania, eloquently urged a constitutional change, a plan of union, designed to bring Great Britain and the Colonies into closer co-operation and at the same time to remove parliamentary supremacy over colonial affairs. This was opposed both by the anti-British extremists and the more numerous moderates. The latter desired neither to shorten the gap between British and colonial authority nor to extend it beyond its position in 1763. To this end the Congress drew up a declaration of rights, prepared addresses to the peoples of Great Britain and of British America, and sent a petition to the King. In addition, they recommended to the colonists an economic boycott of British goods.

Although the boycott was a coercive measure, this was not the first time it had been employed by the colonists, nor was it an act of rebellion. The Congress had no legislative authority and could only recommend the boycott, which was not, in itself, a violation of British law. However provocative the boycott might be, Congress, through its petition to the Crown, offered the British government an opportunity to reconsider its American policy. This policy had been displayed in the acts of repression against Massachusetts, the so-called Intolerable Acts of 1774, and in the Quebec Act of the same year. The Intolerable Acts included the closing of the port of Boston and arbitrary changes in the government of the Massachusetts Bay Colony, and the Quebec Act placed within the Province of Quebec areas northwest of the Ohio River that were claimed by various colonies to be within their charter grants. This policy of repression and, in the colonial view, disregard of colonial rights and liberties, was adopted after extensive debate by large majorities in Parliament and in full knowledge that war with the Colonies would almost inevitably entail war with France and Spain. Virtually every movement of Choiseul and Vergennes in France, Britain, or America was known to the British government. Lord Chatham, Edmund Burke, the Duke of Grafton, and many others warned the government of the consequences of its policy. But the ministry of Lord North, "the most muddle-headed," said a later British writer, "that ever mismanaged the affairs of Great Britain," was impervious to all arguments for conciliation. Having taken its stand, the ministry was not disposed to change its policy in any fundamental way on account of proposals emanating from the American Congress. Lord North made a gesture, in February, 1775, in the general direction of conciliation, but no one was impressed with his feeble movement.

The Second Continental Congress met in May, 1775, subsequent to the outbreak of war in Massachusetts. From then on until independence was declared a little more than a year later, Congress adopted warlike measures, one after another, which, in retrospect, seem to form a chain of necessity leading to an inevitable end. Their confidence in the certainty of foreign aid is one of the primary considerations in relieving the revolutionary leaders of the serious charge of reckless irresponsibility. Although the colonists were spread over a large area containing many hiding places in "forests and swamps," as the Duke of Richmond noted in appealing for conciliation, the great majority of them lived along navigable rivers or within a short distance of the coast. Britain had abundant sea power, if it could have been diverted exclusively to American waters, to seal up American foreign intercourse, and to expose the principal centers of population to the range of naval guns. The colonists had little capacity to produce munitions or other materials of war, no fortified places, almost no financial reserves, only rudimentary military and naval forces, and no central government save the Continental Congress. To these hard realities should be added the fact, which in subsequent years most Americans have been willing to neglect, that the colonists were far from being united in their attitude toward Great Britain. John Adams argued eloquently in the Congress that independence would provide unity, and it did to some extent, but mainly it sharpened the lines of cleavage. The revolutionary lead-ers placed high hope on colonial courage and prowess, as well they should have, and relied somewhat on the influence of British statesmen who were sympathetic to their cause. But except where policy was based on anger and rash inexpediency, no factor was more important than the confidence of the Colonies in foreign assistance. Independence, foreign allies, and colonial union were the three equal parts of Richard Henry Lee's Resolution of June 7, 1776, under which the Congress initiated measures to achieve these ends.

Along with the expectation of foreign aid, the revolutionary leaders placed great stress on the hope that Canada would join in any movement against Britain. The First Continental Congress prepared, in October, 1774, an address to the people of Canada explaining the objectives of American policy and suggesting a unity of interest. This met with some favorable response and was one of the several factors that led to the sending of military forces into Canada under Generals Richard Montgomery and Benedict Arnold. In one way the expeditions against Montreal and Quebec transformed the war from one of colonial defense to one of ag-gression, but Congress acted under the theory that its military activities in Canada constituted friendly invasion for purposes of liberation. News of the capture of Montreal reached Congress in November, 1775, and stimulated great optimism that British power in Canada would be quickly broken and that Canadian delegates would soon be in Congress. Plans were made to send a diplomatic mission to Canada to facilitate co-operation. Benjamin Franklin, perhaps the most ardent proponent of the Canadian venture, was chairman of the delegation, and other members were Samuel Chase and Charles Carroll, both of Maryland. They were instructed simply to encourage Canadian opposition to British rule. Canada was to choose whether or not she would oppose Great Britain by federating with the American colonies. She was to be assured of local autonomy, which would include religious autonomy as well as other rights of self-government.

Whatever chance of success this first diplomatic mission of Con-gress might have had earlier, it arrived in Canada too late to ac-complish its purpose. Montgomery had been killed and Arnold wounded in an unsuccessful attack on Quebec, and this failure, together with sickness and discouragement within the American forces, led the Continental Army to fall back in the face of advancing British reinforcements. The mission returned convinced that, for the time being at any rate, Canada was firmly in Britain's grasp.

Meanwhile, in November, 1775, Congress took a long step toward independence by appointing a Secret Committee of Correspondence whose purpose was to establish contacts "with friends in Great Britain, Ireland, and other parts of the world." This committee, called the Committee for Foreign Affairs after April, 1777, performed the function of a foreign office and lasted until the appointment of Robert R. Livingston as Secretary of Foreign Affairs in 1781. Another committee, first called the Secret Committee and later the Committee of Commerce, was empowered to import powder and munitions and to export goods in order to pay for such imports. In March, 1776, Congress decided to issue letters of marque and reprisal, and in April it opened American ports to all but British ships. An agent of Vergennes, Achard de Bonvouloir, reached Philadelphia in December, 1775, and assured Congress that France was willing to provide technical assistance and to permit the purchase in France of arms and military supplies. French merchants were already in Philadelphia to arrange the private trade in munitions, but Bonvouloir intimated that France would do more than permit the sale of goods if Congress requested French aid and if the King consented. This led to the appointment of Silas Deane as the first agent of the United States to France. He was commissioned by both the Secret Committee of Correspondence and the Committee of Commerce.

Deane's instructions, dated March 3, 1776, were drafted by Franklin, who combined the statement of congressional authorization with a subtle treatise on the fine art of diplomacy. Thus they defy condensation, but in prosaic substance Deane was authorized to make an initial request from France for one hundred fieldpieces, clothing, arms, and ammunition for twenty-five thousand men, and for other goods including articles for the Indian trade. He was to intimate that France might wish to insure the delivery of these articles by naval convoy and that such assistance would encourage the Colonies to separate from Britain and to bestow on France their friendship as well as a large part of their future trade and commerce. He was to inquire whether France would favor an alliance with the Colonies "for commerce, or defense, or both."

THE INTEREST OF FRANCE IN THE AMERICAN REVOLUTION

The Duc de Choiseul regarded the peace that ended the Seven Years' War as only a truce during which France could prepare for a renewal of hostilities against Great Britain. He conducted the peace negotiations shrewdly with the next war in mind, and as long as he held office or had influence, this one great objective received his principal solicitude. His plans, drawn on a large scale, were formed with competence and vision, and were based on the primary assumption that the Bourbon Family Alliance with Spain could be maintained and enlarged. Within seven years after 1763, he had managed to strengthen the naval and military establishments of the two allies and to improve their financial positions. Not the least of his plans involved the prospect of British-American conflict. As soon as the news of the Stamp Act controversy reached France he sent a competent naval officer, M. de Pontleroy, to investigate the political and military situation in the Colonies and to fan the flames of anti-British sentiment. Later (1768) he sent the Baron de Kalb on a similar mission. But at the height of his preparations, and possibly on the edge of war, he was removed from office by Louis XV. This act, said Lord Shelburne, was a "miraculous interposition of Providence." However that may be, war was averted, French foreign policy concerning America became virtually stationary, and Britain gained the opportunity, which it did not embrace, to revise its American policy.

Louis XVI came to the throne in 1774 with the strong desire of restoring the prestige of the Crown. That France's prestige had declined conspicuously during the last days of Louis XV had been dramatically illustrated by the first partition of Poland in 1772 without even the foreknowledge of France. France stood humiliated and alone in Europe save for her one ally, Spain. The new King chose as his foreign minister an able and experienced diplomat, the Comte de Vergennes, whose thinking regarding the international prestige of France was almost identical with that of Choiseul. He believed that the plight of France could be traced to Britain's door and that Britain's power was derived primarily from her colonial commerce. To this extent Vergennes was a child of mercantilist doctrines. Since a preponderant amount of Great Britain's foreign trade was with her American Colonies, it followed that if this trade, or a substantial portion of it, could be diverted to France, or at any rate away from Britain, one important source of British strength would be undermined and she would be less likely to challenge France on the Continent or to seize her remaining colonial possessions. Vergennes believed that Britain was "proud and restless," the natural enemy of France and a perfidious one, and that Britain and France drew nearer to war the longer its outbreak was postponed.

The desire of Vergennes to curb British growth and power was not separate in his thought from the need of France to recover her proud position in Europe in accordance with her tradition of grandeur. This, in turn, was not distinct from the desire to restore the prestige of the Crown in France. All these matters were parts of a single fabric each thread of which led to war with Britain. War might have its "disadvantages" for France, Vergennes admitted, but it was the road to power and glory, and he agreed with Choiseul that "the balance of power lay in America." The outbreak of war in America in April, 1775, gave him the opportunity to promote Spanish resentment against Great Britain and to encourage the spirit of rebellion in America by sending thither a new French agent, Achard de Bonvouloir.

Well before Deane arrived in France, which was not until July, 1776, the French Foreign Minister had matured his plans for assisting the Colonies, had solicited Spanish co-operation, and had largely overcome opposition at home. His ideas and plans were clearly and extensively elaborated in instructions to French ministers abroad and in memoranda prepared for the King and the ministry. Vergennes recommended that active preparation should be made for war with Great Britain, who should be lulled into a sense of security from French and Spanish attack until the most opportune moment had arrived. In the interim all possible assistance should be given to the American Colonies. They should be allowed to sell goods in France and purchase goods and munitions, even from French military stores, and financial aid should be extended to them as a supplement to their own resources. The Colonies should be made to realize, however, that the more vigorously they waged war the more aid they could expect from France. In this way they were expected to earn the assistance they received. France and Spain would secure "political advantages," said Vergennes, equal to their expenditures. Thus the books would be balanced.

Vergennes advanced these proposals against strong opposition, among his opponents being the Minister of Finance, Turgot, who advocated peace and domestic reform. Turgot's program was disliked, however, by the nobility and the Queen, while the ideas of Vergennes were supported by the Ministers of War and Marine and the energetic Beaumarchais. Gradually Louis XVI was won over. In April, 1776, he issued a royal order permitting the sale of "discarded" military supplies, and in May he placed a million livres at the disposal of the fictitious Rodrique Hortalez et Compagnie, established by Beaumarchais as a blind behind which the extensive operations of supplying American needs were organized. In May, also, Turgot was dismissed, and across the Atlantic the American Congress advised the Colonies to form independent governments. Already American privateers were swarming the sea, and many of them entered French ports, "in stress of weather," naturally, or for supplies, or repairs, or under any legal ruse that would cover their presence while they accomplished their business. In August, Spain added a million livres to the funds for secret aid, and by the end of 1776 at least seven shiploads of supplies had reached American shores.

THE FRANCO-AMERICAN ALLIANCE

Those members of the Continental Congress who believed it was both wise and possible to secure a redress of grievances and to effect reconciliation with Britain lost their cause with the decision to proclaim independence. By that time Congress had already instructed Silas Deane to explore the possibilities of a

treaty of commerce or alliance with France. But he was not authorized to negotiate a treaty. Policy decisions were yet to be
made regarding the nature of treaties desired, whether they should
be commercial exclusively, or wartime military alliances, or permanent alliances with territorial guarantees. Some members of
Congress never lost their fears of France and would have been
satisfied if treaties with her could have been avoided or restricted
to commercial subjects. Other members, including John Adams,
realized the need for wartime military alliances, but believed
that the future security of the new American nation would be
found in a European balance of power from which America could
stand apart. Still others, among whom were Silas Deane and
Benjamin Franklin, favored the negotiation of treaties on a wide
scale. They were impressed with the looseness of the American
union and its weakness in contrast with the unity and strength
of Britain and concluded that for the immediate needs and future
security of the colonies, British power should be diffused and
exhausted against as many allies of America as possible. To them
the logic of independence did not admit the doctrine of isolation.

For all practical purposes Congress decided on independence
when it appointed a committee, June 10, 1776, to draft a resolution to that effect. Two days later it appointed another committee
to draw up a Plan of Treaties with foreign powers. Its report,
drafted by John Adams, was submitted to Congress on July 18,
1776, and was adopted with slight amendment on September 17.
During the interim the committee prepared instructions for the
commissioners who were to be intrusted with treaty negotiations.
Although the Plan of Treaties was intended to be a general model,
it was written with specific reference to a treaty with France.

The Plan envisaged bilateral commercial treaties under which
the United States as a neutral would have the greatest possible
freedom of trade when any nation with whom it had a treaty was
a belligerent. Under such circumstances the neutral could trade
with the enemy of the belligerent, either directly or between enemy
ports. Free ships gave freedom to enemy goods, save contraband,
which was enumerated, and neutral goods could be confiscated
in enemy ships. France was to be secure in the fishing rights she
enjoyed under the Treaty of Paris, but she was to be excluded

from acquiring any British possession in North America. This prohibition did not extend to British possessions in the Caribbean. If Britain declared war on France in consequence of the treaty, the United States was to refrain from giving aid to Britain. France was to protect American ships against plundering from the North African states and was to protect American ships in French waters or on the high seas whenever they could join a French convoy. The commissioners were authorized to sign a treaty with France under the terms of the Plan if possible but were given wide discretionary authority. Congress selected Benjamin Franklin, Thomas Jefferson, and Silas Deane as commissioners. Thomas Jefferson reluctantly declined the appointment, and Congress chose Arthur Lee in his place.

The story of Franklin's activity and service to his country as commissioner and later as minister of the United States in France is familiar. Yet repetition has not lessened its interest, nor has scholarly investigation reduced its importance in American diplomatic history. Many explanations have been given for Franklin's immense popularity with all classes in Paris and for his success, but none is satisfactory. There is no way to define the essence of a great personality. It can only be said that the place, the time, the whole vast complex of circumstance and the man were combined and suited to the result. Outwardly, Franklin did nothing spectacular. He found comfortable lodgings in Passy, about two miles from the center of Paris, on the estate of a wealthy friend of the American cause, Le Roy de Chaumont. He dressed simply and went about his affairs with dignity but without ostentation. He spent much time in the libraries of Paris, attended the Academy of Sciences, where he met Voltaire, visited almost everybody of importance, and of every faction, and did not in the least neglect the fashionable salons or the fashionable ladies of Paris, to one of whom he proposed marriage. These pleasant activities fascinated Paris, and possibly Franklin too, and diverted attention from other areas of his serious enterprise. He cultivated the Freemasons, who had large influence on French liberal thought and on the French press, organized extensive propaganda against that of the British ambassador, Lord Stormont, and most of all gained the respect and confidence of Vergennes. Franklin was a superb diplomat, and this was well, for the American cause stood in dire need of the friendship of France.

During the time between the signing of the Declaration of Independence and the conclusion of the French alliance on February 6, 1778, American diplomatic fortunes in France and Spain fluctuated violently in response to the vacillation of ministers, changes in the Spanish government and in its policy toward Portugal, and the tides of war in America. As already noted, French policy toward Britain was posited on the assumption of Spanish co-operation. The Bourbon allies were united in their dislike for Britain, but their other interests were divergent. France had lost her possessions on the continent of North America, did not hope for their recovery, and was willing to assist the British Colonies in becoming a strong and independent state as a weight in the formation of a new balance of power. Spain, however, still retained her vast American empire and feared both the influence of democratic doctrines among her colonial subjects and the expansionist tendencies of the United States. She was in conflict with Portugal in the La Plata area of South America and wanted French assistance in a war of conquest against Portugal, who was an ally of Britain. In addition, Spain had ambitions to recover Gibraltar, Minorca, Jamaica, Florida, and British Honduras.

Early in 1777 it became evident to the Congress and also to the commissioners in Paris that the United States would need more than secret aid in order to win the war. It needed military allies. Acting on their own initiative at first, and later under authority from Congress, the commissioners began to offer positive commitments in the form of territorial guarantees. They offered Spain and France a triple alliance involving a declaration of war by the United States against Portugal and a division among the three signatories of the British possessions in America. Arthur Lee went to Spain to use his influence directly on the Spanish government. He was not allowed, however, to reach Madrid. Vergennes, who had been irresolute for several months, began to realize that France had to make a fundamental decision either to abandon the American enterprise or to extend it into a military alliance with the United States. By July, 1777, he decided on alliance and secured the King's consent subject to Spanish co-operation.

Now Spain became the stumbling block. The death of the King

of Portugal had brought about a change in the ministry, and an armistice between Spain and Portugal in June, 1777, gave prospect of peace between the two states. In addition, Grimaldi had fallen from power, and his place had been taken by the Conde de Floridablanca who had revised Spain's foreign policy. The new Spanish minister disliked or was jealous of France, and feared the growth of democratic influences everywhere. He was willing to assist a Roman Catholic uprising in Ireland and to continue secret aid to America but unwilling to fight Britain for American independence. The Spanish attitude and news of fresh British victories in America dampened French enthusiasm for immediate action.

At this low state in American hopes for an alliance, two events were in the making that brought it to fruition. One was the surrender of General John Burgoyne and his army at Saratoga, the news of which reached Paris on December 3, 1777, and the other was a new movement in Britain for American colonial reconciliation. In December, 1775, Parliament had approved a proposal for reconciliation on the basis of forgive and forget and designated as commissioners to negotiate with the colonists, General Sir William Howe and his brother Lord Richard Howe, military and naval commanders respectively of the British forces sent to New York in 1776. These proposals never had the slightest chance of securing congressional approval, but one or another of the Howe brothers tried to negotiate on the basis of them all through 1776 and 1777. Meanwhile the friends of reconciliation in Parliament kept the issue alive. Lord Chatham, for example, told the House of Lords in May, 1777, that the Colonies could not be conquered, although they might be destroyed, and that peace should be made before Spain and France entered the war. He said that instead of demanding unconditional surrender, Parliament should grant unconditional redress of colonial grievances and should propose a federal union with the Colonies on the basis of complete local self-government. This and other efforts to move Lord North's government failed, but the Saratoga disaster awakened it to the realities of the situation and led to a new policy of reconciliation.

Lord North's position was manifestly difficult. If his proposals for reconciliation were liberal enough to please the parliamentary opposition, they would in all probability alienate his own following.

If he gave primary consideration to national interests rather than to domestic politics, he needed to offer the Colonies something specific and more than they might secure through an alliance with France and the continuation of the war. But Lord North was either politically unable or lacked the strength of purpose to play at once for the highest stakes. He proposed, on February 17, 1778, that Parliament should declare its willingness to refrain from taxing the Colonies for revenue purposes, should repeal various acts passed after 1763, which he supposed were the main sources of conflict, and should authorize the appointment of commissioners to negotiate with the Colonies. His proposals did not yield the *right* of Parliament to tax the Colonies, did not offer repeal of the obnoxious Quebec Act, and left obscure the exact terms on which the commissioners would negotiate. The first draft of Lord North's proposals reached New York on April 14, 1778.

The determination of Vergennes to conclude an American alliance, with or without the adherence of Spain, kept pace with these events. He had to contend, however, with the reluctance of Louis XVI to act without Spanish co-operation. He was obliged to bombard the hesitant sovereign with his entire stock of arguments, some of which he himself was probably not seriously impressed with. The Saratoga victory, the knowledge that Lord North intended to propose some form of reconciliation with the Colonies when Parliament met on January 20, 1778, and the presence in France of British agents, who were known to be in contact with the American commissioners, contributed to his purpose and hastened his action. He was able to persuade the King and the Royal Council to authorize, on January 7, 1778, the negotiation with the United States of two treaties, one of commerce and amity and the other of alliance. Under these treaties the complete independence of the United States would be recognized, French and American possessions in North America and the West Indies would be reciprocally guaranteed, peace could not be concluded by either nation without the consent of the other, and Spain would be allowed to join the alliance. From then on negotiations moved rapidly until the treaties were signed on February 6, 1778.

The Treaty of Amity and Commerce followed with remarkable fidelity the Plan of Treaties of 1776. It has been truly said that although it was signed in France, it was made in America. The principal variation from the American treaty plan was the omission of the political articles because they were covered in the Treaty of Alliance. At the suggestion of France the most-favored-nation principle was adopted, but with the reservation that special concessions made in return for compensation would not be extended without similar compensation. The broad principles of neutral rights as suggested in the treaty plan were retained, and France granted to the United States complete commercial equality. Later on two articles regarding export and import taxes on goods exchanged between the United States and the French West Indies were suppressed by mutual consent.

The Treaty of Alliance contained (1) provisions regarding military co-operation between the signatories if war should break out between France and Britain during the existing conflict and (2) articles of territorial guarantee. The United States was left free to acquire any territory of Great Britain in the "Northern Parts of America or the Islands of Bermudas," and France specifically renounced forever possession of the Bermudas or any part of the "continent" of North America which belonged to Britain before the Treaty of Paris of 1763 or was acquired under it. France was free to secure the British islands in or near the Gulf of Mexico. France guaranteed to the United States forever its independence and whatever territories it secured within the terms of the agreement, and the United States guaranteed to France her American possessions and any additional territory she might acquire under the stipulations of the treaty. Neither party could make peace without the consent of the other, and other nations might join the alliance under mutual agreement. In a separate and secret article, Spanish adherence to the treaties of 1778 was specifically permitted, and if Spain wanted changes in their terms, France could *suggest* other conditions "analogous to the principal aim of the alliance and conformable to the rules of equality, reciprocity, and friendship." The United States would *endeavour* in good faith to adjust alterations proposed by Spain.

ASSISTANCE TO AMERICAN INDEPENDENCE BY SPAIN,
HOLLAND, AND THE LEAGUE OF NEUTRALS

The secret article of the Treaty of Alliance and the whole course of French policy toward America show the importance attached by Vergennes to Spanish co-operation. He repeatedly stated and undoubtedly believed that the success of the entire Franco-American enterprise depended on the assistance of the Spanish fleet. This belief was not fully shared by the French ambassador at Madrid, the Comte de Montmorin, who doubted that aid from Spain would be equal to the difficulties caused by her demands. Nevertheless, Vergennes induced Spain to sign, on April 12, 1779, the secret Treaty of Aranjuez.

Under this treaty France and Spain agreed to make common cause against Great Britain and promised that neither party would make peace without the consent of the other. France pledged specifically to continue the war until Spain had recovered Gibraltar. This was an unrestricted commitment comparable to the agreement with the United States concerning independence. Otherwise France agreed to assist Spain in the realization of her territorial ambitions already noted. Spain agreed not to cease fighting until France had secured the abolition of treaties restricting her from fortifying Dunkirk or, in default of that, some other object acceptable to France. Spain recognized French interests in the expulsion of the British from Newfoundland, the acquisition of the island of Santo Domingo, and the recovery of Senegal.

France did not consult the United States in the negotiation of this treaty and had no right, without American consent, to connect its interests with those of Spain. It is extremely doubtful, however, that a case can be made by the United States against Vergennes on either score. France made no attempt to link the United States with her commitments to Spain, and she could have agreed at any time to peace between Britain and America without violating the Treaty of Aranjuez. In a similar way she could have agreed to peace between Spain and Britain without violating the Treaty of Alliance. France alone was committed both ways. She made no promise to Spain concerning the western boundaries of the United States and none concerning Florida which the United States had not already proposed. There is no reason to accuse France of infidelity to the American cause or to misunderstand her objectives. She entered the war in order to humiliate Great Britain and to reduce her strength, objectives which she believed could be accomplished through American independence. She signed the Treaty of Aranjuez and made large commitments to Spain for this sole purpose.

Among the many reasons that led Vergennes to support American independence was his belief that the United States would adopt more liberal policies concerning the maritime rights of neutrals than Britain had been willing to accept. He realized also that the advocacy by France of such policies might be the means of drawing other maritime states into a concert against the British. Accordingly, France willingly approved the provisions on neutral rights in the Plan of Treaties of 1776 and, after the Treaty of Alliance was signed in 1778, issued maritime regulations embracing these principles together with the additional stipulation that a blockade must be effective to be binding. France announced further that she would observe these principles for the benefit of all neutrals who would exact similar concessions from Great Britain.

This action initiated a movement, embraced first by Denmark and later by Russia, which led to the League of Armed Neutrality of 1780. Russia hesitated to act as long as Britain seemed to be the only offender against the liberal policies, but as soon as Spain interfered with Russian commerce under regulations even more damaging to neutral shipping than those of Britain, Russia announced, without waiting for concerted neutral action, a code of neutral rights which she proposed to defend with naval power and with which she invited other neutrals to associate themselves. These Russian proposals of February 28, 1780, were essentially the same as those proposed by Vergennes. They declared that (1) neutral vessels could navigate freely between the ports and along the coasts of belligerents, (2) free ships could give freedom to enemy goods, save contraband, (3) contraband was to be enumerated in accordance with an existing Anglo-Russian treaty, and (4) a legally blockaded port had to be sufficiently invested to render access "clearly dangerous." The contraband list specified was limited in extent and did not include naval stores.

After some negotiations which effected minor changes in the contraband list, but before the end of 1780, Denmark and Sweden signed conventions with Russia embracing her proposals, and the Netherlands acceded the following January. Later on Prussia, Portugal, the Two Sicilies, and the Holy Roman Empire gave their adherence. At the suggestions of France, Spain adopted the principles of the Russian declaration, as did also the American Congress. Thus, at the end of the war only the independent states of Northern Italy, the Papal States, and Turkey, among the maritime nations of Europe, refrained from joining either the war against Britain or Armed Neutrality. Since the "armed neutrals" never succeeded in forming a precise program of concerted action, their embryonic organization has been called an "armed nullity." This designation underestimates the idea's importance. It furthered and emphasized the isolation of Britain and caused her to modify some of her maritime practices, gave a degree of sanction for the liberal principles of neutral rights advocated by the United States and France, and contributed to the outbreak of war between Britain and the Netherlands.

Under an Anglo-Dutch commercial treaty of 1674, Britain had agreed to a liberal definition of neutral rights which permitted the Dutch to carry goods directly to French ports and specifically exempted from contraband ship's timbers and naval stores greatly needed by France. Dutch carrying trade thrived under this situation, and when Britain interfered, the Netherlands protected their trade with France by naval convoy. The growing Anglo-Dutch tension was acerbated by Dutch-American trade in munitions which reached the United States through the Dutch West Indies, particularly by way of St. Eustatius. After Spain entered the war in 1779, Britain demanded from the Netherlands the fulfillment of a century-old treaty of alliance (1678) which obliged each signatory to assist the other in case of attack. When the States General refused, Britain denounced the alliance, and the commercial treaty of 1674 as well, and ordered the seizure of Dutch vessels carrying enemy property or contraband as defined by "the general law of nations." The Dutch ordered unlimited naval convoy and began to prepare the necessary armament. Britain waited, however, until the States General decided, November 20, 1780, to join the Armed Neutrality before war was declared. From the American point of view the Anglo-Dutch war accomplished a further diffusion of British power, facilitated the negotiation of Dutch loans to the United States, and brought about a favorable commercial treaty in 1782.

With the exception of the Netherlands and France, European courts were indifferent to the efforts of congressional agents sent abroad to secure loans or to negotiate commercial treaties. This was not because Europe was sympathetic to Great Britain, for there was little respect in Europe for a nation which aspired to greatness but was obliged to buy mercenaries from sordid German princes in order to subdue its rebellious subjects. But the ruling classes of Europe were disturbed by Jefferson's glowing phrases in the Declaration of Independence and were aware that freedom, even in distant America, was a challenge to privilege. Benjamin Franklin strongly opposed the sending of amateur diplomats to courts where no arrangements had been made to receive them. John Adams, however, believed that "militia diplomacy" might be successful where regular methods would fail, but the "militia diplomats" who were sent to Prussia, Austria, Italy, and Russia were rebuffed and accomplished nothing.

PEACE NEGOTIATIONS AND THE TREATY OF 1783

Great Britain could have won the war against its American colonists and their allies and collaborators if it had possessed a great military leader who could win victories notwithstanding an ineffective government at home, or a great statesman who could organize a strong government able to persevere in the face of military defeats. It had neither. Although Lord North's ministry survived a serious political crisis in 1779, and the British Army in America was successful in the South in 1780, the surrender of General Cornwallis at Yorktown on October 19, 1781, brought about North's resignation on March 20, 1782. The new ministry headed by the Marquis of Rockingham, and with Lord Shelburne in the Colonial Office and Charles James Fox as Foreign Secretary, was predisposed toward a speedy conclusion of the war.

Beginning soon after the French alliance and continuing until the peace negotiations began, Congress had given frequent and serious thought to acceptable peace terms. This activity was encouraged by the first French minister to the United States, Conrad Alexandre Gérard, who reflected the efforts of France to find an accommodation between American and Spanish interests in order to gain the support of the latter, first for an alliance and later for a more active participation in the war. The congressional debate was characterized by (1) an anti-French faction's opposition to the French alliance, although not to French aid, and this group's distrust of French advice, (2) factional and sectional interests of members, marked particularly by eastern concern over commercial and fishing rights, and western concern over boundaries and the free navigation of the Mississippi River, (3) pressure from the military to appease Spain, and (4) fluctuations between hope and despair for the success of the war. These influences were most evident when decisions had to be made on items considered indispensable to peace.

In its first decision on peace terms, Congress agreed that British recognition of American independence should be a prerequisite for negotiation. It desired that the northern boundary should run along the 45th degree of north latitude to the St. Lawrence, thence to Lake Nipissing and, in a straight line, to the source of the Mississippi. The Florida boundary was to start at the 31st degree of north latitude. Congress was willing, however, for the northern boundary to be adjusted, provided the western part of it did not drop below the 45th degree. The cession of Canada and Nova Scotia, and particularly the securing of "equal and common" rights to the fisheries, were considered of the "utmost importance," but they were not to be demanded at the price of continuing the war. Such were the instructions of August 14, 1779, given to John Adams, who was appointed minister with authority to negotiate peace with Great Britain. They were based on a congressional resolution of February 23, 1779, which affirmed also the right of the United States to the free navigation of the Mississippi River.

Almost simultaneously with the appointment of Adams, Congress selected John Jay as minister to Spain in an effort to secure Spanish adherence to the Franco-American alliance. Jay was authorized to inform Spain that the United States was willing for her to have the Floridas and to guarantee their possession to Spain provided Spain would recognize the right of the United States to the free navigation of the Mississippi River. But Spain remained unwilling to recognize American independence, virtually withdrew from the war, and carried on negotiations with Great Britain regarding Gibraltar.

Meanwhile, during the closing months of 1780 and the beginning of 1781, American prospects for military success and the achievement of independence reached their darkest period. Spain remained aloof save for her own interests, the French treasury was empty and the government discouraged, and American resources for continuing the war were all but exhausted. In this critical situation Congress, on February 15, 1781, authorized Jay to recede from the demand for free navigation of the Mississippi below the 31st degree. This represented the most extreme concession to Spain that Congress was willing to make. Jay presented the proposal reluctantly and warned Spain that if she waited for a settlement of Spanish-American problems until a general peace was made, the United States would not be bound by these wartime offers.

With the same sense of urgency, Congress replaced Adams as sole minister to negotiate peace with a commission which, in addition to Adams, included Franklin and Jay. New instructions from Congress permitted the commission to accept a "long truce" instead of immediate recognition of independence, provided all British troops were removed from American soil, gave the commission wide discretionary authority over other matters, and directed them to be guided by the advice of France.

Peace negotiations between the United States and Britain began with the exchange of letters between Franklin and Lord Shelburne, who soon became Prime Minister and commissioned an agent, Richard Oswald, to negotiate with the Americans in Paris. Oswald was not authorized, however, to grant British recognition of American independence as a preliminary to negotiations. This did not bother Franklin, who was willing to have independence recognized at the end of the negotiations, but Jay was suspicious of French intrigue and of the sincerity of the British, and without letting Franklin know about it, sent a secret emissary to Shelburne with the suggestion that if Britain would acknowledge American independence, the United States would not be bound under the Franco-American alliance to continue the war. He believed that France was secretly working against American territorial interests in the Southwest, and urged Britain to retain the Floridas.

Jay's action may not have damaged American interests, for Shelburne paid little attention to his emissary, but this will always remain an unknown factor. Negotiations with the British were delayed through Jay's action, and on account of this delay the British did not receive a draft of American proposals for a settlement until October 11, 1782, several days after news had reached Britain that Gibraltar had survived a French-Spanish assault. The precarious situation of Gibraltar had been one of the important factors which induced the British government to see if it could drive a wedge between the United States and France. The favorable turn of affairs at Gibraltar, together with the earlier news of a British naval victory over the French in the West Indies, and the arrival of French and Spanish peace proposals almost simultaneously with those from the United States, had a dual effect on Lord Shelburne. Those events stiffened his will to resist peace terms unacceptable to Britain and lessened his interest in separate arrangements with the United States.

Shelburne sent Henry Strachey to Paris to assist Oswald and instructed him to suggest the old Quebec Act line on the Ohio River as the northwest boundary of the United States, to restrict American fishing rights to the high seas, and to secure provisions concerning the payment of American prerevolutionary debts to British subjects and the compensation for losses sustained by Loyalists. Late in October, 1782, John Adams arrived in Paris from the Netherlands and joined Jay and Franklin in the negotiations. With Adams being all but *persona non grata* to Vergennes, Jay still strongly distrustful of him, and Franklin ill much of the time, little attention was paid to the instructions of Congress concerning the reliance that should be placed on French friendship. The

American commissioners were anxious about the outcome of negotiations, and well they might be, for they had virtually thrown over the French alliance when they insisted on prior recognition of independence, and had little left to bargain with save persuasion and the war weariness of the British people.

With these weapons they did very well. The hope of securing Canada had long since been abandoned. The Lake Nipissing line faded too. But Britain gave up the old Quebec Act boundary and all agreed on the "water line" through rivers and lakes from the 45th degree of north latitude on the St. Lawrence to the Lake of the Woods and westward from the northwest corner of that lake to the Mississippi. The navigation of the river was to be free to the subjects of both nations forever. In making these grants, Britain was astonishingly indifferent to the interests of her Indian allies and her Canadian subjects. Congress, in its instructions of 1779, had stipulated the St. John River as the northeast boundary if Nova Scotia were not secured, but the commissioners quickly and wisely accepted the St. Croix River, for the boundaries of Nova Scotia were indefinite, and Britain might well have demanded the Penobscot or even the Kennebec as a boundary river.

It is interesting to note, in comparison with territorial questions, the relative importance given to the right of British creditors to recover prerevolutionary debts and the treatment of American Loyalists. Compromises were reached on these and other relatively secondary problems, and may have been justified, but difficulties arose over most of them later. The provisional treaty, signed on November 30, 1782, was in substance the final treaty, although the so-called "definitive treaty" was not signed until France and Great Britain made peace on September 3, 1783.

Franklin was worried, particularly during the later stages of the negotiations, over the attitude of Vergennes, who had not been seriously consulted or even kept fully informed. The commissioners had talked with him about various problems, and they gave him an incomplete copy of the provisional treaty. Still Vergennes had good reasons for complaint, and expressed it. Nowhere does Franklin's genius shine brighter than in his success in meeting the criticism of Vergennes and at the same time securing a further loan from France.

The treaty was received with general approval in the United States. In Great Britain it was vigorously denounced and strongly defended. Vergennes was surprised at its terms "but not displeased." Leopold of Tuscany said it marked the fall of a great power "completely and forever." But the Spanish ambassador in Paris, the Conde de Aranda, looked into the future and reported his vision:

> This federal republic is born a pigmy. A day will come when it will be a giant; even a colossus, formidable in these countries. Liberty of conscience, the facility for establishing a new population on immense lands, as well as the advantage of the new government, will draw thither farmers and artisans from all nations. In a few years we shall watch with grief the tyrannical existence of this same colossus.

The ambassador did not explain why he thought the new nation, with all the attractiveness that he admitted it to possess, would have a tyrannical existence.

III

THE BEGINNING OF INDEPENDENCE, 1783–1801

HISTORY does not divide itself naturally into chronological periods because there is always some continuity between the forces and events of one period and the next. Nevertheless it is generally possible to observe in retrospect certain logical divisions of history in which an era has the character of an epoch. During the period under consideration, the United States passed from the government of the weak Confederation to that of the stronger Constitution, problems immediate to the treaty of 1783 were settled, treaties of commerce were negotiated, diplomatic and consular establishments were provided, and the French alliance was terminated. When Jefferson came into the Presidency in 1801 he believed that relations with foreign states were tranquil and that the nation could properly turn its attention primarily to domestic matters. Jefferson's hopes proved illusory, and he was soon obliged to give his attention to foreign affairs. Another era was to pass before it could be said that American independence had been fully established. It is proper, however, to characterize this era as the beginning of independence.

COMMERCIAL TREATIES UNDER THE CONFEDERATION

One of the first needs of the United States at the end of the Revolution was to negotiate commercial treaties under which

American commerce and navigation would enjoy the greatest possible freedom and security. This task was impeded by the limitations placed upon congressional authority by the Articles of Confederation. They granted to Congress the sole right to make treaties but provided that no treaty of commerce should be made under which the states would be restrained from imposing imposts and duties on foreign merchandise equal to those imposed by foreign nations on their own people, or restrained from prohibiting the exportation or importation "of any species of goods or commodities whatsoever." Congress was not given the authority to regulate commerce or to levy imposts, and had no power, therefore, to pass retaliatory measures against nations that discriminated against American trade. All attempts to amend the Articles so as to give Congress these powers failed, and this defect in congressional authority was one of the principal causes for the establishment of a stronger central government.

At the end of the war Congress withdrew the authorization it had earlier extended to its agents in Europe to accede to a convention that might be adopted by the Armed Neutrality League for the protection of neutral commerce. Congress declared that although it still approved the principles of the Armed Neutrality, the necessity of having the support of the armed neutrals was no longer needed since American independence had been secured. Congress was no longer willing to become a member of a confederacy which might involve the United States in the politics of Europe. It was anxious, however, to have commercial treaties and drew up a new Plan of Treaties in May, 1784, which represented the hopes of the new nation regarding the freedom of the seas. Drafted by Jefferson, the new plan improved on the Plan of 1776 in the following ways: (1) in case of war between the signatories, the normal commerce of either party should be unmolested and neither side would commission privateers to act against the other; (2) if one signatory was a neutral and the other a belligerent, contraband goods could be purchased but not confiscated; (3) enemy goods, not contraband, were to be free in neutral ships; and (4) a blockaded port was defined as one where an entering ship would be in "imminent danger" of capture.

In accordance with this plan Congress authorized a commission consisting of Franklin, Adams, and Jefferson, who was soon to

replace Franklin in Paris, to negotiate treaties with a large number of European states, and to revise if possible the commercial
treaties with France, Holland, and Sweden. They were successful
in signing only two additional treaties during the Confederation,
one with Prussia in 1785, and the other with Morocco in 1787.
Prior to the Revolution, American commerce had been protected
from the marauding tendencies of the Barbary States by the British Navy. This protection no longer existed, and Congress, with
no sea power at its disposal, had recourse to bribery. Although
the treaty with Morocco was effected at a cost of about $30,000,
the other Barbary States (Algiers, Tunis, Tripoli) were not satisfied with offers that could be made to them, and they continued to
capture American ships and enslave American nationals until the
United States acquired sufficient sea power to provide authority
for its protests and respect for its rights.

British policy concerning postwar commercial relations with the
United States was not fully developed at the beginning of negotiations for peace. Britain had lost some three thousand merchant
ships during the war, her treasury was almost empty, and food
shortages had caused unprecedented suffering among the poorer
classes. She needed to rebuild her merchant marine and to restore
her far-flung trade. At the same time she did not want to impose
so many restrictions on American trade that it would find permanent advantage in French ports. At first British policy seemed to
be in favor of complete commercial reciprocity with the United
States, but it quickly shifted toward commercial restriction. This
shift reflected the triumph in Britain of British shipowners and
shipbuilders over merchants, the West India planters, and the
advocates of free trade.

The British government became convinced that the United
States could become a great maritime rival of Great Britain and
that this development could be retarded by restrictions placed on
American shipping. By Orders in Council of July 2, 1783, and
later by an Act of Parliament, Britain excluded American ships
from the British West Indies, Canada, and Newfoundland, and
either excluded or limited the importation of American products
into these areas. American ships and most American raw materials
were admitted to the British Isles. Manufactured goods were ex-

cluded. Since the Congress of the Confederation had no power to regulate foreign commerce and therefore no way to retaliate against British restrictions, retaliation devolved upon the states. All of them except Connecticut enacted retaliatory restrictions on British trade, but such measures were largely ineffective because Britain could use Connecticut as an entrepôt, and could send selected items to states whose restrictions on such items were least burdensome. The American minister in Britain, John Adams, exhausted his greatest efforts in a futile attempt to break the British navigation system as it affected the United States, and returned home with the strong conviction that one of the first needs of the new American nation was the establishment of a central government powerful enough to undertake trade retaliation.

The negotiation of a commercial treaty with Spain became interwoven with the problems of the right of the United States to enjoy the free navigation of the Mississippi River below the 31st parallel and the controversy over the Florida boundary. Spain's policy was set forth in a document issued on July 29, 1784, to Spanish officials in America. Spain denied that Britain had the right to cede to the United States the free navigation of the Mississippi below the northern boundary of Florida. Britain's right, it was claimed, to the navigation of the Mississippi had been recognized by Spain because Britain held the entire eastern bank of the river. It followed then, in Spain's view, that the United States had no right to the free navigation of the river below the point where she did not own the eastern bank no matter what stipulations were made in a treaty between the United States and Britain. On the boundary matter, Spain was willing to accept the boundary of East Florida as claimed by the United States from the St. Marys River to the Flint, but wanted the boundary of West Florida expanded to include the territory south of the Tennessee and Ohio rivers.

When the Spanish agent, Diego de Gardoqui, arrived in New York in 1786, Congress appointed John Jay to negotiate with him but specified that Jay was not to sign an agreement unless Spain recognized the right of American citizens to navigate freely the Mississippi River and accepted the 31st degree as the northern boundary of West Florida. Gardoqui could not accept these two stipulations and no agreement was possible unless he could effect a shift in American policy. Since Gardoqui was allowed considerable leeway on the boundary question, Jay proposed that this could be left to later negotiation, or to a commission, and that the navigation problem be eliminated by an American promise to *forbear* the navigation of the river for the proposed duration of the treaty, twenty-five or thirty years. For these concessions the United States would secure complete reciprocity in trade with continental Spain and the Canaries, and a Spanish guarantee of American territory.

Jay's proposals initiated the most prolonged, serious, and important debate in the Congress of the Confederation. The northeastern states, having the greatest interest in commerce and the least interest in the growth of the West, were willing to change Jay's instructions to suit his proposals. The five southern states steadfastly refused. Although the pro-treaty forces had a majority in Congress, 7 states to 5, Delaware being absent, they could not muster the nine states necessary to adopt a treaty, and Jay wisely decided that no value would be gained in concluding a fruitless negotiation. Both sides in the great debate realized the necessity for a stronger union in order to deal with the Mississippi question.

THE TREATY OF PEACE AND THE NORTHWEST POSTS

The treaty of 1783 provided that Great Britain would remove her troops from American soil "with all convenient speed." New York was evacuated before ratifications of the treaty were exchanged, but the Governor of Canada, Frederick Haldimand, refused to order the evacuation of British posts along the northern border of the United States when requested to do so by Major General Baron von Steuben, whom Washington had sent to Canada to arrange for the transfer. The most important of the posts were at Ogdensburg, Oswego, and Niagara in New York, Erie in Pennsylvania, Sandusky in Ohio, and Detroit and Michilimackinac in Michigan. The day before George III proclaimed the treaty of peace, his Secretary of State for Home Affairs, Lord Sydney, instructed Governor Haldimand to retain the posts. This was an outright violation of the treaty, apparently in order to use the posts in holding the United States to the provisions regarding the treatment of the Loyalists and the settlement of prewar debts. Lord Sydney looked upon the American Confederation as being weak and contemptible and not likely to last. He was quite willing therefore to hold the posts, to supply the Indians with arms and ammunition—"to enable them to defend themselves"—and to contemplate the possible recovery of at least a portion of lost territory. If Jay had based his case for an accommodation with Spain on the necessity for dealing with one problem at a time, and on the wisdom of selecting the British as offering the greatest threat to American security, he would have had a strong position.

Although the British were the first to violate the treaty, the United States government was unable to implement immediately all of its treaty obligations concerning Loyalists and British debts. All the states had passed laws inimical to Loyalists. Article Five of the treaty required Congress to *recommend* to the states the restoration of the property of Loyalists who had not taken up arms against the United States, and the revision of laws concerning Loyalists in the spirit of justice and reconciliation. Congress fulfilled this obligation by sending the required recommendations to the states. Article Six, however, stated that no further confiscations would be made and no prosecutions commenced against Loyalists, but Congress had no power to compel the observance of these provisions by the states.

Article Four of the treaty provided that British creditors "shall meet with no lawful impediment to the recovery to the full value in sterling money of all bona fide debts heretofore contracted." This, like Article Six, provided an obligation that Congress could not discharge by passing a resolution of recommendation and could not oblige the states to enforce. But by 1786 only Virginia still had laws protecting debtors against suits for the recovery of the debts. Virginia complied with the treaty in December, 1787, although the restrictions were not fully removed until 1789.

It would not be just, however, to say that since both parties to the treaty violated it, they were equally responsible for the growing difficulties between them. Congress, on its part, either carried out its obligations fully, or endeavored to do so in good faith, and was completely successful except in one state. Britain, on the other side, made no effort to fulfill its obligations either with respect to the return of property carried away when its armies evacuated eastern ports or with respect to the return of the north-western posts. The treaty was violated by the express orders of the British government; it was violated in the United States only against the express will of Congress.

THE NEW FEDERAL GOVERNMENT

American historians have tended to emphasize the failures and weaknesses of the Confederation and the reasons, therefore, for the establishment of a more centralized government. The majority of early Americans, however, were satisfied with the general character of the Confederation because they thought first of all in terms of individual human freedom and believed that freedom was best preserved in the wide diffusion of authority. The problem of the framers of the Constitution was to discover what additional powers indispensable for the national welfare should be granted to the central government and what institutional arrangements could be devised to prevent a government which held such powers from perverting them into tyranny. The framers of the Constitution believed they had solved this problem through the creation of a "republican" rather than a "democratic" government whose powers, though extensive, would be strictly enumerated and limited, and whose exercise of power would be circumscribed by a system of checks and balances. In keeping with this spirit and purpose, the Constitution divided authority in both foreign and domestic affairs between the executive, legislative, and judicial branches of the central government and reserved to the states or to the people all authority not precisely granted. To what extent the character of the Constitution has been gradually altered by decisions of the Supreme Court, or the doctrine that in foreign affairs the central government possesses authority not found in the Constitution but inherent in sovereignty, is beyond the scope of this account.

The process of treaty-making gave the framers of the Constitution considerable difficulty. They wanted treaties to be the supreme law of the land on exactly the same level as federal statutes. They realized, however, that it was difficult to enumerate the possible subjects of treaties or to confine their negotiation to the same legislative process as other laws. At the same time, if the authority to make treaties were delegated to the executive branch, or to the executive and the Senate, the check normally exercised over legislation by the House of Representatives would be lacking. They solved this problem by vesting in the executive the power to "make" treaties with the advice and consent of the Senate, provided two thirds of the senators present concurred. This two-thirds rule for Senate approval was the check, or makeweight, to replace the safeguard normally provided by the House.

Although the Constitution granted exclusive authority over foreign affairs to the federal government, it did not succeed in making a clear distribution of this authority between the three branches of the federal government. It is quite simple in theory to make the distinction that a legislature makes laws, the courts interpret them, and the executive enforces them, but under the Constitution the lines of separation are frequently obscure. Congress was given power, among other things, to provide for the common defense, to regulate commerce with foreign nations, to define and punish piracies and felonies committed on the high seas and offenses against the law of nations, to raise and support armies, to provide and maintain a navy, and to declare war. "Executive power," a term not defined in the Constitution, was vested in the President. In addition he was made Commander in Chief of the Army and Navy of the United States, was authorized under conditions already noted to make treaties, empowered to nominate, and, by and with the advice and consent of the Senate, appoint ambassadors and other public ministers and consuls, and to receive such officials from other countries, and he was given the duty to take care that the laws be faithfully executed. The judicial power was extended to all cases in law and equity arising under treaties made by the United States, to cases affecting ambassadors and other public ministers and consuls, to admiralty and maritime jurisdiction, and to controversies to which the United States should be a party or controversies between a state, or the citizens thereof, and foreign states, citizens, or subjects.

Throughout American history the influence in foreign relations of the separate branches of government has fluctuated. The existence of a popular and strong-willed President, a great national emergency, or weak and indifferent leadership in Congress, have often contributed to the extension of executive action, while other circumstances have led to a preponderance of legislative authority. The Supreme Court has generally abstained from placing a restraining hand on the expansion of federal power in foreign relations when this power has come into conflict with the rights reserved to the states. The definite trend has been toward the expansion of centralized government and within that area the growth of executive power.

PRESIDENT WASHINGTON AND THE GROWTH OF POLITICAL FACTION

Washington truly deserves to be called "the Father of His Country." As a soldier he contributed greatly to the success of the revolutionary cause. He presided with infinite patience over the Constitutional Convention, and by his great prestige aided the ratification of the Constitution by the states. His dignity of bearing as President, his resoluteness in times of stress, his unimpeachable character and patriotism, and his command of the universal esteem of the people enabled him to hold the nation together during its initial years when the follies of faction might have torn it asunder.

The basic conflicts in the United States over domestic as well as foreign policy during the Federalist era reflected the growth of two political groups. These groups held fundamentally different views of the national interest, or when in agreement over broad objectives, differed regarding the policies best designed to achieve them. The most influential person in the Federalist group was Alexander Hamilton, although it could not properly be said that he dominated in all respects the policies either of Washington or John Adams. The Democratic-Republicans, more commonly known simply as Republicans, were under the leadership of Jefferson in close co-operation with James Madison. One group was not more patriotic than the other, or necessarily more attached to the Constitution than the other. They had opposing views of the national welfare at a particular time and also some diversity of outlook regarding the direction in which they would like to see the new American nation develop.

Hamilton distrusted democracy and the diffusion of authority, and favored a centralized national government. He devised policies that would benefit a banking, industrial, and mercantile aristocracy. These policies included a protective tariff to aid American industry, maritime laws favorable to American shipping, taxation to support a large federal establishment, and a larger army and navy. This domestic program depended, he believed, on close relations with Great Britain, with whom the United States had the most natural ties of trade and finance. Consequently he both disliked and feared the French alliance because it might be a cause of disturbing relations with Britain.

Jefferson and his followers feared the growth of centralized power, and opposed domestic policies based on class interest. Although they were neither anti-British nor pro-French, they were sympathetic to the ideas of the French Revolution, which appeared at first to be democratic, favored the French alliance because they believed France could be used as a counterpoise to British supremacy and arrogance, and supported the use of economic retaliation against Britain as a means of securing American rights on the seas and the freedom of its soil from British occupation.

THE DEPARTMENT OF STATE

In organizing the executive branch of the government under the Constitution, Congress established first the Department of Foreign Affairs. It intended to establish also a department of home affairs which would supervise relations between the states and the federal government, keep the records and the great seal of the United States, direct the mint and the patent office, and attend to other duties. It decided later, however, to combine home affairs and foreign relations under a single department which it designated the Department of State. The duties of the Secretary of State regarding foreign affairs were to be whatever, in conformance to the Constitution, the President directed. President Washington wanted to hold himself above party or faction, and to secure as heads of the executive departments persons known to him and to the nation as possessing outstanding competence and fitness for their positions. He invited Thomas Jefferson to become the first Secretary of State. Jefferson preferred to remain as minister to France, but under Washington's gentle urging and the advice of his intimate friend, James Madison, he accepted the post.

RELATIONS WITH BRITAIN: THE NORTHWEST POSTS AND THE JAY TREATY

As soon as Jefferson took up his duties as Secretary of State, he was immediately faced with the necessity of finding some way to remove the British from the northwest posts. Not only did British garrisons occupy the posts, but British officers encouraged the Indians of the Northwest to resist the advance of American settlement. British agents intrigued with separatist movements in Kentucky and Vermont, and Britain continued to discriminate against American shipping. It was not until September, 1791, after Britain had been aroused over a threat of American economic retaliation, that a minister, George Hammond, was accredited to the American government. Hammond defended the British failure to comply with the treaty of peace primarily on the allegation that the United States had failed to fulfill its obligations with regard to Loyalists and debts to British creditors. In reply, Jefferson composed one of his most lengthy, carefully documented, skillfully argued, and competently written state papers. He had shown the draft of his paper to the Attorney General and to Hamilton, and had secured the hearty approval of Washington. Hammond was at a loss for an answer to Jefferson's note and sought the advice of Hamilton, with whom he had established close co-operation. According to the evidence supplied later by Hammond, Hamilton declared that Jefferson did not represent the views of Washington, and advised Hammond to disregard the Secretary of State. Hammond's account of this may not be accurate, but he made no attempt to answer Jefferson's note in detail and no progress was made during Jefferson's tenure of office with respect to British-American relations. Jefferson left the Department of State at the end of the year 1793.

Notwithstanding Hamilton's intrigues and Jefferson's resignation, a crisis was approaching in British-American relations by the beginning of 1794. In addition to the policy of Britain regarding the northwest posts and her continued discrimination against American trade and ships, there was added, particularly after the outbreak of her war with France in 1793, new violations of what the United States regarded as its rights on the seas—including the impressment of American seamen, the seizure of foodstuffs as contraband, and the capture of American vessels engaged in French colonial trade. As time passed, indignation against Britain grew among the people, and Congress was disposed at the very least to enact retaliatory economic measures against British trade. Although Washington was normally sympathetic to the Hamiltonian program, he was not indifferent to his duties, and he had set about establishing a military force in the Northwest capable of driving the British out if that should be necessary.

In this situation, Hamilton and his followers devised the plan of sending a special envoy to Britain in the hope of securing an accommodation that would avoid hostilities. Washington agreed, and John Jay was selected as the envoy. He stood high in Federalist circles, was an experienced diplomat, and represented the prestige of the nation since he was Chief Justice of the Supreme Court. Edmund Randolph, who had succeeded Jefferson as Secretary of State, was less influential than Hamilton in the formation of Jay's instructions. The instructions touched upon all the points of controversy between the United States and Great Britain, but, with the exception of a demand for the evacuation of American territory and a stipulation that nothing should be agreed upon contrary to American obligations under its treaties with France, Jay was given wide discretionary authority.

In several respects the time was opportune for the United States to secure a favorable settlement with Britain. Congress was willing to enact retaliatory economic measures against British trade. The European coalition against France was showing signs of weakness which might leave Britain to face France alone. Sweden and Denmark had formed, in March, 1794, the nucleus of a new Armed Neutrality which the United States could join and promote. A strong policy would have made the utmost use of these opportunities to bring pressure on Britain, but a strong policy might also lead to war with Britain, which the Federalists wished to avoid at virtually any cost. The result was a treaty entirely satisfactory to the British but disappointing to those in the United States who favored a stronger stand against British policies. Britain promised to evacuate the northwest posts, which she was obligated to do anyhow under the treaty of peace, but nothing was said about impressments, and the United States virtually abandoned, as far as Britain was concerned, the rights it had claimed regarding neutral commerce. Although a provision in the treaty prevented it from being in direct conflict with American obligations to France, the spirit of the treaty was hostile to the French alliance. Otherwise, the treaty was significant for the establishment of arbitral tribunals for the settlement of American-Canadian boundary problems, the dispute over prerevolutionary debts to British creditors, and American claims against Britain for illegal seizure of goods on the high seas. In this connection the treaty established a precedent in American foreign policy for one form of peaceful settlement of disputes.

When the provisions of the treaty became known in the United States, the Federalists defended it as the best settlement that could be effected at the time. The Republicans vigorously denounced it as a surrender to Britain and a disregard of France. After a sharp debate, the Senate gave its advice and consent to the ratification of the treaty, but Secretary Randolph opposed some provisions of the treaty and President Washington hesitated. The nation seethed with agitation from both sides. In this critical state of affairs, the President ratified the treaty, having decided that a new treaty more favorable to the United States could not be negotiated and that peace with Britain was the paramount national interest. Some historians have argued that since the treaty settled none of the major conflicts with Britain over maritime rights, and since it permitted Indians and citizens of both nations to trade without restriction across the American-Canadian border and thus enabled the Indians of the Northwest to secure arms from Canada, it contained the seeds of the War of 1812. Others have defended the treaty along Federalist lines, to the effect that a disastrous war with Britain might otherwise have occurred.

RELATIONS WITH SPAIN

In the years that followed the abortive negotiations with Spain during the Confederation, the United States had been unable to secure Spanish approval of its southern boundaries or its right to the free navigation of the Mississippi River, or to negotiate a trade agreement. Spain continued in its efforts to secure territory north of the boundary of West Florida, tried to make treaties with the Indians of the Southwest, and attempted to plant settlements in the disputed area where it retained frontier posts. Spain was playing, however, a losing game, for Americans were rapidly moving into the area, and the United States under the Constitution was gaining in the power to defend its territory and its rights. Spain decided to make peace, a decision which may have been influenced also by events in Europe.

Along with Great Britain, Prussia, Austria, and other states, Spain had been a member of a coalition against revolutionary France. The coalition was impressive in size but disunited, and France had not only defended its territory but had carried the war beyond its frontiers, among other places into northern Spain. When Prussia made a separate treaty with France early in 1795, Spain decided to follow the same policy. Spain may have realized that since it was no longer an ally of Britain in the European coalition, and since the Jay mission indicated a *rapprochement* between the United States and Britain, it would be isolated in case of hostilities with the United States. At any rate, it decided on peace and in the Treaty of San Lorenzo of 1795 agreed to virtually everything the United States requested. Spain accepted the 31st parallel as the northern boundary of West Florida, granted the free navigation of the Mississippi River along with the right of deposit below the Florida boundary, accepted American ideas of neutral rights, promised to prevent Indians in Florida from raiding American territory, and granted limited commercial privileges.

RELATIONS WITH FRANCE

The French hope of attracting a large portion of American trade which had formerly gone to Britain was largely unrealized. Notwithstanding the liberal terms of the Franco-American commercial treaty and, in contrast, the discrimination against American trade by Britain, American trade soon returned mainly to its prerevolutionary channels. The primary reasons for this were the availability of British credit, the ties of language and custom, and the industrial supremacy of Britain. From its beginning the French Revolution produced divided sentiments in the United States, but probably the majority of the people thought of the Revolution as a democratic movement. Moreover, French friendship and British hostility were fresh in their minds, and the French alliance was regarded as the cornerstone of American foreign policy. As soon, however, as the Revolution in France took a more radical turn after 1791, and when France became engaged in a war with Britain as well as with other European states, new problems arose: (1) the possibility that the United States might be drawn into the war through the French alliance, (2) questions regarding American neutral rights, and (3) the interest that the new French government developed in the recovery of some part of the former French empire.

Washington requested the views of his "cabinet" regarding American obligations under the alliance and the desirability of proclaiming neutrality. Hamilton argued that the alliance was no longer in effect because the French government with which it was made no longer existed. Jefferson could point out, however, that treaties were made with states not governments and that otherwise all American treaties would be void after each change in administration. Washington accepted this analysis, but agreed with Hamilton that the United States should proclaim its neutrality. Jefferson was as anxious for the United States to remain neutral as was Washington and Hamilton, but he opposed issuing a statement to that effect. His reasons were both legal and practical. Since Congress, he said, had the sole right to declare war, it also had the sole authority to declare neutrality. He believed also that a declaration of neutrality tended to favor Britain over France, but most of all that such a proclamation would deprive the United States of the opportunity to keep the two nations in suspense regarding American policy and to play one against the other with the prospect of securing concessions from both.

This debate was a part of a series of related events that took place between 1793 and 1796, which included the Jay mission to Britain, as noted earlier, the James Monroe mission to France to retain French friendship, the mission of Edmond Genêt from France to the United States, the Thomas Pinckney mission to Spain which resulted in the Treaty of San Lorenzo, and the Presidential election of 1796. During this time France played a devious as well as a complicated diplomatic game because her situation in Europe as well as in America was fluid. She did not want to invoke the American alliance if her action would drive the United States into the arms of Britain; she did not want to continue liberal trade arrangements with the United States if Britain were allowed to disregard American neutral rights; she wanted to use the United States as a base of operations against Spanish America if peace negotiations with Spain fell through; and, although she was seeking financial aid from the United States, she promoted American domestic dissension and intrigued with dissident elements on the southwestern frontier in the hope of securing a part of her former empire.

With these varied and somewhat contradictory objectives in mind, the first envoy of the new French Republic to the United States, Genêt, had both open and secret instructions. Jefferson was willing to use Genêt to further his own efforts in dealing with the activities of Spain on the southwestern frontier, but the French envoy overplayed his role of intrigue and his conduct became intolerable to Jefferson as well as to the Federalists, who were less well disposed toward France. As a result Genêt failed in every way. The United States secured his replacement, ratified the Jay Treaty with Britain, agreed to the Treaty of San Lorenzo with Spain, and remained firmly neutral in the European conflict.

Meanwhile, Monroe met with difficulties in France partly because the French government was dissatisfied with its failures in America, partly because Monroe was not kept fully informed of American negotiations with Britain, and partly because of his own indiscretion in expressing hostility to the Jay Treaty. He was quickly recalled, but France, now under the Directory, refused to receive his successor, severed relations with the United States, and

began the seizure of American ships in violation of treaty agreements. President Adams tried the expedient of sending a commission rather than a single envoy to France in the hope of restoring
friendly relations. The commission was not officially received by
the Directory, but its agents, later known in published despatches
as "Messrs. X, Y, and Z," indicated to the commission that it
would be received if it would offer a bribe to the Directory, would
arrange a loan from the United States to France, and would offer
an apology for some remarks about France made by President
Adams in a message to Congress. Since these terms were unacceptable to the commission and further negotiations proved futile,
diplomatic relations with France were not restored. With this
failure and the continuance of French seizures of American ships,
the United States Navy and armed merchantmen were authorized
by Congress to capture French armed vessels, including privateers,
that endangered American commerce. The "naval war" of 1798–
1800 that followed did not develop into a general conflict because
President Adams wanted to avoid that eventuality if possible and
because Franco-American diplomacy took a new turn with the rise
of Napoleon to power in France.

Napoleon desired peace with the United States because he was
still preoccupied with a war in Europe and was about to launch a
movement for the re-establishment of a French empire in America
through the restoration of French power in Santo Domingo and
the acquisition from Spain of Louisiana. Diplomatic negotiations
were initiated by France and eventually led to the treaty of 1800.
During the negotiations the United States sought compensation
for French spoliations of American commerce, the abandonment
of the Treaty of Alliance, and a new commercial treaty based on
the provisions of the treaty of 1778 but without special privilege
to France. France was willing to accept the American proposals
except for compensation; she was quick to point out the weakness
of the American position in wishing to annul the treaty it was
using as a basis for its claims, a treaty that Congress had already
declared void. In the end the United States gave up its claims for
damages in exchange for the annulment of the Treaty of Alliance
and a new commercial treaty. France, therefore, drove a hard

bargain, but looking back over his career in later years, Adams felt that the negotiation of the treaty of 1800, and thus possibly the avoidance of war with France, was perhaps his greatest service to his country.

WASHINGTON'S FAREWELL ADDRESS

Washington's Address to the nation near the end of his Administration is probably the most famous document of American foreign policy, comparable only with Monroe's message to Congress in 1823. Chronologically, of course, it preceded the Adams Administration, but philosophically it represented the foreign policy of the whole Federalist era. First printed in a Philadelphia newspaper on September 19, 1796, it announced Washington's intention not to seek a third term and stated his convictions concerning policies that should be followed in the national interest. Since 1796 many political leaders and commentators have used the Address for their own purposes, playing upon the great prestige of Washington and excising words or phrases to suit their contentions. Others have minimized the lasting significance of the Address by emphasizing its relationship to the contemporary problems and anxieties that weighed upon Washington's mind. Naturally it reflected the context of the times, but it was neither parochial nor ephemeral.

Washington advised the nation to avoid sectional and partisan discord, to obey federal law and support the Constitution, and to remedy any defects in either by changing the laws in the one case and by formal amendment in the other. He urged support of education and the safeguard of the public credit by using it sparingly. Eloquently he urged his countrymen to avoid involvement in the political affairs of Europe, whose primary interests, he felt, were alien to those of the United States. Security should be achieved by unity at home, *temporary* alliances whenever absolutely necessary, and the maintenance of a strong military position. He urged commerce and friendship with all nations on the basis of good faith and respect for treaties. He opposed "permanent inveterate antipathies" against some nations and "passionate attachments" with others where common interests might be imagined but did not exist in reality. Jefferson repeated much of Washington's advice in his first inaugural address, particularly when he warned against "entangling alliances," supported the public credit even more vigorously than Washington, and advocated orderly change in the laws or the Constitution.

IV

THE REALIZATION OF
INDEPENDENCE, 1801–1829

When Jefferson assumed the Presidency in 1801, he did not contemplate any radical change in American foreign policy. He ratified the treaty of 1800 with France, which had not reached its final stages under President Adams. Problems with Britain regarding trade, neutral rights, and impressments still existed, but Jefferson thought renewed efforts should be made to deal with these matters through the arts of diplomacy, and the prospect of success appeared greater after Britain and France made peace in 1802. Since relations with Spain and other European states were tranquil, Jefferson intended to give his primary attention to domestic affairs. Soon, however, a crisis arose over Louisiana, and within a month after that issue was settled, war broke out again between Britain and France which brought with it renewed violations by both nations of American rights on the seas. Foreign affairs occupied the remainder of Jefferson's Administration and nearly all of the Administration of James Madison. Difficulties developed with Spain over the Floridas, and scarcely had this problem been solved when the United States faced a possible challenge from Europe over the independence of Latin America. Although the Monroe Doctrine was issued in 1823, the United States did not feel free from European entanglements until well into the Administration of John Quincy Adams, which ended in March, 1829. Thus, it was almost three decades after 1800 before the United States could feel reasonably secure from European involvement.

THE LOUISIANA PURCHASE

In the territorial settlement following the French and Indian War, Britain acquired Spanish Florida and an adjoining coastal strip which had been a part of French Louisiana. This strip extended from the western Florida boundary, the Perdido River, to the Iberville River and a chain of lakes that formed the eastern boundary of the "island" of New Orleans. The northern boundary of this former French area was fixed by Britain in 1763 at the 31st degree of north latitude, and the area was named West Florida. This designation will be used hereafter in discussing the complications that arose under subsequent treaties in which substantially the same area became involved. At the same time that Britain acquired the Floridas, Spain received New Orleans and all of French Louisiana west of the Mississippi River. Later, at the end of the American Revolution, Spain recovered her former colony of Florida and secured also West Florida. As noted earlier, Spain hoped to extend the boundary of West Florida northward, but agreed, in the Treaty of San Lorenzo (1795), to the 31st degree of north latitude, and agreed also to the free navigation of the Mississippi River by the United States.

Spain believed that the Floridas and Louisiana would form a buffer against the possible expansionist tendencies of the new American republic, but soon became disillusioned with this prospect as far as it related to Louisiana. Few Spanish settlers moved into the area, it proved to be an economic liability rather than an asset, and Spain realized it could probably not be held by force if the United States decided to seize it. Spain was predisposed, therefore, to accept the French argument that Louisiana would be more of a buffer against the United States in the hands of France. Induced by this reasoning and the promise of territorial compensation elsewhere, Spain agreed to restore Louisiana to France. The promise of restoration was made in a secret treaty signed by Spain the day following the conclusion of the Franco-American treaty

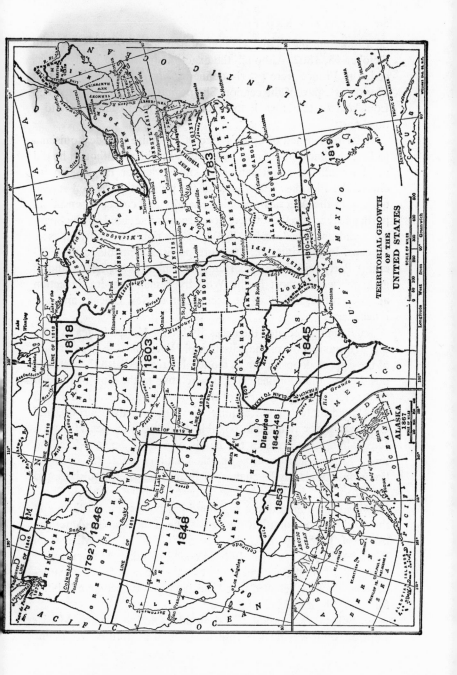

TERRITORIAL GROWTH
OF THE
UNITED STATES

of 1800, but the actual cession of the area was delayed until October 15, 1802. Although the exact boundaries of Louisiana as ceded to France were poorly defined, France did not claim West Florida as a part of the cession. She promised Spain either to keep Louisiana or to return it to Spain and never to alienate it to a third party.

Jefferson learned of Spain's "secret" promise to cede Louisiana to France almost as soon as he became President, although he did not have official confirmation or know whether the cession included the Floridas. Knowledge of the prospective cession spread quickly to the American people generally and caused a sensation, particularly in the West where concern was increased by the Spanish withdrawal, in October, 1802, of the right of deposit at New Orleans. In this situation, the more partisan elements in the Federalist Party seized the opportunity to embarrass Jefferson and to gain political support in the West by demanding drastic action against France, including the occupation of New Orleans and war if necessary.

Jefferson appreciated the necessity for the United States to have the free navigation of the Mississippi River and the convenience of the right of deposit near its mouth. He realized also the strategic positions of the Floridas and Cuba relative to the Gulf of Mexico and therefore to the security of the Mississippi outlet. He believed the United States should acquire New Orleans, the Floridas, and Cuba whenever it became possible to do so in a peaceful way. Meanwhile these areas in the hands of a weak Spain offered no threat to American security or other national interest. The situation would obviously be changed if France acquired Louisiana and the Floridas. She already had a base in the Caribbean, Santo Domingo; she might desire to extend her possessions further; and she would not be bound by the provisions of the Spanish-American treaty of 1795 regarding the free navigation of the Mississippi River. Although Jefferson fully intended to take whatever action was needed in the national interest, he did not become panic-stricken since he believed that Louisiana would become a liability for France as it had been for Spain.

In Jefferson's opinion the desirable solution for the Mississippi question was for the United States to acquire New Orleans and the Floridas. In this way American interests would be secured and the need for any further expansion involving Cuba or the remainder of Louisiana could be met when the need arose. Since he thought time was on the side of the United States, he did not think the desired areas should be seized, thus provoking war, provided France would agree to American navigation of the Mississippi on the same terms formerly accepted by Spain. If France refused this minimum request, Jefferson was willing to make an alliance with Britain and to use force against France if necessary. First, however, all possible diplomatic pressure on France and Spain should be attempted, and he sent James Monroe as a special envoy, accredited to both nations, to indicate the gravity with which the United States viewed the matter.

Napoleon's reasons for deciding to sell all of Louisiana to the United States will probably always remain in doubt. The decision to sell was made arbitrarily and personally by Napoleon without the approval of his ministers or previous consultation with the Chamber of Deputies. He may have been influenced by his distrust of the French Navy's ability to protect overseas possessions, his disappointment over the difficulties of establishing French authority in Santo Domingo, his strong predisposition to be more interested in spreading French influence in the Middle East than in the American hemisphere, or by his desire to renew hostilities against Great Britain. If the latter was the primary factor, Jefferson's strong diplomacy in threatening an alliance with Britain, and Napoleon's realization that France could not hold Louisiana against the United States while waging war with Britain, may have been decisive. At any rate, the offer was made and quickly accepted by the American envoys in France, and the purchase price of $15,000,000 was agreed upon.

Jefferson approved the action of his envoys although they had not been authorized to purchase all of Louisiana. The Secretary of State, James Madison, approved, as did all the Cabinet, and Congress was willing to do its part in bringing the treaty of cession into effect. Jefferson was disturbed, however, over the constitutionality of such an acquisition of territory. He made a distinction apparently between acquiring a small area or a place of great strategic importance, such as New Orleans, and the addition of an area as vast as Louisiana, equal in extent to the original United States and destined to provide new states to the Federal Union, thus altering the relative political position of existing states. No provision of the Constitution explicitly authorized such an act, and Jefferson felt that the great principle of strict construction of the Constitution should be adhered to, and would be promoted in its lasting effect if it were applied in this important instance. He favored, therefore, a constitutional amendment conferring on the federal government the right to acquire territory. All of his principal political advisers opposed this policy. They feared the opposition of those Federalist Party members who wanted Louisiana to remain permanently a dependency rather than an integral part of the United States as the treaty of cession provided; these Federalists might be able to prevent or postpone the acceptance of the amendment by the necessary number of states, and such delay might thwart the great opportunity the treaty provided. Some of his advisers were less strict constructionists than Jefferson and professed to see a clear constitutional sanction for the purchase. Under these pressures, Jefferson gave in, although the argument of expedience prevailed in his mind over that of constitutional legality.

The only remaining problem was to discover the exact extent of territory included in the treaty of cession, for it did not contain a detailed description of the boundaries of Louisiana. The area was the same as that which Spain had retroceded to France and which in turn France ceded to the United States. France described the area by quoting from the Spanish treaty of retrocession, namely:

> . . . with the same extent it now has in the hands of Spain, and that it had when France possessed it; and such as it should be after the treaties subsequently entered into between Spain and other states.

After considering this wording, the American envoys in France decided that West Florida was included, and although they were probably not aware of it, Spain had considered West Florida as a part of Louisiana. Certainly West Florida was a part of Louisiana as France possessed it. Thus, if the United States acquired what

France had possessed and what Spain held as Louisiana, West Florida was included in the Louisiana cession. The question then was whether the last part of the description provided a problem. The only treaties that Spain had entered into which might have a bearing on the subject were those with Great Britain, the United States, and France. Since the treaties with the United States and Great Britain provided no ambiguities or contradictions, the only relevant treaty was that of San Ildefonso (1800). This was the treaty of retrocession of Louisiana from Spain to France and the description of Louisiana as quoted above in the treaty cession from France to the United States was lifted almost verbatim from the Treaty of San Ildefonso. This treaty, therefore, could not logically have been one of the treaties "subsequently" entered into. But if by hypothesis it could be included, it did not exclude West Florida from the Louisiana cession.

For these reasons the description of Louisiana in the treaty of cession was not necessarily ambiguous. Based on the text of the treaty, the United States had an excellent claim to West Florida. The issue became clouded by Spain's denial that West Florida was included in the retrocession treaty, and by the decision of France not to claim the area although it intended to claim that Louisiana extended on the southwest to the Rio Grande River. Neither Napoleon nor his ministers would clarify what they thought the treaty of cession meant regarding West Florida. Jefferson believed that West Florida was included in the Louisiana Purchase and was probably willing to occupy the area if no peaceful agreement with Spain could be reached, but he preferred to purchase the area twice, so to speak, once from France and once from Spain, rather than to quarrel with Spain, from whom he hoped to acquire East Florida, or to resort to force.

Jefferson pursued his conciliatory policy until the end of his Administration. Congress passed the Mobile Act in 1804 authorizing the establishment of a customs district for Mobile, but Jefferson established the port of entry on the Mobile River north of the disputed area, avoided conflict, and permitted Spain to retain nominal control of Florida with small garrisons at Mobile and Baton Rouge. He was unable to effect an agreement with Spain before its government was overthrown in 1808 by Napoleon, who did not want a settlement of the Spanish-American question. After 1808, when Spain was in disorder at home and her American empire in revolt, the United States could have pursued a "large policy" and could have taken Cuba, Florida, or any other area of the Spanish-American empire it desired. Neither Jefferson nor Madison contemplated such a large policy, but soon after Madison became President, he was faced with the necessity for a decision concerning West Florida. American settlers had been going into the area, particularly into the section around Baton Rouge. Late in 1810 they overthrew the weak Spanish government there and requested the United States to assume control. The United States did not want to restore by force a government which it held had no legal right to be there, nor did she want to permit the West Florida question longer to remain undecided. Consequently Congress added a part of the area to the State of Louisiana and most of the remainder to the Territory of Mississippi. A settlement, however, of the whole Florida question with Spain was not reached until 1819.

THE FREEDOM OF THE SEAS

As noted earlier, one of the main objectives of American foreign policy after the Revolution was the negotiation of a satisfactory commercial treaty with Great Britain which would include provisions covering the rights of neutrals on the high seas. This objective had not been accomplished in the Jay Treaty and remained unfulfilled at the time Jefferson became President. Jefferson let the matter drift for a time, partly because the need was less urgent during a temporary peace between Britain and France and partly because he was preoccupied with the Louisiana question. The need for a treaty became more urgent after Britain and France renewed hostilities in 1803. Britain and the United States were at odds regarding virtually every principle advocated by the United States regarding its neutral rights. These involved the definition of contraband and blockade, the right of Great Britain to seize American ships trading with French colonial ports, and the doctrine of "free ships, free goods," namely, that noncontraband goods could not be seized by a belligerent on a neutral ship, that the flag, so to speak, covered the goods.

On this matter the British would not budge, although their negotiators were willing to make vague promises that British officers would exercise greater discretion in distinguishing between British and American nationals. The American negotiators, contrary to their instructions, signed a treaty that did not deal with the basic issue and which Jefferson would not accept. Although negotiations continued, new events muddied further the waters of British-American relations, and led eventually to Jefferson's experiment with economic pressure.

One of the new factors in the situation was the famous *Chesapeake-Leopard* affair, which aroused anti-British feeling in the United States to a greater degree than at any time since the Jay Treaty or, as some people thought, since the Battle of Lexington. The American frigate *Chesapeake,* which had sailed from Norfolk on June 22, 1807, for the Mediterranean station, was not expecting trouble and was not prepared for action when it was fired on by the British frigate *Leopard* for refusing to permit its crew to be searched for British deserters. Twenty-one of the *Chesapeake*'s crew were killed or wounded and four were impressed as alleged British subjects, two of whom were later proven to be American-born citizens. Jefferson immediately ordered all British ships out of American waters, put into effect a Non-Importation Act which Congress had authorized earlier, and almost certainly could have had war if he had called Congress into immediate session and requested it. Instead he summoned Congress to meet after the first heat of resentment against Britain had cooled, and proposed the Embargo.

Meanwhile other events besides the *Chesapeake* affair and the failure of diplomacy had led Jefferson to this decision. Beginning in 1806, Great Britain and France had issued a series of decrees and counter-decrees that had the effect of subjecting any American merchant ship to capture that attempted to enter a British or European port. Theoretically the decrees were aimed by the belligerents against each other, but they worked a major hardship against the United States. Since the sea power of France and her allies was weak after Trafalgar, American merchants could have traded with Britain without much danger from France if the United States had been willing to ignore impressment and other

British violations of American maritime rights. This was what many American merchants and leaders of the Federalist Party desired. Jefferson was not tempted. He realized that Britain was the principal cause of American maritime troubles and believed the situation offered so much opportunity for the exercise of sufficient economic pressure—peaceful coercion—that Britain would feel obliged to abandon her arrogant practices on the seas as a lesser evil than the economic distress which the pressure produced.

Several considerations appeared to support this view. If Britain was already under considerable economic strain because of the war, if France could actually close Europe to British commerce under the so-called Continental System, and if the United States would then cut Britain off from its major source of supply from the Western Hemisphere, British distress might soon become intolerable. The idea that economic pressure might be a substitute for war, when diplomacy based on reason and justice had failed, had long been held by Jefferson, and Congress was willing to support his view. An embargo on all American foreign trade might be onerous, but it would be much less damaging both to life and property than war. Accordingly, in December, 1807, Congress closed American ports to all foreign ships for the purpose of carrying American goods abroad and restricted all American ships to the American coastwise trade, thus in theory depriving Britain and France of all American goods, markets, and shipping services.

The Embargo failed for a number of reasons which could not be clearly foreseen at the time of its enactment. The least of these, but the most humiliating from the standpoint of American patriotism, was the successful evasion of the law by American traders who managed to smuggle goods out of the country by sea or to transport them across the Canadian border. As originally enacted, the law contained loopholes that permitted some trade with Europe. Although Congress eventually closed most of the gaps in its enforcement, compliance with the law was never absolute, particularly in New England, where hostility to the law reached almost to the point of rebellion and secession.

More important was the fact that the Continental System, which Napoleon had boasted would absolutely seal Europe against

British trade, leaked like a sieve, partly through smuggling but mostly by connivance between the avowed belligerents. Soon after Napoleon invaded Spain, Spanish colonial ports were opened to British trade, and almost at the same time Portuguese colonial ports were opened also. Britain was unusually fortunate in having an excellent food crop during the summer of 1808 when the Embargo was at its height. In addition to these factors, the people in Britain who were most quickly affected by food shortages and other economic pressures were the poorer classes who had the least voice in the government, while the shipping interests thrived on the absence of American competition, and the Admiralty, which was the main stronghold for the policy of impressment, held firm against concessions to the United States.

Notwithstanding these facts, the Embargo caused real hardship in Britain and might have been successful if it had been continued for another year or two. There was much support for the Embargo in the nation, and Jefferson's party was successful in the election of 1808, Madison being elected to the Presidency. It was notable also that the agricultural areas of the South and West that suffered the most distress from the Embargo gave Jefferson his greatest support, while the maritime and industrial areas that suffered less made the greatest complaint. The reasons were as much political as economic in both cases, for the opposition to the Embargo came mainly from the Federalists who had opposed it from the beginning. This group denounced enforcement measures, defended Britain as the champion of freedom against the tyranny of Napoleon, while their extreme leaders advised the British not to give in to the United States and, as noted earlier, talked of rebellion. The results of this agitation, the growing economic pinch which the Embargo entailed, and its failure to secure quick results combined to cause its repeal at the end of Jefferson's Administration. Congress enacted in its place the Non-Intercourse Act, which prohibited trade with France and Great Britain, thus continuing a measure of economic pressure while avoiding the appearance of surrendering the principle of the Embargo. Since American goods could reach these countries through indirect channels, however, the act was a partial victory for those who opposed the more complete restriction or any restriction of trade with Britain.

President Madison, like Jefferson, believed that the violation of American rights on the seas should not be endured indefinitely and was probably ready for war whenever it was clear that negotiation and economic pressure had reached the limits of their effectiveness. He was willing, however, as Congress virtually forced him to be, to give the Non-Intercourse Act a trial, and for a time during the summer of 1809 it appeared that economic pressure had been at least partially successful against Great Britain. The British government sent a new minister to the United States, David M. Erskine, with instructions to withdraw under certain clearly specified conditions the British decrees of 1807 inimical to American neutral commerce, and, if agreement was reached, to put it into effect without referring back to the British government for approval. The issue of impressment was not included in Erskine's instructions, but Madison had been authorized by Congress to revoke the Non-Intercourse Act against either France or Britain in case either one or both ceased to violate American neutral commerce. Under these circumstances negotiations were undertaken with Erskine, and an agreement was reached involving the mutual revocation of restrictive decrees, including a date for the agreement to go into effect. On that date American ships were to be released for British trade.

The agreement was a complete fiasco, damaged relations between the two nations, and proved to be the last real opportunity for a peaceful settlement. Erskine's instructions allowed him the "liberty" of communicating to the American government *in extenso* the exact conditions under which he was given the authority to revoke the British decrees, but they did not require him to make such a communication and he decided against it. He thought the agreement was within the spirit of his instructions, satisfied British as well as American desires, promoted peace, and would be acceptable to the British government. Madison thought the same, for he supposed that in signing the agreement and setting a date for it to become effective, Erskine had acted in complete accord with his authority. Such was not the case. The instructions required Erskine, before he could sign an agreement, to secure from the United States a specific recognition of the British right to interfere with American neutral commerce in ways the United States would not accept, and also to secure an American promise to retain its restrictions on trade with France no matter what France did in removing its obnoxious decrees, a promise that Madison was prohibited by Congress from making. The British government not only denounced the agreement, but seized also some of the American ships that had been released by the United States when it supposed the agreement was valid.

Erskine was recalled and replaced by a minister less friendly to the United States, who accused the American government of knowing the precise instructions of Erskine and of connivance with him in evading them in the agreement. When the minister repeated these charges after being admonished of their falsity, Madison refused to have further negotiations with him and he soon returned home. The American minister in London returned home also, leaving the two nations on the eve of the war without high-level channels of communication. Meanwhile Congress tried an oblique approach to economic pressure by passing Macon's Bill No. 2, which removed the restrictions under the Non-Intercourse Act but provided that if either France or Britain removed its interference with American neutral commerce, nonintercourse should be resumed with the other. Almost immediately France pretended to remove its restrictions and, believing this had been done, the United States restored the interdict on trade with Britain. As American patience ran out, grievances against France were not fully eliminated, but Britain remained the principal offender against American commerce and the sole offender regarding impressments. War or surrender to British violations of American rights on the seas seemed to be the only alternatives.

While these events were taking place in Congress and in diplomacy, other causes arose in the United States for a warlike sentiment against Great Britain. The advance of American settlement in the Northwest was meeting increasing resistance from the Indians, and the belief grew in that area that the British in Canada were supplying the Indians with arms and were encouraging them to oppose further land concessions to settlers. As a result, the conquest of Canada was advocated primarily as a means of dealing with the Indian problem. In the South some people thought a war with Britain would give the United States an excuse and an opportunity to secure East Florida. It is very difficult to estimate the relative importance of the so-called expansionist movement, for the people of the West and South had other reasons for developing a warlike attitude. They had a strong sense of individualism and apparently for this reason a greater antipathy against impressments than was manifest along the Atlantic seaboard where seamen were not held in high esteem. In addition, these areas had suffered economic distress, along with other parts of the nation, from the various acts restricting American commerce. It seems probable that the influence of the expansionist factor as a determinant for war could easily be overestimated. Congressmen from the West and South did not provide more than one third of the votes for war in the House of Representatives, while Congressmen from north of the Delaware River provided a majority of such votes. By the time Congress met in 1812, a majority of its leaders were ready to support a declaration of war as a consequence of their belief that for a long time Britain had in effect been making war on the United States. President Madison had arrived at the same decision.

One of the ironies of the War of 1812 was that, unknown to Congress, the British were preparing the revocation of the decrees of 1807 just at this time, the orders being revoked just five days after the declaration of war. This resulted from long-standing hostility on the part of some British leaders to the restrictive decrees against American commerce, the economic strain imposed on Britain by the war in Europe, the effect of American economic pressure and the knowledge that the United States was moving toward war, and the apparent belief that American hostility was derived more from British policies concerning commerce than from impressment. Since the vote for war in the Senate was by a small majority, it is possible that war might have been avoided if the British action had been known earlier, but this must remain purely speculative. The reasons for supposing that delay in declaring war would have prevented it are no more impressive than the reasons that would indicate a different conclusion. Britain thought the United States might be willing to reconsider its war policy as soon as it knew the decrees had been revoked, and the United States thought Britain might reconsider its impressment policies when it was faced with actual hostilities. Neither idea was valid and in the end, therefore, as in the beginning, impressment was the fundamental issue in the conflict.

In the same year that war was declared, negotiations for peace had a feeble beginning in an offer of mediation by Britain's new ally, Russia. Believing that Britain approved this offer, Madison accepted. It turned out that Britain had not approved Russian mediation, but the British Foreign Secretary, Lord Castlereagh, desired peace and proposed direct negotiations. Again the United States accepted, and after many delays discussions between representatives of both nations were begun at Ghent in August, 1814, and lasted until a treaty of peace was signed late in December of the same year. From the beginning Britain negotiated from a position of strength. The war in Europe had temporarily ended with the first overthrow of Napoleon, and Britain was able to send seasoned veterans to America. A British army was being prepared in Canada to invade the United States from the north, while an expedition of large proportions was making ready to invade from the south at New Orleans. The Spanish King, Ferdinand VII, now restored, was requesting Britain to secure for Spain the return of West Florida and Louisiana, and Canadians thought of extending their domain into the Mississippi Valley. Britain's demands reflected her confident attitude, and included cessions to Britain of various segments of territory along the American northern border, the creation of an Indian buffer territory out of the American Northwest, and the recognition of British maritime policies. The United States rejected all the British demands and in turn demanded that Britain agree to abandon impressments.

For a time no prospect of agreement seemed possible, but gradually conditions changed and both sides began to retreat until peace was made with neither side securing its original position. Britain was influenced by the known desire for peace among the war-weary British people, the success of the United States on the Great Lakes and on Lake Champlain, the depleted condition of the British treasury, and some uneasiness over conditions in

France and at the Congress of Vienna, where the peace of Europe was being arranged. The British government authorized the acceptance of a treaty, agreed to by the United States, without waiting to know the fate of its expedition to New Orleans. On the American side, Madison was influenced by the prospect that peace in Europe would terminate interference with American commerce and would end any excuse Britain had for impressments. The willingness of Britain to withdraw all of her original and somewhat arrogant demands indicated to Madison that Britain did not intend to pursue her past policies with respect to American rights on the seas, although she might not be willing for political and prestige reasons to renounce its alleged rights. The military position of the United States remained weak even though the invasion from the north had been delayed, and the internal unity of the United States in promoting the war had been progressively eroded by New England Federalists whose extreme elements threatened secession. Added to these factors was Britain's apparent willingness, brought out in the negotiations, to establish arbitral commissions to settle Canadian-American boundary problems, to agree to treaties on commerce and fisheries, and to accept a mutual limitation of armaments on the Great Lakes. The treaty that was possible, therefore, would represent peace with honor to the United States if not with complete victory. The opponents of the war soon passed for the most part into political obscurity; its supporters believed it was a second war of independence.

To a considerable extent the contemporary controversy over the justification for the War of 1812 has been reflected among writers and historians who have attempted to evaluate it. One side has characterized it as a needless war, ended by a treaty which settled nothing. This side argues, in addition, that the policies of Jefferson and Madison aided the dictator Napoleon when Britain, the natural ally of the United States, was defending democratic principles, and that although American defense of the freedom of the seas had merit, the American contentions were not established rights under international law. On the other side, the war has been justified for reasons stated by Jefferson and Madison, and emphasis is given to facts or events which were either the direct or indirect result of it.

Britain never again impressed American seamen. The boundary commissions provided for by the treaty of peace settled some boundary problems and continued the precedent set by the Jay Treaty for this type of peaceful settlement. An Anglo-American treaty of commerce was concluded, and a treaty limiting armaments on the Great Lakes was the first step in making the American-Canadian border the "unguarded frontier" which has been the pride of both nations. In addition, British intrigue with American Indians was broken forever. The defeat of the British at New Orleans and the peace settlement ended the hopes of Spain for the recovery of West Florida and Louisiana, and contributed indirectly to the Spanish-American treaty of 1819, under which the United States acquired East Florida, a satisfactory western boundary between Louisiana and Mexico, and whatever rights Spain had to the Oregon Country. The war brought about the death if not the burial of the Federalist Party, and, for a time at least, promoted in the minds of the American people a sense of national unity and pride. Perhaps all these claims for advantages gained by the war cannot be traced directly to it and are not wholly justified, but neither is the view that the war was a failure and settled nothing.

LATIN AMERICA AND THE MONROE DOCTRINE

After the War of 1812, the United States concerned itself mainly with domestic affairs. The war had revealed defects in the national structure, in its highly decentralized banking system, weak military establishment, lack of good roads, and dependence on Europe for manufactured goods. In the wave of nationalism produced by the war, constructive measures were taken to remedy these limitations. Madison's Secretary of State, James Monroe, followed him in the Presidency, John Quincy Adams became Secretary of State, and the nation settled into what has been called "the era of good feeling." Monroe was re-elected in 1820 almost without a dissenting vote in the electoral college.

The calm in foreign relations was disturbed during the latter part of Monroe's Administration by developments growing out of the revolutions against Spain in Latin America and the possibility that European powers might attempt to assist Spain to recover her colonial empire. The revolts in Spanish America had deep roots of discontent with Spain's rule and misrule, and were influenced by the examples of the American and French revolutions and the philosophical ideas that characterized them, but the occasion for the revolts was the overthrow of the Spanish monarchy by Napoleon. This left the Spanish colonies with the options of accepting French authority, of remaining loyal to local Spanish rulers who were disliked, of establishing temporary governments pending the possible restoration of Ferdinand VII, or of deciding on complete independence. Gradually and through many vicissitudes, heroic struggles, victories and defeats, the colonies chose and achieved independence. During this time the United States was preoccupied with maritime rights, the War of 1812, and subsequent negotiations with the restored Spanish monarchy over the Floridas and the western boundary of Louisiana. It gave Latin-American movements for independence no official assistance, but the enforcement of United States neutrality laws was sufficiently lax that goods and military supplies often reached the revolutionary governments through individual American initiative.

These new governments achieved some regional military co-operation in their struggle against Spain, but their revolts did not begin or end at the same time, and they did not attempt general political unity. As a result, independence was gained singly and at different times. The United States observed these movements with sympathy and was disposed to recognize as independent new Latin-American states as soon as their governments had authority over their areas, a reasonable prospect of permanence, and the support of a majority of their people. Such a policy was in keeping with the American revolutionary doctrine. By 1818, Monroe was ready to consider the recognition of states that met these conditions, but he proceeded with caution and preferred to act in co-operation or in concert with the principal European nations. He found, however, no favorable response in Europe, and reached the decision early in 1822 to act independently. This decision was the product of several factors that also contributed to the Monroe Doctrine.

The extremes of the French Revolution in its later stages and the long wars with Napoleon produced in Europe a temporary reaction against whatever tendencies had existed earlier toward more responsible and democratic governments. This reaction was observed in the United States and gave impetus to an idea which already existed, namely, that the United States—and, in view of the Latin-American revolutions, probably the Western Hemisphere—was moving in the direction of political and social liberalism in contrast to the political systems of Europe. Secretary of State John Quincy Adams stated the idea bluntly and clearly in his reply to an invitation from Russia to the United States to adhere to the Holy Alliance. This "alliance" consisted only in an agreement to a statement of benevolent principles, but the United States refused the Tsar's invitation. Secretary Adams, in replying to the Tsar, said the United States approved the principles of the alliance and would observe them, but "for the repose of Europe as well as America, the American and European systems should be kept as separate and distinct from each other as possible." The same concept had been expressed by Washington, Jefferson, and others, and was emphasized by Henry Clay in 1821, when he said the Americas should be a "counterpoise" to the alliance of European powers.

Although the British government was relatively conservative following the Napoleonic Wars and Britain was a member of the European concert of powers, she did not fully share the desires of some of these powers to intervene in the affairs of other states in order to preserve what was called the principle of legitimacy— the rule of hereditary or existing governments—and particularly did not approve European assistance to Spain to recover her American empire. When a movement in this direction seemed to be developing in Europe, the British government suggested to the United States in August, 1823, the issuance of a joint declaration of policy concerning Latin America. The proposed declaration expressed the view that Spain would be unable to recover its colonies although it should be given the opportunity to do so by "amicable negotiation," that Britain and the United States did not desire possession of any portion of them, but would not observe "with indifference" the transfer of any part of them to any other European power. The recognition of them as independent states should be left to "time and circumstance." The American minister in London, Richard Rush, was willing to agree to this declaration if the provision concerning recognition were removed, but when the British government was unwilling to make this change, he referred the question to his superiors at home. Obviously the minister could not agree to a statement on recognition contrary to a policy already adopted by the United States.

President Monroe and the majority of his Cabinet shared the views of the American minister to Britain, and they were approved also by ex-Presidents Jefferson and Madison, whose opinions were sought by Monroe. There should be no objection, it was thought, to a joint statement with Britain if the statement conformed to what was already *American policy*. On the contrary, British adherence to American policy concerning Latin America would greatly strengthen it among the governments of Europe. Secretary Adams believed, however, that if any statement were issued by the United States concerning the danger of European intervention in Latin America, it should be issued independently rather than jointly with Britain. Since the discussion of this issue had been prolonged and the time had come for Congress to meet, in December, 1823, Monroe adopted a dual policy. He decided to issue an independent statement on Latin America in his message to Congress and at the same time to permit his minister in London to issue a joint statement with Britain on essentially the same terms the minister had proposed before. Meanwhile the British government had become impatient of American delay regarding a joint statement, had sent a memorandum to France opposing European interference in Latin America, and thereafter indicated no interest in a joint statement with the United States.

In his message to Congress, Monroe was concerned also with another matter involving the Western Hemisphere. The United States had acquired, in the Spanish-American treaty of 1819, whatever rights Spain possessed to the territory west of the Rocky Mountains and north of the 42nd degree of north latitude with the northern boundary of this area, known as the Oregon Country, undefined. Britain had claims to a northern portion of this area and had agreed in a treaty with the United States that the na-

tionals of both nations could enter any part of the territory pending a boundary settlement. At the same time, the southern
boundary of Russian Alaska had not been agreed upon, and by
1821 Russia had shown a disposition to expand its territorial
claims southward along the Pacific Coast. Being concerned about
this matter as well as about Latin America, Monroe included both
problems in his message to Congress of December 2, 1823, and
since he made his reference to Russian expansion indirectly, and
in broad terms which included other European states, it has become customary to link both statements to form one policy, the
Monroe Doctrine.

Regarding the expansion of European nations in the Western
Hemisphere, Monroe asserted "as a principle in which the rights
and interests of the United States are involved," that the American continents were no longer "subjects for future colonization
by any European powers." The reference to Latin America was
more extensive, and its full force and meaning are not easily
conveyed through brief analysis. Monroe made it clear, however,
that the "political system" of the European powers as shown in
their governments was "essentially different" from that of America, and that any attempt on their part to extend their system to
any portion of the Western Hemisphere would be considered
"dangerous" to the peace and safety of the United States, and that
any attempt of Europe to oppress or to control the destiny of any
Latin-American state whose independence had been recognized
by the United States would be considered by the latter as un-
friendly and would not be regarded with indifference. The United
States, Monroe said, had not taken part and did not intend to take
part in the wars of European states "in matters relating to themselves" or to interfere in their "internal concerns," and would
recognize their *de facto* governments as legitimate, but in the
Western Hemisphere the circumstances were "eminently and conspicuously different."

The Monroe Doctrine was not put to the test by European
powers, and Congress was not put to the test of implementing it.
When the Republic of Colombia asked the United States what it
intended to do if Europe intervened in Latin America, the
American government gave an evasive answer but indicated it

would act in co-operation with Great Britain on the basis of prior agreement. After John Quincy Adams had succeeded Monroe in the Presidency, an attempt was made by Latin-American states, at a meeting in Panama, to form a defensive military alliance. Britain and the United States were invited to the conference. Adams hoped the conference could be persuaded to issue a declaration proclaiming the principles of the Monroe Doctrine and liberal principles of the freedom of the seas and of commercial reciprocity. In this way the concept of inter-American consultation and solidarity would be tacitly established. This hope did not materialize at the conference, but it formed the germ of an idea that later grew into reality. The Monroe Doctrine, however, had been declared, was destined to become the most cherished instrument of American foreign policy, and in the sense that it affirmed the inherent right of American self-defense has never been abandoned.

V

THE DIPLOMACY OF TERRITORIAL
AND COMMERCIAL EXPANSION

THE FOREIGN POLICIES of the United States from the beginning of
the Administration of Andrew Jackson in 1829 to the Civil War
were characterized by the settlement of boundary problems along
the Canadian border, territorial expansion to the Pacific Coast and
trade expansion to the Orient, the growth of American concern
over events in the Caribbean area, and the extension of foreign
commerce. With the minor exception of some of the boundary
problems, these areas of activity formed either a sequence of
events or in other ways were connected. The movement of American settlers into Texas led eventually to its separation from
Mexico and its annexation to the United States. This prompted the
Mexican War and quickened the acquisition of California, which
in turn gave an impetus to trade expansion in the Pacific with
its relationship to American policies in the Far East. The establishment of the United States on the Pacific Coast increased the desire for a canal across Central America and created greater concern over events in the Caribbean area. All of these items were
connected with vehemently controversial domestic issues, including the building of a transcontinental railroad, the admission
of new states and the government of territories, and the increasing

sectional conflict over slavery. The era was one of great social economic, and political change along with rapid expansion.

THE NORTHERN BOUNDARY OF THE UNITED STATES

Problems over the northern boundary of the United States arose as a result either of inaccurate geographical knowledge or inexact description of the boundaries in treaties that defined them. These problems extended over almost a century, from 1784 until 1872, and caused extensive negotiation, but, with one small exception, were settled peacefully by new treaties or by arbitration. The possible exception was the Aroostook War, a bloodless controversy in 1839 between rival claimants to territory along the Maine border, which ended in a truce until a settlement could be effected. The boundary drawn in the treaty of 1783 was often called a "water boundary" because the greater part of it ran through rivers and lakes. Beginning at the mouth of the St. Croix River, the boundary was to be the mid-channel of that river to its "source," and thence by a straight line to the highlands that separated the waters flowing into the Atlantic Ocean from those flowing into the St. Lawrence River. It was to follow the highlands to the "northwestern-most head" of the Connecticut River and along its mid-channel to the 45th degree of north latitude, thence to the St. Lawrence River and through its mid-channel to Lake Ontario. From there the boundary was to run through the middle of the Great Lakes and their connecting water passages, through rivers and lakes to the northwestern-most point of the Lake of the Woods, and thence in a straight line due west to the Mississippi River. Difficulties arose immediately over this description of the boundary. No river was known locally as the St. Croix, and after that was located, agreement had to be reached concerning which one of its branches led to its "source." It was difficult to follow the "highlands" indicated unless it was known where they ended, that is, on what branch of the Connecticut River was its "northwestern-most head." Surveys that were relied upon as determining the 45th degree of north latitude were inaccurate, and the United States erected a fort which later proved to be north of the correct line. Various water routes suited the description of the boundary from Lake Superior to the Lake of the Woods, and to complete the comedy of errors, the line due west from the northwest corner of that lake did not intersect the Mississippi River.

The latter problem was settled in 1818 by a treaty between the United States and Great Britain which placed the boundary along the 49th degree of north latitude from the Lake of the Woods to the "Stoney Mountains." Other portions of the boundary were agreed upon from time to time by commissions established by the Jay Treaty of 1794 and the Treaty of Ghent of 1814, but two sections caused serious controversies and remained unsettled until the Webster-Ashburton Treaty of 1842. Under that treaty, agreements were reached that were favorable to American claims in the area between Lake Superior and the Lake of the Woods but unfavorable along the border of Maine. It seems probable that Webster could have secured a larger portion of the area in dispute along the Maine border if he had been more diligent in searching for favorable evidence. The treaty, however, was the last step in establishing the boundary of the United States from the mouth of the St. Croix River to the Rocky Mountains. The United States and Great Britain created an International Boundary Commission in 1908 which made an elaborate survey of the boundary, and since then minor problems relating to the boundary have been settled either by treaty or by reference to a permanent boundary commission which was established between the United States and Canada.

THE ACQUISITION OF OREGON

The United States had claims to the Oregon territory based on the explorations by its citizens along the coast, the famous Lewis and Clark Expedition of 1804–1806 to the Columbia River, the establishment of an American fur-trading post near the mouth of that river, and the rights to the area it had secured from Spain in the treaty of 1819. British claims to the region were based on explorations and commercial activities. After Russia agreed in 1824 to make 54° 40′ north latitude the southern boundary of Alaska, the United States and Britain were the only claimants to

Oregon, and they agreed in the treaty of 1818 that the whole territory should be open for a period of ten years to the traders or settlers of both nations alike. Although a demand for all of Oregon became a political issue with the slogan "Fifty-four Forty or Fight" in the presidential election of 1844, the American government never seriously proposed that its territory should extend north of the 51st parallel, and by 1826 was willing to accept the 49th parallel as the boundary. On its part, the British government did not seek territory south or to any considerable extent east of the Columbia River, and even then was willing to grant to the United States an enclave on the Olympic Peninsula north of that river. The area in dispute, therefore, was not the whole of Oregon, but a relatively small part of it north and west of the Columbia River.

Failing to reach a settlement over the area remaining in dispute, in 1827 the two nations extended indefinitely the so-called joint occupation agreement of 1818 with the provision that it could be revoked by either party on one year's notice. From 1827 until about 1840, diplomatic negotiations regarding Oregon were negligible while other events tended in some cases to weaken and in others to strengthen the interests of both nations in the area. Aside from a desire to retain free access to the Strait of Juan de Fuca for commercial purposes and to control Vancouver Island, which guarded the strait, British economic interest in the area south of the 49th degree was largely in the fur trade, which rapidly declined after 1830. The Hudson's Bay Company controlled this trade and had a post at Fort Vancouver just north of the Columbia River. The British government tried to strengthen this company and to attract settlers to the area, but its efforts were unsuccessful, and prior to 1846 the company moved its post to Vancouver Island. During the same period American interests in Oregon tended to increase, particularly after routes were found for wagon trains to cross the Rocky Mountains; American settlers began to occupy the Willamette Valley. By 1840, western politicians had begun to make the Oregon Question a political issue.

Meanwhile other factors indirectly influenced the attitude of the United States regarding Oregon. As will be noted later, the annexation of Texas became a problem for the United States after Texas achieved its independence in 1836. British intrigue regarding Texas, together with indications of British interest in California as well as in Oregon, gave impetus to American expansionist tendencies in those areas in order to counteract possible British expansion. Secretary of State Daniel Webster, who had opposed the annexation of Texas and was anxious to settle all outstanding differences with Great Britain, attempted in 1842 to secure a tripartite solution for the whole western territorial problem. He had weakly or inadvertently surrendered to Britain considerable territory in Maine in the treaty of 1842 and now wanted to surrender more. He proposed to concede to Britain the disputed part of Oregon, save for a coastal strip, in return for British support in Mexico for the purchase of Upper California by the United States. This scheme had no real chance of success, for although President Tyler consented to it, he was interested in the annexation of Texas as well as in the acquisition of California, while Britain was trying to prevent the annexation of Texas to the United States. Mexico was uninterested in the proposal and it is highly improbable that Congress would have approved it. The matter was dropped as soon as Webster was replaced as Secretary of State by Abel P. Upshur in 1843.

In the election of 1844, western expansion became a serious political issue. The Whig Party nominated Henry Clay for the Presidency and appeared to oppose expansion, but the Democratic Party took a different stand. It nominated James K. Polk and declared in its platform that the title of the United States to the "whole of the Oregon territory" was clear and that no part of the area should be ceded to Britain. It is very doubtful, however, that the election of Polk constituted a mandate from the people for this broad policy, for other issues, including slavery, received greater attention during the political campaign. However this may be, when Polk became President he did not feel bound by the platform statement on Oregon and soon indicated to Britain that he would adhere to the earlier American position of accepting the 49th parallel as the boundary of Oregon with adjustments to satisfy British commercial interests in the Strait of Juan de Fuca.

The British government had observed the growing intensity of feeling in the United States over the Oregon issue and had decided to accept a settlement along the lines of Polk's proposal, for Britain clearly had larger economic interests in the United States than in the disputed territory. It had experienced great industrial and commercial expansion during the first part of the nineteenth century and needed to sell manufactured goods abroad and to purchase agricultural products. The low tariff policy of the Democratic Party suited British as well as American interests. The British government felt, however, that it should secure political immunity on the Oregon issue from the Opposition in Parliament before it would be politically expedient to surrender territory it had so strongly claimed for so many years. The opposition leaders were willing to make this arrangement, and the British minister in Washington was instructed to negotiate on the basis of Polk's general proposal. An agreement should have been effected in 1845, but the minister mismanaged the matter, appeared to reject the American proposal, and suggested arbitration, which Polk declined. This stiffened Polk's attitude, caused a flurry of excitement in Congress, and might have had serious results had the British government not been quick to redress its minister's error. It did this by drafting a treaty in London in line with American proposals, placing the boundary along the 49th parallel to the sea and through the mid-channel of the Strait of Juan de Fuca, thus placing Vancouver Island in British possession. Since Polk needed to be politically wary also, he sought and secured the consent of the Senate before he signed the treaty. Later it was found that two passages through the Strait of Juan de Fuca would satisfy the wording of the treaty, the San Juan Islands being at stake between these two channels. This problem was eventually referred, under the Treaty of Washington of 1871, to the German Emperor, who decided on the northern passage, thus accepting the American contention and placing the San Juan Islands within American territory.

It has frequently been suggested that while the United States had a stronger position than Britain in the controversy over the Maine boundary, the score was evened somewhat in the Oregon settlement, where the United States had the weaker position regarding the area north of the Columbia River. This is not necessarily true. American rights in the first instance were based on treaty agreement, but in the second instance neither nation had rights under a treaty signed by the other. Neither nation had substantially settled or occupied the area, and the logic of the situation was probably on the American side at least to the following extent: When Britain agreed in the treaty of peace of 1783 that the boundary line west of the Lake of the Woods should be due west from its northwestern-most point to the Mississippi River, it was logical thereafter to extend this line to the sea. The United States, in the treaty of 1818, accepted the more southern line of the 49th parallel and made, therefore, a concession to Britain, making it more reasonable from the American point of view to extend that line to the sea. Yet in the perspective of history, all minor considerations fade before the great achievement of peaceful settlement notwithstanding the clamor of partisans and the exigencies of politics.

THE ANNEXATION OF TEXAS

The United States had a respectable claim that the area between the Sabine and Rio Grande rivers, later commonly known as Texas, was a part of the Louisiana Purchase. France and Spain had never drawn a definitive boundary between their respective territories either on the east or the west of Louisiana. On the eastern side, the Perdido River was a boundary by usage and perhaps tacit consent, but no such line existed on the west. The United States recognized this fact in its discussions with Spain over the western boundary of Louisiana, and although it asserted its claim to Texas, it held that since no boundary had been agreed upon, it was a proper subject for discussion. In the negotiations leading to the Spanish-American treaty of 1819, the United States used its claim to Texas as part of its makeweight in exchange for East Florida, and the boundary between the United States and Texas was set along the southern and western banks of the Red and Sabine rivers respectively. Thereafter, the United States had no legal claim to Texas as a part of the Louisiana Purchase and made none. After American emigrants had settled in Texas, the United States offered more than once to purchase from Mexico an area west of the Sabine River that would extend either to the

Nueces or the Rio Grande rivers, but these offers were rejected, and the proposed Nueces River boundary in this connection had no direct relationship to the claims of Texas as an independent state that its southern boundary should be the Rio Grande River.

Since Texas was largely uninhabited by people of European origin, it offered attractive opportunities for American settlers, and a group of them secured permission from the Mexican government in 1823 to settle there under conditions of liberal land grants and virtual self-government. Mexico not only permitted but also encouraged American immigration. Until about 1830, immigration was relatively rapid and no serious problems arose between the American settlers and the government of Mexico, although some friction existed. After 1830, however, the situation began to change and a series of events and incidents during the next six years led to the movement in Texas for independence. One of the major factors in this situation was the influence of an anti-American British agent in Mexico who warned the Mexican government that continued immigration of American settlers to Texas and the relative lack of Mexican emigrants to the area would soon result in a preponderantly American population whose natural tendency would be to separate themselves from Mexico and seek union with the United States.

Accepting this view, the Mexican government began a series of acts which caused the result it sought to prevent. It first restricted and later abolished further immigration into Texas from the United States, attempted to divert Texas trade from American to Mexican ports, abolished slavery throughout Mexico, and tried gradually to extend Mexican law and the influence of the Roman Catholic Church to Texas. Of these measures, the restriction on immigration was most irksome to Texans, but neither this nor the other acts of Mexico caused an immediate movement for independence, partly because some of the restrictions were temporarily suspended and others not well enforced, and partly because many Texans thought an accommodation with Mexico could be reached on matters of serious concern to them. A change in their attitude came with the rise to power in Mexico of Antonio López de Santa Anna, who set out to crush ruthlessly local self-government in all Mexico, including Texas. Early in March, 1836, on the eve of an "invasion" of Texas by an army under Santa Anna, Texas declared its independence. This movement, hastily organized and militarily weak, might well have failed if the Texan people had not been greatly aroused over Mexican atrocities at the Alamo and Goliad, or if Santa Anna had been a more competent leader. As it was, a nondescript army under Sam Houston completely defeated Santa Anna's forces and captured him at the battle of San Jacinto, less than two months after Texas had declared its independence. During the next few years considerable political confusion existed in Texas, and it might have been recovered by Mexico had not greater confusion and disorder existed there.

Almost as soon as independence was achieved, the Texan government sought annexation to the United States. President Jackson was sympathetic to the Texan Revolution but acted cautiously and did no more during his term of office than to recognize Texan independence. During the next several years, through Van Buren's and Harrison's administrations, and the first part of Tyler's, Texas stood knocking at the door of the United States without being admitted. Among the causes for this situation were (1) the influence of the antislavery agitation which claimed that the whole Texan movement—American emigration to the area, the revolt against Mexico, and the request for annexation—was a southern plot to expand slavery, (2) the desire to avoid trouble with Mexico, in view of its refusal to recognize Texan independence and its constant threat to recover the area by force, and (3) the preoccupation of the American government with pressing domestic issues.

Other factors, however, were leading to a change in American policy. Chief among these were (1) intrigues on the part of Great Britain and, to a lesser degree, France, (2) the influence of American investors in Texan bonds and land script, (3) the growing ability of Texas to maintain its independence, and (4) the replacement of Webster as Secretary of State with a succession of two secretaries who agreed with President Tyler's pro-annexationist policy. The intrigue of the British government was prompted by its desire to thwart the expansion of the United States, to court the good will of Mexico as a part of its own expanding influence in the

Caribbean area, and to support an independent Texas as a cotton-producing competitor to the United States. British policy was influenced also by fanatical abolitionists who thought slavery could be abolished in Texas, which could then be used as a base for agitation against slavery in the United States. Britain proposed, therefore, an agreement between herself, France, Mexico, and Texas, under which Mexico would agree to Texan independence in return for a guarantee that Texas would not join the United States. These various influences, added to the basic fact that Texas had been requesting annexation, led Tyler to sign with Texas an annexation treaty which was defeated in the Senate by a large majority, with every Whig senator but one voting against the treaty. This brought the issue into the presidential election of 1844. After Polk was elected, but before he assumed office, Congress passed a joint resolution permitting annexation.

Meanwhile, a Texan government, angry over American delay regarding annexation, had negotiated independently in 1845 a treaty with Mexico similar in terms to the one proposed by Britain but without European participation. As a result of these movements, Texas had the options of maintaining its independence free from commitments regarding its future, of accepting either of the two treaty agreements, or of annexation to the United States. There was no doubt at all about its desire. By an act of its congress, supported by a state convention and referendum, Texas chose annexation and became an American state in February, 1846.

THE MEXICAN WAR

The Mexican government probably realized that Texas could not be recovered when it signed the treaty of 1845 agreeing to Texan independence, but it was politically difficult and perhaps impossible to admit this to the Mexican people; it was necessary to represent the treaty as a demonstration that Texas would remain independent as a buffer against the United States. When Texas chose annexation, the government decided, therefore, to declare this an act of aggression against Mexico. It broke relations with the United States, sought an alliance with Britain, and began more vigorously to prepare an army for the invasion and recovery of Texas. In order to defend Texas, the United States sent a small army under General Zachary Taylor, who took a position sufficiently north of the Rio Grande River to indicate in the American view a purely defensive posture. This view of Taylor's mission represented the crux of American relations with Mexico.

The United States looked upon the Texan question as exclusively a boundary matter. It held that Mexico no longer had the shadow of a reasonable or logical claim to Texas, but was willing to consider the location of the boundary in a different light. It supported the claim of Texas that the Rio Grande River was the proper boundary, but preferred to avoid trouble with Mexico, to negotiate over the boundary, and to offer Mexico compensation, not exactly as a purchase of disputed territory but rather as a reward for peaceful settlement. The award would provide Mexico with a way out of its dilemma and a political excuse for making an agreement.

In principle, this was not a new policy of the United States. It had followed a similar course in the treaty of 1800 with France, in the treaty of 1819 with Spain, and in the treaty of 1842 with Great Britain, when Maine was given compensation for the loss of territory it claimed. Whether the United States could have effected a boundary settlement agreeable to all, as in the case of Maine, if Mexico had been willing to negotiate, is a futile question. The hard fact was that although the Mexican government agreed to receive an American envoy, John Slidell, for the purpose of negotiation, it refused to confer with him when he arrived in Mexico. This government was soon overthrown by a faction which refused any negotiation whatsoever and claimed that the former government had been trying to avoid a necessary and glorious war. And this war, it bears repeating, would not be for a satisfactory boundary settlement or for the recovery of disputed territory, but for the whole of Texas. In the Mexican government's view, the presence of an American army anywhere in Texas was an aggressive act. In this situation, Polk moved Taylor's army to the Rio Grande River, and may have decided then that no peaceful solution of the boundary was possible.

While these developments were in progress, largely during

1845 and the early months of 1846, indirectly related events were taking place regarding Oregon, as noted earlier, and California. It would be difficult to determine when the United States first had a serious interest in the acquisition of California. But no matter when the interest started, it had become extensive by 1845 and was the product of diverse causes. Prominent among them were the growth of American commerce in the Pacific area, the expansion of the American people across the continent and into Oregon and California, and the activities of the British. By the time American interest in California had developed, the golden age of Spanish colonization there had passed, and the Spanish population, probably under nine thousand, were diffused mostly along the coast and had very little attachment to the government in Mexico. At least one thousand Americans were in California by 1846, more were coming, and only a few years would need to elapse before California would fall to the United States by the desire of its people as Texas had done. The United States was willing to purchase California, as it had been willing to purchase Texas, but it did not need to seize the area or to promote a war with Mexico to secure it.

American concern over California was based on the activities there of the British. The British government was resentful at the failure of its Texan policy and was at odds with the United States over Oregon. It probably had no intention of military intervention in California, but it at least considered this possibility, and let it be known that if California became independent, Britain would oppose its annexation to the United States. President Polk counteracted the British policy in two ways. In his message to Congress, December, 1845, he strongly reaffirmed the Monroe Doctrine, and particularly applied it to North as well as South America. In addition, he informed the American consul in Monterey, California, that if California wanted to be an American state, it would be accepted. It seems highly probable that concern over British interests in California was a major factor in Polk's unwillingness to let the Mexican problem remain long unsettled for he had no assurance that Mexico might not offer California to Britain in return for military aid.

It is not possible to discover to what extent, if any, the unstable

Mexican government was influenced in its Texan policy by a knowledge of the whole situation in California and by a possible belief that somehow California would not be lost, or, if lost, would not be acquired by the United States, if a settlement of the Texan boundary question were avoided. However this may be, Mexico assumed the initiative, declared war on the United States on April 23, 1846, and sent a skirmishing force which crossed the Rio Grande River and clashed with American troops two days later. As soon as this was known in Washington, Congress declared war with only 14 dissenting votes in the House and 2 in the Senate. The government of California surrendered with only token resistance to a small American military expedition, and General Taylor won victories in northern Mexico. Nevertheless, the war lasted almost two years, partly because the United States tried to make peace after each successive victory. In the treaty of peace of 1848, the Texan boundary was settled at the Rio Grande River, and the United States acquired the area from Texas westward to the coast. It agreed to pay Mexico $15,000,-000 and to liquidate American claims against Mexico amounting to over $3,000,000. Shortly thereafter (1853), the United States purchased a small strip along the border, the Gadsden Purchase, for $10,000,000. In all, the United States gave Mexico for a boundary settlement and for the area west of Texas almost the exact amount it had offered before the war. Webster and fourteen senators wanted to return California to Mexico, and Sam Houston and eleven senators wanted additional territory, but Polk was willing to have the treaty of peace as signed, partly because he feared a reopening of negotiations would encourage a growing movement in the United States and in Mexico for the annexation of all Mexico.

THE CARIBBEAN AREA

The right of free navigation of the Mississippi River was one of the important objects of American diplomacy from its beginning. This right was secured from Britain, guarded thereafter in diplomatic relations with Spain and France, and firmly established by the purchase of Louisiana. The approaches to the mouth of the river from the Caribbean Sea through the Gulf of Mexico were important also, and this was one of the reasons for American interest in East Florida and concern over Cuba. Even Jefferson, who opposed a large policy of expansion toward Latin America, made an exception of Cuba. He was content for Cuba to remain in the hands of Spain, but opposed its transfer to any other European power, and looked forward to the time when the United States might acquire Cuba peacefully and with the consent of all concerned. This remained the basic policy of the United States regarding Cuba until after the Civil War, although the policy was expanded a little, emphasized in different ways, and failed as to peaceful acquisition.

The expansion of the basic policy consisted mainly in extending the nontransfer principle to Latin-American states when movements existed in Colombia and Mexico for the annexation of Cuba. On several occasions, however, the United States reaffirmed its basic policy in statements to Spain and other powers. In 1840, for example, it informed Spain that it would oppose "at all hazards" Spain's voluntary transfer of Cuba to another power, but would come to Spain's assistance if any other power tried to seize Cuba. Later, in 1852, when Cuba was disturbed by filibustering expeditions, Britain and France proposed to the United States a tripartite protectorate for Cuba under which the three powers would deny any intention of taking Cuba themselves and would oppose its acquisition by any other power. The United States rejected this proposal, declared that the "condition of Cuba was an American question," and pointed out that Cuba, being close to the United States and at "the doorway" of an isthmian route to California, was far more important to the United States than to any European state. The United States had already offered Spain $100,000,000 for Cuba, but this had been rejected. As the United States became more interested in a canal, and as unrest in Cuba grew and filibustering expeditions continued, another attempt was made to purchase Cuba, this time for $130,000,000. Spain still refused and the United States let the matter rest, for by 1856 the movement to acquire Cuba had become a partisan political issue, notwithstanding the fact that the basic Cuban policy had been held with remarkable consistency by every Presi-

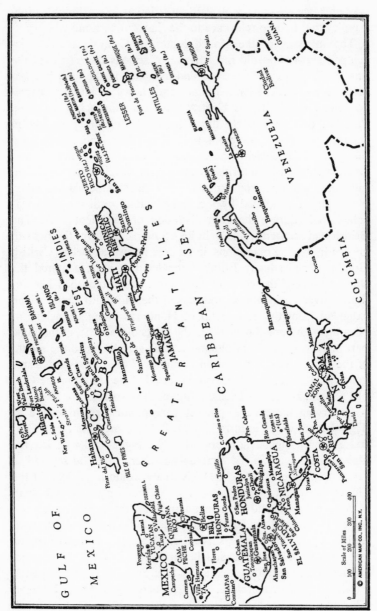

Caribbean Area

dent and every Secretary of State since Jefferson's Administration, a policy that had no relevance to the slavery question.

The interests of the United States in Central America developed slowly and did not become of serious concern until the 1840's after British expansion and influence in the area had become extensive. The United States had shown an interest in various canal routes across Central America—through Nicaragua, Panama, and particularly the Isthmus of Tehuantepec—but in general had been indifferent to Central American affairs even though numerous events there involved violations of the Monroe Doctrine. Meanwhile British commercial development, political influence, and territorial expansion in Central America had taken place almost unnoticed by the United States until attention was called to it during the Administration of President Polk. The British had secured from Spain an economic enclave, the right to engage in logging operations, in an area known as Belize (British Honduras). Gradually Britain extended this area, acquired the Bay Islands off the coast of Honduras, and established her authority over an indefinite area called the Mosquito Coast which extended from the eastern tip of Honduras along the whole of Nicaragua and possibly as far as the limits of Panama, at that time part of New Granada (Colombia). This area included the mouth of the San Juan River, eastern terminus of the proposed Nicaraguan canal route. In 1849, Britain seized Tigre Island in the Gulf of Fonseca, key to the Pacific terminus of this route.

Observing these developments (except for British seizure of Tigre Island, which occurred later), Polk's representative in Central America signed a treaty with Nicaragua under which the United States guaranteed Nicaraguan sovereignty and secured in return exclusive canal rights. This treaty would have brought the United States into direct conflict with Britain over the San Juan River canal route and the ownership of the Mosquito Coast. Since the treaty reached the United States late in Polk's Administration, he left the problem to his successor. Meanwhile Britain extended her commercial interests and her influence in Central America, particularly in relation to Costa Rica, El Salvador, and Nicaragua. President Taylor, therefore, and his Secretary of State, John M. Clayton, were confronted with a serious crisis. They decided, for reasons not clearly known, not to make a firm stand on the basis of the Monroe Doctrine as in the case of Cuba, or as was done later by President Cleveland, but to seek an accommodation with Britain, resulting in the Clayton-Bulwer Treaty of 1850. Under this treaty, Britain agreed to make no *further* territorial advances in Central America, and the United States surrendered its right to maintain or control any means of transportation, ship canal or otherwise, across Central America. Both nations agreed to promote the building of a canal and to guarantee its neutrality and security. The Senate accepted the treaty probably without fully understanding its import with respect to previous British expansion.

The treaty soon produced a controversy with Great Britain over its meaning and a debate in the United States over its wisdom. Britain held firmly to an interpretation of the treaty that did not require British territorial retrenchment, while the United States held that Britain was required to relinquish all her acquisitions in Central America except her enclave at Belize. Based on the wording of the treaty, Britain had the better case but, after almost a decade of debate, decided that her larger interests were not being served by this controversy and made agreements with the relevant Central American states returning to them the areas in dispute. The wisdom of the United States in surrendering its freedom to build and control a canal is another matter, and the fact that the United States was able, at the beginning of the next century, to secure a revision of the Clayton-Bulwer Treaty does not affect the argument. It is important to note, however, that the policy of having an American canal exclusively under American control did not develop in the United States until after the Civil War.

Shortly before these events in Central America reached a serious stage, New Granada (Colombia) had begun to fear British expansion into the Panama area and, failing to secure an agreement with Britain, suggested to the United States in 1846, that it should guarantee the neutrality of the Isthmus of Panama and the "sovereignty" of New Granada over it. In return for this, New Granada would grant to the United States the same rights of transit across the Isthmus of Panama, and under the same conditions as to tolls, that Colombia would reserve for herself by any means of communication then existing or that might be constructed. The United States agreed to this treaty. Its guarantee clauses were unique, but the treaty did not give the United States a right to build a canal or exclusive privileges in the use of one that might be built.

It can be observed that the policies of the United States in the Caribbean were somewhat mixed. Cuba was considered to be an American question, while the control of a canal across Central America became a British-American question. The United States was willing to guarantee the sovereignty of Colombia over the Isthmus of Panama, but unwilling to guarantee Nicaraguan sovereignty over her canal route. Nevertheless, the nontransfer principle was supported and the Monroe Doctrine reaffirmed, and at the end of the era both principles remained intact.

COMMERCIAL EXPANSION INTO THE PACIFIC

The basic policies of the United States in the Pacific area prior to 1860 were inherently consistent and essentially the same as those encompassed later under the term "the open door." They embraced the principles of nonaggression, nonalliance with European powers, reasonable protection of American life and property, and equal commercial opportunity. These principles were strained in a few instances under the pressure of circumstances, but they were not seriously disregarded or abused, and the only addition to them was the extension of the nontransfer principle to the Samoan and Hawaiian islands.

The first American ship to engage in trade with China entered the port of Whampoa, near Canton, in 1784, one year after the treaty of peace with Great Britain. In the years that followed, trade between the United States and China increased until United States traffic in the Far East was second only to that of Britain. In its earlier period American-Chinese commerce was stimulated by its connection with the northwest fur trade. Ships from the Atlantic Coast sailed around South America, reached the Northwest, exchanged part of their cargoes for furs, and traded these, along with other American goods, for oriental products. This trade was generally profitable but hazardous. The long voyage was dangerous, disease among the crews was a constant threat, pirates were prevalent along the Chinese coast, and trade negotiations with Chinese factors, unregulated by treaty and often venal, were difficult. In addition, when conflicts arose between Chinese and American nationals, and the latter were subjected to Chinese law, the Americans frequently felt that justice had miscarried as the result either of the judicial processes or the nature and severity of punishment. For these reasons the United States sought to place its trade with China on a treaty basis, but it failed to do so until after Britain had obliged China in 1842 to make a commercial treaty, the Treaty of Nanking.

Stimulated by this treaty, the considerations mentioned above, and pressure from American merchants, the United States sent an envoy to China in 1844, who negotiated the Treaty of Wanghia. Under this treaty, the United States secured access to four Chinese ports and the right of residence in these areas, a fixed schedule of tariffs, and the right of American citizens to be tried in their own consular courts, commonly called extraterritorial jurisdiction. China also extended to the United States the "most-favored-nation" treatment, conferring on the United States any privilege that had been or would be given to any other nation. American rights under this treaty were continued and slightly extended in a subsequent treaty signed in 1858, the Treaty of Tientsin. It became customary later in the century to refer to these treaties and similar agreements with other powers as "unequal treaties," and this designation is correct since China did not secure equal privileges in the treaty states. Yet it is fair to note that China welcomed rather than opposed the Chinese-American treaty of 1844, because as China's chief statesman and principal negotiator informed the Emperor at the time, it was to China's advantage to make treaties with nations besides Britain, and because the United States did not seek territorial acquisition.

American trade and intercourse with Japan had a different beginning from that of trade with China. China was willing to trade with foreigners, but considered them inferiors, barbarians, and disliked the implications as well as the limitations of agreements with them. In contrast, Japan had first opened its ports to foreign intercourse around 1542, but from 1624, in a violent reaction against the growth of foreign influences, had forced all foreigners to leave Japan and banned all foreign connections, except for a regulated and restricted trade with the Dutch at Deshima, an island in the harbor of Nagasaki. American interest in Japan, aside from the general desire to extend foreign commerce, was derived from the inhumane treatment of seamen from American whalers who were shipwrecked or otherwise forced to seek refuge on Japanese coasts. Having failed in numerous attempts to open negotiations with Japan on this matter since about 1820, the United States decided on more forceful action, the expedition of Commodore Matthew C. Perry. The United States did not demand from Japan a commercial treaty or any rights that could not properly be called humanitarian. It wanted permission for American ships to make repairs and secure supplies in Japan, and assurances that American seamen stranded on Japanese shores would receive humane treatment until they could be removed. Perry's use of force was restricted to an entrance into Japanese waters and the insistence that a letter from the President be delivered to the Emperor. He was authorized, however, to inform the Japanese that if the American request concerning ships and seamen was rejected and thereafter any American subject, forced to land in Japan, was treated in any cruel or inhumane way, Japan would be "severely chastised." Perry had no authority to engage in reprisals, and intended, if he met with failure, to retire to some nearby base and await instructions.

The reasons that led Japan to accept in essence the American proposals are too complex to be considered here. Much of the incentive already existed, and Perry's expedition was only one of the stimuli rather than the compulsion for action. Russia had been trying for a hundred years to secure a commercial treaty with Japan and had decided to make a new attempt the year before Perry's expedition. The Russian squadron arrived in 1853 while Japan was considering the American proposals, and this may have been a decisive influence in Japan's decision to make a treaty with the United States. Under Perry's treaty of 1854, the Treaty of Kanagawa, two Japanese ports were opened where American ships could secure supplies, remove any stranded seamen, and trade if local authorities permitted. An American consul could reside in Japan, and the United States was granted the most-favored-nation treatment. This was a beginning. In 1858, the two nations signed a more extensive commercial treaty, opening additional ports, permitting trade under regulated tariffs, establishing American consular jurisdiction over its nationals, and allowing an American diplomat to reside in Tokyo.

Coincident with these developments in the Far East, the United States expanded its commercial interests elsewhere in the Pacific. The head of a naval exploring expedition in the South Pacific signed articles of agreement with chiefs of the Samoan Islands opening those islands to American commerce. Similar arrangements were made with the King of the Hawaiian Islands in 1826, and American settlers and traders flocked to Hawaii in such numbers and gained so much economic influence that by the 1840's the United States regarded the Hawaiian Islands with special interest and let it be known that it would oppose their transfer to any other power.

Commercial expansion continued in other parts of the world. A reciprocal trade treaty, the first of its kind, was signed with Britain in 1854, greatly facilitating trade between the United States and Canada, and a large number of commercial treaties were entered into with states of Latin America, North Africa, the Middle East, the Far East, and Europe. The United States Navy was enlarged and given the duty of protecting American commerce from pirates and of providing a kind of police service in areas where trade was permitted but not always protected by local officials. This great commercial expansion was assisted by the low tariff policy of the United States and by the rapid development of its shipping industry. At the same time, the United States progressed industrially as well as agriculturally and, by the end of the period under survey, appeared to be on the eve of great cultural and intellectual advance. All this was interrupted, and in some respects terminated, by the Civil War.

VI

THE CIVIL WAR AND ITS AFTERMATH

THE CIVIL WAR and the issues that grew out of it, or were connected with it, constituted a distinct era in American foreign relations. The war produced problems that were not settled by the end of hostilities and required more than a decade for their solution. Gradually the war era flowed out like an ebb tide, and when the tide returned, it brought with it the era of imperialism. If a date must be set to mark the transition from one to the other, the year 1880 is as good as any. The foreign policies of the war era were concerned primarily with the freedom of the seas and hemispheric problems, but the consequences of the war had far-reaching influences on American economic development and eventually on the rise of imperialism.

THE FAILURE OF COMPROMISE AND THE NATURE OF THE WAR

One of the major tragedies of American history was the failure of statesmen to find acceptable solutions to the growing sectional issues that preceded the Civil War, and particularly their failure to do so between December, 1860, when the first southern state seceded from the Federal Union, and the clash of arms at Fort Sumter in April, 1861. The last of the attempts at compromise concerned foreign policy and was initiated by Secretary of State

William H. Seward. While he was still a senator from New York, but after he had reason to suppose he would be selected by President Lincoln as Secretary of State, Seward had contributed substantially to the failure of the first promising compromise proposal. One of the rational explanations for his conduct in this instance is the supposition that he thought he could find another opportunity for compromise after he had become Secretary of State. He saw this opportunity in a threat that had arisen to the Monroe Doctrine. It was known at the time he assumed office that Great Britain, France, and Spain were preparing to invade Mexico for the redress of grievances, and that Spain was preparing to take over the Dominican Republic.

By this time, the Gulf states and a southern tier of Atlantic seaboard states had seceded and had formed a central government, but the northern tier of slave states had not joined the Confederacy and were reluctant to do so. In this situation, Seward formulated a set of proposals which he presented to the President. Although they were not elaborated in detail, they outlined a comprehensive policy. Seward proposed that steps be taken to make it clear both in the South and in the North that the issue of secession was not one of party or slavery but was one of patriotism, of preserving the Federal Union. One step in this direction would be to avoid any hostile movement in connection with Fort Sumter, regarded on both sides as a key to the existing uneasy truce. At the same time the hemisphere would be alerted to the danger from European intervention, and the United States would declare war on France and Spain, and possibly on Britain, unless their movements for intervention were ended. Whether this conciliatory policy toward the embryonic Confederacy, coupled with a strong foreign policy, would have succeeded in reuniting the nation cannot be known, for Lincoln dismissed the proposal without consulting his Cabinet. After hostilities had started, both Lincoln and Congress declared that the war was not for the purpose of abolishing slavery, but was solely for the preservation of the Union, but by that time any chance for compromise had been lost.

The United States never declared war on the Confederacy, or recognized its legal existence, or considered as legal any of the state ordinances of secession. In its view, the conflict was an insurrection, and the "war" was a domestic police action against individuals who were violating federal law. In like manner, the blockade of Confederate ports which the President proclaimed as soon as the war started was a part of the police action, and any individual, acting under the pretended authority of the Confederate States, who molested a vessel of the United States was to be treated as a pirate. In practice, however, the United States conducted itself as if it were at war. Captured Confederate privateersmen were treated as prisoners of war and not as pirates, Confederate soldiers were exchanged as prisoners of war, Congress passed laws and the President acted in ways that were legal under the Constitution only as war measures, and the United States defended its maritime policies under the rules of international law. Foreign nations that acted at all did so on the basis of American practice rather than its theory, recognized the belligerent status of the Confederacy, but not its independence, and proclaimed neutrality.

PROBLEMS OF THE FREEDOM OF THE SEAS

During the Civil War at least four major problems arose that concerned the historic position of the United States regarding the freedom of the seas. These related to blockade, contraband, the doctrine of continuous voyage, and the sale of warships by neutrals. During all its history the United States had held to the position that a blockade had to be effective in order to be legal. What constituted effectiveness was difficult to define, but the United States had favored a rigorous definition. The blockade must be so invested that a ship would be in imminent danger of capture if it attempted to go through the blockade. This stringent concept of effectiveness had been adopted by European nations in the Declaration of Paris of 1856, and the United States had offered, as soon as the Civil War started, to subscribe to the Declaration.

At the beginning of the war, the United States had only a few steam-driven ships that could be used for blockading purposes, while the Confederate coastline extended over three thousand miles, had 189 rivers that emptied into the sea, and contained numerous bays, inlets, and interior channels. The United States

voyage. It made a distinction between journeys where both parts were by water and those where one part was overland. Concerning the former, it held that both the goods and the vessels carrying them could be captured or destroyed, but in the latter situation only the goods could be seized. The British government accepted the American position on continuous voyage partly because it was in line with its own traditional policy and partly because of a calculated consideration that its long-range national interests might be served by the American use and support of the policy. As it turned out, this proved to be the case, for Britain used the doctrine to great advantage when the United States was a neutral during the early years of the First World War.

A more serious problem involving the rights and duties of neutrals arose over the sale of "warships" to the Confederacy. British laws prohibited the sale to a belligerent, while Britain was a neutral, of warships or of merchant ships equipped as warships. The laws of Britain, and in her view the duties of neutrals, did not prohibit the sale of merchant ships to a belligerent such as the Confederacy, or the sale of guns and other warlike equipment, provided such goods were sold and transported separately. Obviously the merchant ships would be subject to capture if they attempted to go through a legal blockade, and the equipment would be subject to capture as contraband anywhere on the high seas. This policy was in conformity also with earlier American practice and court decisions. The Confederate government, in strict conformity with both British law and American practice, undertook to have ships built in Britain, ostensibly as merchant ships but constructed so as to be easily transformed into warships, and to purchase separately equipment for them. A typical example, and the most famous case, was that of a ship later named the *Alabama*.

This ship was constructed in a British port, outwardly as a merchantman, and she sailed for the British Bahamas without any warlike equipment on board. At the same time, another merchant vessel sailed for the same area with guns and ammunition. The two ships held a rendezvous on the high seas outside British territorial waters, where the warlike goods were tranferred to the *Alabama*. Having passed through the paper blockade into Charleston harbor, the *Alabama* was reconstructed into a warship, sailed through the blockade again into the Atlantic, where it engaged in the capture or destruction of United States merchant vessels. American agents in Britain were aware the *Alabama* was being constructed as a potential warship and protested this as a violation of British neutral duties. The British government eventually became convinced of this probability and decided to hold the ship, but acted too late to prevent its departure. Later the government adopted the view that international law did not prevent a neutral from selling warships to a belligerent any more than it prevented the sale of munitions, and that, in any case, no warship or merchant ship equipped as a warship had left a British port for the Confederacy. The United States held that the sale of warships to a belligerent was a nonneutral act, and that in reality the *Alabama* was built as a warship. This controversy between the two nations was not settled during the Civil War, grew in importance after the war, and was finally disposed of by an arbitral agreement which will be considered later.

Although the problems of the freedom of the seas were important when they arose, and in some instances later, they were both influenced and overshadowed by the British decision not to intervene in behalf of the Confederacy. From the beginning of the war, and continuing with decreasing confidence until its end, the Confederacy hoped for British recognition of its independence and for intervention. This hope was based on a number of considerations but primarily on the belief, which proved to be a delusion, that "cotton was king." The idea had been fostered by writers in Britain as well as in the United States and was virtually an article of faith in the South. It was supported by substantial reasons. The British textile industry had experienced phenomenal growth in the two or three decades before the war, provided employment for a large segment of the population, and furnished one of the most important items in British foreign trade. Far more than half of Britain's supply of raw cotton came from the United States. The South believed that Britain could not long endure the economic stress which a curtailment of its principal cotton supply would produce, and, in addition, that Britain would welcome the establishment of the Confederate States, whose free-trade policy suited them better than the protectionist policy of the Lincoln Administration, and whose existence would weaken the United States both as a possible threat to Canada and as a competitor in world trade.

The reasons why Great Britain remained neutral, enormously diverse and interwoven, were economic, political, and humanitarian, were influenced by European events and by miscalculation, and at significant times were relevant to the military status of the conflict in America. In this complexity of factors, it is probably impossible to designate a single primary cause for British policy or even to separate the greater from the lesser influences. At the beginning of the war, the British government thought the Confederacy would be successful and that intervention in its behalf was not necessary even if Britain had been inclined to intervene. As the war progressed and economic questions became more important, it became increasingly clear that intervention to secure a greater amount of Confederate cotton was not essential for British prosperity. The cotton textile industry was hard pressed by the end of the war and its decline probably produced temporary unemployment for as many as 400,000 people, but many of them found opportunities in the thriving woolen and flax industries, while the decline in the cotton textile industry was more than offset by prosperity in other areas of British economy. Moreover, the decline in the cotton industry was quite gradual. Britain had a large surplus of cotton when the war started, received cotton constantly, particularly after the first year of the war, from the Confederacy because of the ineffective blockade, secured cotton in increasing amounts from other areas, and her cotton merchants profited so enormously from the increase in cotton prices that they were sorry to see the war end.

Other economic factors aided in the dethronement of King Cotton. Britain was partially dependent on the United States for its food supply, its sale of munitions and other goods to the North was of great significance, and its shipowners watched with growing satisfaction the virtual disappearance from the seas of the American merchant marine, a result produced by the Confederate commerce destroyers or the fear of them. War with the United States over the paper blockade or any other matter would have gained for Britain nothing but a better cotton supply, for which it could easily afford to wait.

Two additional factors in Britain's decision against intervention entered the situation in 1863. One was the issuance by President Lincoln of the Emancipation Proclamation and the other was the outbreak of a revolt in Poland. The Emancipation Proclamation was the product more of domestic than of foreign policy but the latter was not absent from the considerations that produced it. From the beginning of the war, some people in Britain thought the principal reason for the secession movement was the preservation of slavery, but the United States government had consistently made its sole war objective the preservation of the Union. When it decided to make the abolition of slavery an additional objective, antislavery groups in Britain had a better case for urging their government on moral grounds to refrain from aiding the Confederacy. Near the end of the war, in a last desperate attempt to gain British assistance, the Confederacy offered to abolish slavery. By that time, however, British policy of neutrality was firm.

The Polish revolt had given Britain an additional reason for not becoming engaged in war with the United States. Russian-Polish relations were controlled to some extent by a treaty to which Britain was a signatory, and it was possible that a European war might result from the situation in Poland. This provided a reason, in addition to all the others, for Britain to refrain from intervention. France, as a counterpart of her Mexican enterprise discussed below, favored intervention during the whole of the Civil War, and at times urged such a policy on Britain, but France was not bold enough to act alone, and Britain remained aloof from French intrigue.

EUROPEAN INTERVENTION IN MEXICO

During the decade of the 1850's, a revolutionary movement arose in Mexico leading to the War of the Reform, which extended over the last two years of the decade. This movement, under the competent leadership of Benito Juárez, sought social, political, and economic changes that would benefit the masses of the people and reduce the powers and privileges of the wealthy aristocracy, including the great landowners, the Roman Catholic Church, and the Army. When it became clear that the reform movement might be successful, the conservative forces were willing to invite European intervention. Spain, France, and Britain had reasons for intervention since the government of Juárez had suspended payments on debts owed to their nationals. Great Britain had an additional grievance against Mexico because guerrilla bands, nominally under the control of Juárez, had seized British funds and had committed acts of violence against British citizens. Spain's interest in intervention was increased by the prospect, held out by Mexican monarchists, that a Spanish prince would be placed on a Mexican throne. French financial interests in Mexico were less than those of the other two powers, but Napoleon III was led to believe that France could gain supremacy in Mexico through a puppet ruler and thereby secure prestige in France and possibly in Europe, and in effect could re-establish French influence in the Western Hemisphere.

The danger of European intervention in Mexico was known in the United States, and before President Buchanan left office, he authorized the signing of a treaty with Mexico that would have provided Juárez with funds to meet European demands, and in return the United States would have secured, among other things, the right of intervention if Mexican independence were endangered. This treaty was defeated in the Senate partly because of the growing sectional controversy. When Lincoln became President, he also authorized a treaty with Juárez that would have had some of the features of Buchanan's treaty, but by this time the European movement, under French leadership, was well under way, and, as noted, French interest was not the redress of grievances or the collection of debts. This was the situation, referred to earlier, that Secretary Seward wanted to take advantage of in the hope of effecting reconciliation with the states in secession. When Lincoln rejected this proposal and the war started, the United States was not in a good position to take a strong stand in support of the Monroe Doctrine. The three European nations offered the United States an excuse for remaining neutral by declaring that their reasons for intervention were strictly the redress of grievances, and that they had no intention of securing territory from Mexico or of interfering with its sovereignty. They requested the United States to join in the enterprise. In rejecting this proposal on the basis of its traditional policy of avoiding alliances with foreign nations, the United States reaffirmed its interest in the independence of Latin-American states, and called particular attention to the declaration of the three powers concerning noninterference with Mexican sovereignty. The door was kept open, therefore, for action later if Mexican sovereignty was endangered.

This position was steadfastly maintained by the United States during the Civil War, even though it became increasingly difficult to do so. By 1862 French designs on Mexico were clear, and both Spain and Britain withdrew from the original enterprise. When France placed by force of arms the Austrian archduke Maximilian as a puppet ruler of Mexico, there could be no doubt but that the Monroe Doctrine had been flagrantly violated, and this produced widespread demand in Congress and elsewhere in the United States that some action against France should be taken. Latin-American states were alarmed also over events in Mexico, and two of them, Peru and Chile, became involved in a controversy with Spain when that country gave some indication of trying to recover a part of its former American empire. These two nations proposed to the United States concerted Pan-American action against Spain and France. The American government rejected this proposal and managed to prevent serious interference on the part of Congress with its established policy.

As soon as the Civil War was ended, however, the demand in the United States for action against France was more pronounced. Secretary Seward, who remained in office after Andrew Johnson became President on the death of Lincoln, was convinced, however, that military force would not be needed to effect the overthrow of the Maximilian government. Maximilian had proven to be a vacillating and incompetent leader who had alienated whatever meager support he had in Mexico and was being sustained in power wholly by French forces that had never been able to liquidate Mexican resistance under the leadership of Juárez. The United States had continued to recognize the Juárez government, and after 1865 was willing to supply him with military aid. Meanwhile Napoleon's Mexican venture had become a serious drain on his treasury and had met with increasing opposition in France. Napoleon was probably ready by 1865 to abandon the enterprise as soon as he could do so without disastrous loss of prestige. Seward correctly decided that a policy of strong and constant diplomatic pressure, aided by a hint of force if that should become necessary, was all the United States needed to do. French troops were removed from Mexico in March, 1867, and before the year was over Maximilian's government had fallen and he had been executed.

While these events were in progress, Spain decided to relinquish its attempt to control the Dominican Republic and to reestablish its power in South America. This development, together with the failure of European intervention in Mexico, created in the United States the impression that the Monroe Doctrine had been sustained, and it became during the years that followed more and more the bulwark of American hemispheric policy. The Mexican civil war which had preceded European intervention and the long struggle against Maximilian had left the country bankrupt, disorganized, and desolate. The death of Juárez in 1872 initiated a new period of factional strife ending in the establishment of a dictatorship under which order was restored, but the old privileged classes were allowed to regain much of their former influence.

POSTWAR BRITISH-AMERICAN RELATIONS

Viewed in perspective, the United States had considerable reason to be grateful for British conduct and restraint during the Civil War and the years that immediately followed. The British government resisted domestic and foreign pressures for intervention in behalf of the Confederacy, withdrew from the Mexican venture as soon as it observed French intentions, and remained calm during the acrimonious postwar controversies that disturbed British-American relations. This view, however, was not taken by the United States government or by influential and often irresponsible politicians in Congress, and it is quite possible that the two nations were very near to serious conflict at various times before the majority of their differences were settled by the Treaty of Washington and the *Alabama* claims arbitration that followed

One of the most extraordinary events among those that clouded British-American relations was the conduct of the United States in permitting the growth on its soil of an Irish Republican movement headed by the Fenian Brotherhood, who between 1866 and 1871 made raids across the Canadian border. The Fenians were a group of fanatics who formed the fantastic scheme of establishing in the United States a military force for the conquest of Canada, after which they would presumably launch an attack on Britain for the purpose of securing the independence of Ireland. The first leaders of the movement came to the United States in the 1850's and agitated for their cause and collected funds. They held a convention in Chicago in 1863, organized a "government" of the Irish Republic, and started the recruiting of an army. After the Civil War, they held conventions in Cincinnati and Philadelphia, trained their "armies" openly, and began to assemble them at various points along the Canadian border, particularly at Buffalo, Rouses Point, and St. Albans. In June, 1866, a raid was made across the border near Buffalo, but after the "Battle of Limestone Ridge," the Fenians made a hasty retreat to the safety of American soil. During the same year an abortive raid was organized at Eastport, Maine, and two additional raids were attempted later. The movement did not die out until after 1870. The Canadian government was not disturbed over the danger of being overthrown, but it was greatly inconvenienced by the necessity of protecting its long border against the marauding bands.

The tardy and largely ineffective measures taken by the American government in this episode can be explained partly by the whole complex of factors that influenced the American postwar attitude toward Britain. Many Americans thought that British wartime policies had favored the Confederacy, and believed also that Canada had been lax in not preventing a raid across the border by a group of escaped Confederate prisoners. In addition, a new cause for friction had arisen over American fishing rights along the Canadian coast. It is probable, however, that the most important reason for the conduct of the United States regarding the Fenian raid of 1866 was the status of domestic politics. The whole southern reconstruction policy of the so-called Radical Republicans was at stake in the congressional elections of that year, and, in turn, the success of this policy would determine the fate of political and economic policies advocated by the Radical group. President Johnson opposed the Radicals and in this matter was supported by the Democratic Party. The domestic conflict was bitter, and both groups believed the 1868 election would be close. For this reason neither group was willing to take a strong stand against the Fenians for fear of losing votes by appearing to favor Great Britain.

Notwithstanding the contributions of the Fenian raids and other matters to British-American disharmony, President Johnson attempted on two occasions to reach a general settlement with Britain. The opportunities were provided by successive changes in the British government, but both attempts failed, the first because an agreement signed by the American minister in London was unsatisfactory to the President, and the second because a new agreement was rejected by the Senate. These failures tended to increase the tension between the two nations, which was heightened by the growing sentiment in the United States in support of extreme demands on Britain for damages allegedly resulting from British policies during the Civil War. The demands involved compensation for damages inflicted directly on American ships by the *Alabama* and other Confederate cruisers built in Britain, indirect damages for losses to American shipowners who kept their ships at home because of danger from the Confederate ships, and general damages occasioned by a prolongation of the war as a result of British recognition of Confederate belligerency. The chairman of the Committee on Foreign Relations of the Senate, Charles Sumner, hinted that Britain might make a beginning at compensation by the cession of Canada to the United States. Obviously there could scarcely be any limit to claims under such theories of British responsibility.

This was the situation when Grant assumed the Presidency in 1869. Both the President and his Secretary of State, Hamilton Fish, appeared to accept the views of the extremists concerning British-American relations, and it seemed possible that the two nations were drifting into war. Neither nation appeared willing to change its position or to make the first move toward a new attempt at agreement. During the year 1870, however, events in

America enabled the government to be more receptive to renewed negotiations and events in Europe contributed to a change in British policy. In America, a conflict between the President and Senator Sumner reduced the latter's influence with the government, which thereafter became a little more flexible in its attitude toward Britain. At the same time, Great Britain began to realize more fully than she had before her vulnerability as a great maritime nation if the United States as a neutral should supply her enemies with warships. The Franco-Prussian War and the growth of Russian influence in the Black Sea area sharpened British sensitivities to this danger. If, however, Britain conceded the American position that a neutral was obligated not to furnish warships under any guise to a belligerent, the United States would be bound to this policy and Britain understood this might be of more worth to her in the future than the cost of direct damages caused by the Confederate cruisers. What was required, therefore, was to find a way to renew negotiations on the basis of an understanding that Great Britain would accept responsibility for the Confederate cruisers while the United States would withdraw its claims for indirect damages.

In order to accomplish this purpose, Britain sent a special representative to the United States who entered into informal discussions with Secretary Fish. No official record was kept of these discussions, but Britain let it be known that she would agree to refer the principal controversies between the two nations to arbitral tribunals, and would accept a stipulation on the duties of neutrals in line with the American position concerning such ships as the *Alabama*. Specific promises were not made by the United States regarding claims for indirect damages, but the British thought there was a clear understanding that this issue would not be pressed. As a result of these conversations, a formal conference was held which drew up the Treaty of Washington of 1871. Under the treaty, the *Alabama* claims were to be referred to an arbitral board, and agreement was reached that a neutral was obligated, among other things:

> . . . to use due diligence to prevent the fitting out, arming, or equipping, within its jurisdiction, of any vessel which it has reason-

able ground to believe is intended to cruise or to carry on war against a Power with which it is at peace: and also to use like diligence to prevent the departure from its jurisdiction of any vessel intended to cruise or carry on war as above, such vessel having been specially adapted, in whole or in part, within such jurisdiction, to warlike use.

Under this rule, it was clear that Britain would be liable for damages inflicted by ships such as the *Alabama*. The treaty did not mention indirect damages, but again, as in the earlier informal conversations, Britain believed there was a tacit agreement on this matter and that claims for indirect damages would not be made.

Whether the American negotiators in the pretreaty conversations or at the Washington conference deliberately misled the British regarding indirect damages must remain speculative. The only certain fact is that with the approval of the President and the Secretary of State, the representatives of the United States before the *Alabama* claims tribunal, which met in Geneva, Switzerland, presented extreme claims for indirect damages without any indication of their limitation. This produced a sensation in Britain and the most serious crisis that had as yet arisen over the *Alabama* problem. The British government could easily have been overthrown if the Opposition had made the matter a partisan issue, the most ardent British friends of America were unable to defend American policy, and Parliament was ready to act in defense of British interests. On the American side, Congress reacted strongly to the British position and apparently was willing to support the Administration if it chose to hold fast to its demands for indirect damages.

With no immediate solution of the problem in sight, the British government suggested the adjournment of the tribunal pending the drafting of a new convention specifically covering the question of indirect damages. Realizing this would return the whole dispute to its former dangerous status, the tribunal decided to intervene, although it had no legal authority to do so, and issued a statement to the effect that in its opinion indirect damages had no basis in international law. This provided a face-saving opportunity for the United States to back down on its extreme claims. Hearings before the tribunal were resumed, and eventually the United States was awarded $15,500,000 in direct damages. While Great Britain's payment of this award was a victory for the United States, it represented on the British side a calculated policy of national interest. Thereafter the United States was morally bound in its relations with Britain to respect the principles regarding the duties of a neutral on which it had so vehemently insisted. During the First World War, for example, Britain was immune from the danger that Germany could secure warships from the United States.

In addition to making possible a settlement of the *Alabama* claims, the Treaty of Washington was significant in other ways. It established a tribunal to settle American claims against Britain resulting from a dispute over the northeast fisheries and drew up a new fisheries treaty, opened several American-Canadian boundary rivers to the free navigation of both parties, referred a northwest boundary dispute regarding the San Juan Channel to an arbitrator, and provided a trade agreement between the United States and Canada. It gave impetus to the idea of arbitration as a method of peaceful settlement, and provided one of the links in a chain of events that drew the United States and Britain closer together during the remaining interval before the First World War.

EXPANSIONIST TENDENCIES

Secretary of State Seward (1861–1869) was an expansionist whose interests included the possible acquisition by the United States of Alaska, Cuba, the Virgin Islands, Hawaii, and probably some areas in the Far East. His activities, however, were mainly confined to Alaska and the Virgin Islands. Russian interest in disposing of Alaska arose on the eve of the Crimean War and resulted partly from the decline in profits from the fur trade in Alaska and partly from the fear that Britain might seize the area in the event of war between the two nations. The possibility of selling Alaska to the United States was considered several times during the 1850's, but American domestic controversies tended to overshadow all other affairs. At the end of the Civil War, Seward renewed discussions about Alaska with the Russian minister in Washington and a treaty was signed in 1867 whereby Alaska was purchased for $7,200,000.

Negotiated in considerable secrecy, the treaty produced an immediate controversy. Ardent expansionists who would have welcomed the acquisition of Canada and other areas favored the purchase on general principles. Others, who saw no advantage in acquiring Alaska and were concerned with its costs, opposed the purchase. With almost complete irrelevance, coupled with considerable demagoguery, the argument was advanced that in some manner the acquisition of Alaska would indicate opposition to Britain and support of Russia who allegedly had shown friendship for the United States by sending a portion of her fleet to American waters during the Civil War. Actually, the visit of the Russian ships had been for the purpose of having them out of the Baltic and in a position to prey on British commerce in case Russia and Britain got into war over Poland. The acquisition of Alaska did not satisfy a public demand or a national interest. It did reflect the circumstances of the time: Seward's expansionism, anti-British agitation, and the activities of a pressure group probably backed by Russian funds.

During the Civil War, the United States Navy developed an interest in acquiring a coaling station and naval base somewhere in the Caribbean area. This interest suited Seward's expansionism and led him to propose the purchase of the Danish West Indies. Denmark finally agreed in 1867 to sell two of the islands, St. Thomas and St. John, for $7,500,000. By that time, however, the Navy's interest had largely disappeared, for the Civil War was over and the danger of conflict with France over Mexico was no longer imminent. The treaty of purchase met opposition in the Senate from those who had favored the acquisition of Alaska since there was no anti-British connection in this instance, and the House of Representatives took the unusual action of resolving that it would not vote the necessary appropriations if the Senate approved the treaty. The treaty became a victim also of the controversy between Congress and President Johnson during his last year in office. President Grant did not revive the issue partly because he became more interested in the acquisition of the Dominican Republic.

The initial movement for the acquisition of the Dominican Re-

public arose from the same circumstance that prompted the movement to purchase the Danish West Indies, the desire for a naval
base in the Caribbean. An attempt to acquire a naval base at
Samaná Bay had been unsuccessful, but the Dominican government offered to negotiate for the transfer of the whole republic to
the United States. Nothing was done about this while Seward was
in office, but President Grant became interested and, after some
irregular diplomatic negotiations, approved a treaty of annexation.
This met with immediate opposition both in the Dominican Republic and in the American Senate. The Dominican government
was able to suppress its opponents through military support furnished by the United States, but the Senate could not be managed
in the same manner. Senator Sumner, who had supported the
purchase of Alaska, led the opposition to the treaty in the most
vigorous possible way and was able to prevent the approval of the
treaty notwithstanding the use by President Grant of the full force
of his office in its behalf. The open breach between Sumner and
Grant on this issue was one of the significant reasons for the
decline of Sumner's influence in opposing reconciliation with Britain over the *Alabama* claims.

The United States almost came into conflict with Spain over a
ten-year revolution in Cuba that was virtually coincident with
Grant's Administration. The United States remained strictly neutral, but Spain felt that the rebels would have been suppressed
more quickly had they not secured supplies of arms and ammunition from the United States, where public sympathy for them was
manifest. Since the rebellion continued with increasing violence
and destruction of property, and since Spain seemed to be making
little progress in restoring order, the United States warned Spain
that it might intervene unless the island was pacified soon. The
existence at the same time of the controversy with Britain over the
latter's neutral duties may have delayed American action in the
Cuban case. At any rate, Spain brought the rebellion to an end
before the United States decided to act.

Viewed as a whole, the post-Civil War era was one of retrenchment in foreign affairs. Aside from the purchase of Alaska, the
expansionist schemes of both the Johnson and Grant administrations failed and no new ones were attempted until after 1890. The

potential conflicts with France and Spain did not materialize, and the controversy with Great Britain was settled. The United States looked inward, raised its tariff walls, permitted its merchant marine and Navy to decline, and to a considerable extent expanded its industrialism at the expense of its agricultural economy.

VII

EXPERIMENTS IN IMPERIALISM AND
WORLD POLITICS, 1880–1913

THE TITLE of this chapter indicates the unique feature of American foreign policy during the era covered, but it does not characterize the period as a whole. Of the presidents who held office during this time, only one of them, Theodore Roosevelt, was an avowed imperialist who dabbled extensively in world politics. Presidents Harrison and McKinley were weak leaders who were not themselves disposed to imperialism, Cleveland was interested mainly in domestic reform, was anti-imperialistic, and acted vigorously in foreign policy only in connection with the Monroe Doctrine, and Taft made no effort to expand imperialism or to play a large role in world affairs. The United States had only a fleeting moment of imperialism as the term is used here: the acquisition of territory without the consent of the people concerned and without according them the full rights of American citizens. Even at the high tide of imperialism at the end of the Spanish-American War, the movement came far more from a few dominant leaders than from the people at large. The fact that McKinley was successful in the election of 1900 over his anti-imperialistic opponent, William Jennings Bryan, is not proof that the majority of the people chose imperialism. The issues in the election were too complicated and confused to permit that conclusion. Yet, notwithstanding these considerations, the era has a degree of unity. The Monroe Doctrine was guarded and notably strengthened, the imperialistic impulse arose and declined, and Theodore Roosevelt's policies were consistent with imperialistic concepts. The era definitely came to an end with the Presidency of Woodrow Wilson, even though he could not immediately liquidate the foreign policy legacies of the three previous decades.

STRENGTHENING THE MONROE DOCTRINE

The impetus given to a renewed interest in the Monroe Doctrine by the French invasion of Mexico continued after that episode was closed. One indication of this was the growing concern of the United States over affairs in Central America and, among other things, over the construction of an isthmian canal under exclusive American control. The older American policy, initiated by Henry Clay and continued through the negotiation of the Clayton-Bulwer Treaty of 1850, was for the United States to promote the construction of a neutralized canal under some form of international control. In the 1860's Secretary of State William H. Seward changed this policy and negotiated with Colombia a treaty giving the United States the exclusive right to construct and control a canal across the Isthmus of Panama. This treaty was not approved by the Senate, and a similar treaty negotiated under the Grant Administration likewise failed to secure Senate approval. Both treaties would have been in conflict with the Clayton-Bulwer Treaty, but since neither one went into effect no difficulty with Britain arose over them. President Cleveland returned to Clay's policy, but did little to promote it, and in general strong national interest in a canal controlled by the United States had to await the Spanish-American War.

The most serious issue involving the Monroe Doctrine came during Cleveland's second Administration and involved a dispute over the boundary between British Guiana and Venezuela. The problem was of long standing because the dividing line between the two areas had never been defined. Britain acquired Guiana in 1814 from the Dutch whose rights there had been recognized by the Spanish in 1648. Britain made various futile attempts to reach a boundary agreement with Venezuela prior to 1880 when that country appealed to the United States for assistance against Britain, who was accused of expanding her territorial claims. The United States was not greatly concerned at first and did little more than offer its good offices and suggest a settlement by arbitration. The American government, however, was becoming more interested in the problem by the time Richard Olney became Secretary of State in 1895, and Olney was influential in bringing about a further policy shift.

The reasons for this change from mild to the most serious possible concern over the issue remains speculative. It may be that Olney's explanation should be taken at face value: that he studied the history of the dispute and became convinced that Britain was aggressive, that the Monroe Doctrine was involved, and that the United States should take a firm stand. It is possible, however, that other considerations contributed to his conclusions. The dispute between Britain and Venezuela had already attracted considerable attention in the press and in Congress where inflammatory anti-British speeches had been made. Since this attack on Britain had come primarily from Republican Party leaders, it is possible that Olney wanted to show prior to the presidential election of 1896 that the Democratic Party did not countenance a soft attitude toward British infringement of the Monroe Doctrine. It is possible also that Olney was influenced by the recent landing of British troops in Nicaragua for the redress of grievances against British subjects and by the continued existence of other unsettled controversies with Britain, including one over the Alaskan boundary. The only solid fact, however, is that President Cleveland and Olney agreed on a drastic policy.

Acting on this decision, the United States sent to Britain one of the most remarkable documents in the history of American foreign relations. It stated bluntly that the boundary issue between Britain and Venezuela involved the Monroe Doctrine and therefore the interest of the United States, that the Doctrine was in effect American public law which the United States would enforce against any or all powers, and that the boundary issue had to be settled by peaceful means. The United States did not take sides on the substance of the dispute in favor either of Britain or Venezuela, but stated simply that no European power would be allowed to expand its territory by force at the expense of an American state or interfere with the sovereignty of such a state. When Britain rejected the American suggestion of arbitration, Cleveland wasted no further effort on diplomatic correspondence, but instead requested authority from Congress to establish a commission to determine the boundary with the understanding that when it was impartially defined the United States would maintain it.

This policy removed the issue from diplomacy into action, and Britain had to decide whether the issue either of territory or principle was worth a serious conflict with the United States. It did not take Britain long to decide that her national interests would not be served by such a conflict, for her greater interests in Europe, the Far East, and Africa would possibly be endangered. Britain decided, therefore, to recognize indirectly American preponderance of power in the Western Hemisphere, and agreed after suitable arrangements had been made, to settle the dispute by arbitration. Thereafter in her relations with the United States Britain acted in conformity with this major decision of policy. She soon removed her fleet from the Caribbean, let the United States know that she regarded Cuban affairs as an American problem, and after the Spanish-American War accepted modifications of the Clayton-Bulwer Treaty to permit the United States to build and control an isthmian canal.

Soon after the turn of the century, a new alleged threat to the Monroe Doctrine arose in connection with the intervention of European states in Latin America for the collection of debts. Intervention for this reason had taken place during the nineteenth century and the United States did not deny in principle the right of states to take such action. It had been disturbed, however, when France intervened in Mexico and Britain in Central America, over the possibility that temporary intervention might lead to permanent occupation. The new elements in the situation after 1900 were the policies of the United States concerning the isthmian canal and the rise of Germany to the status of a world power with the desire of securing influence and possibly a foothold in Latin America. Theodore Roosevelt decided, therefore, that if a situation arose in Latin America which might lead to foreign intervention, the United States should take measures to effect a settlement if a dispute had arisen or to prevent one from arising. He applied this policy in Venezuela in 1902 and in the Dominican Republic in 1905. In the latter case, the United States took over the collection of customs receipts and their distribution partly to the Dominican government and partly to foreign creditors. Whether the Cleveland and Roosevelt policies were in fact corollaries to the Monroe Doctrine, as they are often called, or more properly separate policies designed to protect the Doctrine under new circumstances does not seem important. Their effect was to maintain the principle of American preponderance of power in the Western Hemisphere. They were not designed to secure for the United States special privileges in Latin America or to interfere with the sovereignty of Latin-American states, although it has been asserted that in some instances American policies permitted these results.

THE ROOTS OF IMPERIALISM

An important distinction exists between the observation of events and ideas out of which a historical movement developed and the conclusion that the movement was inevitable. Events may be causal only in the sense they make a movement possible, for an element of choice exists at every stage in a historical process. This was the case with all the factors that are usually considered as bases of American imperialism. They include the growth of American sea power, the expansion of industrialism and the competition for world markets, and the development of various theories concerning the proper place of the United States in world affairs. It is possible to discover some of the deep roots of imperialism in the pre-Civil War era and in the expansionist movements that followed, but the imperialistic urge that characterized the last part of the nineteenth century was of more recent origin. Among its earliest manifestations was the movement that began in the late 1870's for a larger Navy.

After the Civil War, the Navy had been allowed to decline primarily because there was no strong national sentiment for the United States to become a great sea power. The traditional view of the Navy's role was to protect American commerce from pirates, to create respect for the American flag in ports of the world where local law was capricious or ineffective, and to defend the United States against invasion. Since the United States had no extracontinental area to defend and had no reason to expect invasion, a large Navy was not needed. By the end, however, of the 1870's various people in the Navy Department of the government, in Congress, and in private life began to urge the increase of the Navy and to advance most or all of the theories later connected with imperialism.

They argued that the growth of American industrialism demanded a constant supply of raw materials from abroad and the expansion of markets, that a greater proportion of American goods should be carried on American ships, and that a Navy was needed to protect this commerce. It was said also that the Navy was not strong enough to defend the Monroe Doctrine, that a nation must expand in order to live, and that expansion would produce conflict with other nations unless American potential power was sufficient to cause respect for its interests and policies: weakness invited attack, strength insured peace. Congress responded during the 1880's to these and perhaps other arguments and authorized the construction of a larger Navy. From then on American naval power was steadily increased, and the government developed new naval doctrines consistent with the idea of the United States becoming a world power.

Meanwhile the United States had expanded its commercial interests in the Pacific area, particularly in regard to coaling stations and naval bases in the Samoan and Hawaiian islands. The interest in Samoa began as early as the 1830's, but did not become significant until the period under review. The United States acquired in 1878 the right to establish a coaling and naval station in the harbor of Pago Pago, but this right was not exclusive. The American policy regarding Samoa was to respect its independence and to seek no special commercial or political privilege. When controversies eventually arose between American nationals in Samoa and those of Britain and Germany, the United States agreed to a tripartite supervision of the islands but opposed their acquisition by Germany or their division among the three powers.

American interest in Hawaii began in connection with the China trade, grew after 1820 when American missionaries went to the islands, and became extensive enough by the 1850's to foster a movement for their annexation. This movement was abandoned, and prior to 1884 American policy toward Hawaii was to protect its independence against acquisition by any other power but, as in Samoa, to seek no special privilege. This policy was terminated by the American-Hawaiian treaty of 1884, ratified in 1887, which granted to the United States the exclusive right to establish a naval base at Pearl Harbor.

By this time the so-called "native" population of Hawaii had become a minority, while those of oriental origin had increased, and those of American ancestry had secured almost complete control of the economy and government of the islands. It was not strange, therefore, that the dominant business and commercial leaders should seek the annexation of Hawaii to the United States during Benjamin Harrison's Administration, when the American government favored such a policy and American trade restrictions became unfavorable to Hawaiian interests. With the probable connivance of the American diplomatic representative in Hawaii and the protection of a contingent of marines from an American warship, insurgents overthrew the Hawaiian monarchy, established a republic, and signed a treaty of annexation to the United States. The Harrison Administration ended, however, before the treaty was acted on by the Senate, and President Cleveland, who disapproved of American actions in the Hawaiian revolution, withdrew the treaty from the Senate and set in motion an investigation of the whole affair. He was unable, however, to restore the monarchy in Hawaii save by force, which would have required congressional approval that was not forthcoming. Annexation became a political issue in the presidential campaign of 1896, when Henry Cabot Lodge and other imperialists denounced the Cleveland policy as unpatriotic. Yet the significant fact was that little national enthusiasm existed for annexation or for the idea of imperialism. Annexation was not accomplished until after the beginning of the Spanish-American War, when the argument prevailed that the possession of Hawaii was essential for the security of American forces in the Philippines. Even then, annexation was secured by joint resolution of Congress rather than by treaty, which required a two-thirds majority vote in the Senate.

THE SPANISH-AMERICAN WAR

The origins of the Spanish-American War were so numerous and so enormously diverse that any attempt to select a primary cause would be hopeless. The diversity ranges from the extraordinary incompetence of the Spanish Army in its attempt to suppress a revolution in Cuba to the statement of Assistant Secretary of the Navy Theodore Roosevelt that he intended to have a war. In the previous American foreign wars during the nineteenth century, and later in the two World Wars of the twentieth century, the United States could show substantial reason why it had no alternative to war save surrender of its rights, duty to its citizens, or national security. None of these things could be said of the Spanish-American War, nor could it be said that it was in defense of the Monroe Doctrine. Spain did not attack the United States, did not threaten American security, did not propose the transfer of Cuba to some other power, and did not want a war with the United States if it could be avoided with honor. Spain realized that Cuba was lost to her and was willing to accept all or virtually all American demands regarding Cuba. If the United States had no just cause for war against Spain over Cuba, it had far less reason to attack Spain in the Philippines under the incredible theory that the Spanish fleet in the Far East could cross the Pacific Ocean and attack cities on the West Coast of the United States, near which Spain had no coaling stations or supply facilities. If, by some hypothesis, this was a danger, an American fleet stationed in Hawaii would have been adequate protection. Yet the Spanish-American War was popular in the United States, its military leaders were proclaimed as heroes, some of its leading proponents were accorded political reward, and the war was hailed as bringing the United States into the list of world powers.

The explanation of American policy in this instance seems to be a confluence of factors, some historical, some fortuitous, some the result of disingenuous planning, and some the peculiar political context of contemporary American affairs. It had been noted that from the time of Jefferson, Cuba had been thought of as having special importance to the United States, at first with respect to its position in relation to the Mississippi River and later with respect to American interests in a canal somewhere across Central America. Special interest in Cuba was shown also, among other instances, in the Grant Administration when the United States threatened to intervene in the civil war in Cuba that began in 1868. Historically also, the United States had taken a dim view of Spanish rule in Cuba and had been disposed to think that Cuba should be annexed to the United States or should be independent. These influences provided fertile soil for the cultivation of the idea, when a new Cuban rebellion broke out in 1895, that this rebellion was of major concern to the American people. Spain contributed to this idea by her utter incompetence in suppressing the rebellion quickly and by using methods that appeared to be inhumane, although the United States used similar methods later in the Philippines. Various American newspapers took the opportunity to promote sensational accounts of alleged Spanish atrocities in Cuba, while they did not provide the American people with clear information regarding Spain's efforts to avoid a war with the United States.

Among the many fortuitous circumstances and events were the publication of a stolen private letter of the Spanish minister to the United States, Dupuy de Lome, in which he made critical comments regarding President McKinley; the sinking of the battleship *Maine* in the harbor of Havana in February, 1898, although no proof existed that Spanish authorities were responsible; a weak President and a senile Secretary of State, who did nothing to stem the influence of those who wanted war with Spain for imperialistic reasons; and possibly the fact that many politicians were pleased to have an issue which directed public attention from the serious and important domestic problems connected with the political campaign of 1896. But above all, there existed a small, influential group of politicians with imperialistic ambitions who seized an opportunity they partly created to further their designs. Out of this maze two factors stand out above the others. The American people favored intervention in Cuba and therefore a war with Spain, but they thought intervention was an act of liberating Cuba from an iniquitous Spanish empire. Not the acquisition of territory, nor economic advantage, nor imperialism in any form, nor the desire to have the United States become a world power was a significant factor in their thought. They acquired their beliefs from the avowed intentions of their leaders that the war was only for Cuban liberation, from a sensation-seeking press, and from their traditional thinking regarding Spain and Cuba. The second major fact is that the imperialists sought the war not for the reasons that influenced the majority of the people, nor because they were puppets of "big business," but because they coveted power and influence.

Under the treaty of peace with Spain the United States acquired the Philippines, Puerto Rico, and Guam. Because Puerto Rico was small and close to the United States, no public concern appeared to exist over its acquisition. The Philippines, however, were a different matter. They were distant, were occupied by eight million or more people who were not ready for self-government, and would be a liability rather than an asset to American security. The anti-imperialists realized these conditions and tried either to prevent the annexation of the islands or to secure a pledge in the treaty of peace that the Philippine people would be granted independence as soon as they were able to assume the responsibilities of self-rule. The anti-imperialists failed, however, in both objectives, and for a complex of reasons. It seemed clear that Spain was incapable of restoring her dominion over the Philippines, for her Navy had been destroyed and her Army was incompetent, and an independence movement existed in the islands strong enough to thwart the return of Spanish rule. At the same time, Germany, Japan, and Britain were interested in acquiring some or all of the islands. The argument was strong, therefore, that the United States should not abandon the islands to disorder in the one case, or in the other to the results of possible conflict among the powers for their possession.

It was noted earlier that the annexation of the Hawaiian Islands was a part of the Spanish-American War excitement. During the same period the United States agreed to a treaty with Germany and Britain for the division of the Samoan Islands, the United States being allotted, among others, the island of Tutuila with the harbor of Pago Pago, but the annexation of American Samoa was arranged with native rulers. The United States occupied vacant Wake Island during the war with Spain. Thus the United States acquired a new overseas empire, and it became necessary for the Supreme Court, in the so-called Insular Cases, to devise a strained if not a spurious interpretation of the Constitution which would permit American imperial rule over the areas in question.

THE PANAMA CANAL

The acquisition of an overseas empire increased American interest in an isthmian canal and the determination of the government to have this canal completely under American control. In order to accomplish this, it was necessary to secure an alteration of the Clayton-Bulwer Treaty, to decide on the most desirable canal route, and to acquire a right of way through the country concerned. Britain placed no serious obstacle in the way of American canal interests, although Secretary of State John Hay was obliged to negotiate a second treaty with that country in order to satisfy the Senate. The United States had already secured the right to construct a canal through Nicaragua, and an aggressive group in Congress strongly advocated the selection of that route. If the route through Panama was selected, it would be necessary to secure an agreement with Colombia and to acquire the rights of a French company, then called the New Panama Canal Company, which had a lease until 1904 on the Panama route. Since this company was bankrupt and had no chance of completing the canal before the expiration of its lease, its only hope of realizing something from its expenditures was to sell its partially completed canal to the United States. After an extended debate over the merits of the two routes, Congress enacted a compromise measure authorizing the government to build a canal across the Panama route provided a satisfactory agreement could be reached with Colombia and the rights of the French company could be secured for $40,000,000. Otherwise the canal was to be constructed across Nicaragua.

This touched off a series of diplomatic and other events that constituted, as far as the United States was concerned, one of the least defensible episodes in its diplomatic history, damaged its reputation with regard to the fulfillment of treaty obligations, and could not be justified on the basis of national interest or honor. The United States had a treaty with Colombia dating from 1846, under which the United States "guaranteed" to Colombia the sovereignty and neutrality of the Isthmus of Panama. When a new treaty giving the United States the right to build and control a canal proved difficult to negotiate on terms satisfactory to both parties, President Roosevelt had the clear alternatives of continuing negotiations or of turning to the Nicaraguan route. Instead he talked privately of the possibility of a secession movement in Panama and of asking Congress for authority to seize the area. The French company, with $40,000,000 at stake, did not want to take chances on the seizure policy since many members of Congress favored the Nicaraguan route. Accordingly it organized a revolution in Panama and set up a "republic" which the United States quickly recognized and protected by preventing Colombia from landing troops to put down the revolution. The Panamanian government granted to the United States the perpetual right to control a zone across Panama through which a canal would be built. Colombia vigorously protested this flagrant abuse of power by the United States, but Roosevelt refused to apologize or to submit the dispute with Colombia to arbitration. Secretary of State John Hay and his successor, Elihu Root, defended the President's acts with sophistries unbecoming to their character, Congress was subservient to the President, and the people at large were apathetic, or misinformed, or lacking in sustained indignation. Presidents Taft and Wilson were thwarted by Roosevelt's partisans in the Senate from making amends to Colombia, and it was not until petroleum had been discovered there that an indirect apology was made by the United States along with a compensating grant of $25,000,000.

THE FAR EAST

The policies of the United States regarding China and Japan remained relatively constant from the negotiation of the first commercial treaties until the Spanish-American War. With one fleeting exception, the United States sought no territory or sphere of influence and no commercial privilege beyond the most-favored-nation treatment.

Its relationship with Korea, however, was a separate matter. The government of China regarded Korea as a dependency, or in western terms, a quasi-independent area that owed allegiance to China. At the same time, the commercial treaties between China and the Western powers did not extend to Korea, where all foreign commerce was excluded. Japan had attempted to acquire Korea in the sixteenth century, considered it independent of China, and recognized its sovereignty in 1876. The United States and Korea signed a commercial treaty in 1882. Although the United States officially considered Korea as independent, the treaty was negotiated in China with the assistance of the Chinese government, and contained the following provision:

> If any power deals unjustly or oppressively with either government, the other *will exert their good offices* [Italics supplied] to bring about an amicable agreement.

The Chinese government favored the Korean-American treaty as a barrier against Japanese expansion into Korea and wanted the treaty to contain a specific American protectorate. The wording noted here was adopted instead, but Korea regarded the treaty as quasi-protectoral, and both Presidents Arthur and Cleveland, along with various American official representatives in Korea, indicated that at the very least the United States would use whatever moral influence it had in support of this interpretation. This is the most conservative statement that could be made about American obligations under the treaty, for some historians hold that it was regarded by both parties as guaranteeing Korean independence.

THE OPEN-DOOR POLICY

The most important developments in the Far East toward the end of the nineteenth century were the growth of Japan as a great power and its expansionist designs on China, the acquisition of spheres of influence in China by Germany, France, Great Britain,

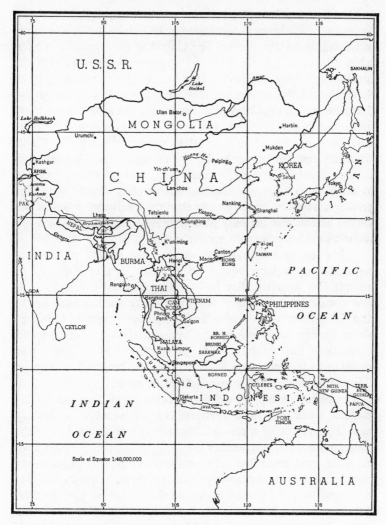

Far East

and Russia, and the expansion of the United States into the area. Although Britain had a large sphere of influence in China, it did not favor its dismemberment. Britain inquired, in March, 1898, whether the United States would co-operate in opposing the restriction of "freedom of commerce of all nations in China either by imposing preferential conditions or by obtaining actual cession of Chinese coastal territory." The United States rejected this offer when it was made, but became more concerned about the possible breakup of China after John Hay became Secretary of State in September of the same year. Hay shared Britain's view that the dismemberment of China was imminent, believed the national interest of the United States was involved, and decided in September, 1899, to suggest to the various powers interested in China what has become known as the open-door policy. He requested Britain, Russia, Germany, France, Italy, and Japan to agree not to establish in China any commercial or other economic special privilege. This was nothing more than the traditional policy of the United States, and the only new feature of Hay's action was the request to other powers to concur in this policy.

It is open to interpretation whether the several powers accepted the open-door request. In their replies they appeared to accept; Hay assumed they had, and proclaimed it as a fact. A few months later the Boxer Rebellion broke out in China, partly as a domestic and partly as an antiforeign movement, and brought about foreign intervention. Hay immediately issued his Second Open Door note in July, 1900, in which American policy was stated to be the protection of its interests in China and respect for Chinese territorial and administrative integrity.

The policy of the United States regarding China was fundamentally weak. American treaty rights in China included consular jurisdiction, rights of trade under specific conditions, and any right China might confer on another nation. A strong policy would have been for the United States to remind other powers of its treaty rights and of its determination to defend them. Not only was this not done, but the United States weakened its position further. After the Boxer Rebellion had been suppressed, Russia seemed most reluctant to evacuate the Manchurian territory of China it had occupied. Japan and Britain were alarmed over what appeared to be Russian expansionism, and Britain asked the United States if it would co-operate to maintain the territorial integrity of China. The United States said it would not do so either acting alone or in concert with other powers. Britain turned to Japan and made an alliance in 1902, which in effect protected Japan from any other power if she got into a conflict with Russia.

This was the status of affairs in the Far East at about the time Theodore Roosevelt became President with his vast ambitions to play a large role in world affairs. Since he was more devoted to action than to logical analysis, it is doubtful that he began with a set of principles and suited his policies to them, but more likely that he decided on courses of action in specific cases and found later he could explain his actions by a general doctrine, the "balance of power." At any rate, he decided that Russia was the most aggressive of any of the powers with Far Eastern interests and that China was unable to protect itself against Russian advance. It followed then, in Roosevelt's opinion, that Japan should be allowed or encouraged to improve her strategic position and her power in order to hold Russia in check, while Britain under the Anglo-Japanese alliance would restrain Germany or France from aiding Russia. Roosevelt would have favored an open Anglo-American-Japanese alliance, but thought Congress would not approve. He accomplished virtually the same objective by letting Japan know informally and secretly that the United States would not fulfill its treaty obligations to Korea if Japan should take over that country, and that the United States would remain neutral in case of a Russo-Japanese war. This abandonment of Korea was confirmed in the secret Taft-Katsura memorandum (1905) which Roosevelt agreed to prior to the signing of the Treaty of Portsmouth, which ended the Russo-Japanese War.

Japan was notably successful in her war with Russia, but was unprepared for a long struggle and became anxious to make peace because the very success of its military advance into Manchuria had left her army in a precarious position. Russia was willing to make peace also, but not on terms she considered intolerable. This gave Roosevelt the opportunity of playing secretly the role of mediator between the two belligerents. The crisis in peace negotiations came over Japan's demand for a large indemnity and the whole of Sakhalin Island. Although Roosevelt remained pro-Japanese to the end of the war and approved the Japanese demands, he also wanted to restore peace, and when Russia stood firm against paying any indemnity but offered to divide Sakhalin, letting Japan have the southern half, he urged Japan to accept the Russian proposal. In view of the military situation, Japan was quite willing to accept, but needed a scapegoat for political reasons at home; the Japanese people were allowed or encouraged to believe that the United States had prevented Japan from securing the full fruits of its victory. The ensuing anti-American agitation in Japan was one of the reasons that led Roosevelt to send the American fleet on a world cruise, 1907–1909, one of its ports of call being Yokohama. No unfortunate incident occurred while the fleet was in Japanese waters, but its visit served only to increase Japanese desire for a larger navy and was probably one of the factors that caused Japan and Russia to undermine Roosevelt's whole balance-of-power doctrine by making a series of agreements between 1907 and 1912 that marked out their respective spheres of influence in northeastern China.

Meanwhile China lay helpless while its sovereignty was violated by Japan and Russia and while it observed the Japanese acquisition of Korea with the consent of Britain and the United States. The growth of sentiment in China against foreign influence, coupled with dissatisfaction over American exclusion laws barring Chinese immigration was shown during the years 1894–1896 in a movement to boycott American trade. The movement was not sponsored by the government of China, which took measures to suppress it, nor was it in violation of international law or of American treaty rights in China. Nevertheless, Roosevelt was greatly aroused over the matter, made military preparations to invade China, and probably would have done so if the movement had not been of brief duration because of government hostility and its own inherent weakness. Aroused over Japanese and Russian encroachments, the Chinese government made a feeble attempt in 1908 to promote a Chinese-American-German alliance, but this was thwarted by Roosevelt and his pro-Japanese Secretary of State, Elihu Root, who negotiated the Root-Takahira Agreement, which implied the recognition of Japan's special sphere of influence in Manchuria.

The result, therefore, of Roosevelt's Far Eastern policy was to decrease somewhat Russia's influence, to increase considerably

Japan's strategic position and power, to neglect and partially abandon the open-door policy, to weaken the moral position of the United States through the disregard of its duties to Korea, and to undermine the American constitutional structure through the making of secret agreements without the knowledge, let alone the consent, of Congress. The balance-of-power fallacy was clearly exposed by the Russo-Japanese *rapprochement* and was abandoned by President Taft, who tried to replace it with an international banking agreement designed to prevent a single power from controlling foreign investments in China. This economic policy, based on a concert of powers rather than on a balance-of-power doctrine, was sound in theory and might have been successful if Russia and Japan had not opposed it and if Britain and France had been willing to support the United States against them.

Since world politics, as the term implies, is not restricted to geographical areas, events in Europe and in the Far East influenced each other. During the late years of the nineteenth century and the early years of the twentieth, the principal powers of Europe formed a series of diverse agreements, sometimes called alliances and alignments, the exact designation and substance of which do not need to be considered here. Fundamentally they divided Europe into two combinations with France, Great Britain, and Russia on one side and Germany, Austria, and Italy on the other. How strong the combinations were was uncertain at the time of the outbreak of the Russo-Japanese War, and the German Emperor decided to test their strength while that war was still in progress. He found an opportunity to suggest a European conference over affairs in Morocco, where France and Britain had made an agreement without consulting other European powers. Germany requested the United States to support the idea of a conference—which France in particular opposed—and to take part in it, thus giving Germany a chance to observe the strength of the Anglo-French entente and the closeness of Anglo-American relations. Germany represented to the United States, however, that its main interest was in supporting the principle of the open door in Morocco.

President Roosevelt was reluctant at first to intervene in European politics because he feared strong hostility in Congress.

He decided, however, that danger of a European war existed and that he should accept the German invitation to promote a conference. Having reached this conclusion, he carried on personal diplomacy with France, Germany, and Great Britain, not only secretly as far as Congress and the American people were concerned, but also without the knowledge of Secretary of State John Hay or the American ambassadors in the three countries primarily involved. He secured a promise from Germany that she would follow American leadership if a conference met and should reach an impasse, and this information was communicated to France. How much Roosevelt influenced French policy cannot be determined because French opposition to a conference was weakened by the fall from power of the French Foreign Minister, Théophile Delcassé, who opposed the conference. At any rate, Roosevelt used his influence in favor of a conference which met in Algeciras in southern Spain in January, 1906, with the United States as a member.

Meanwhile Elihu Root had replaced John Hay as Secretary of State in July, 1905, and was more sympathetic to Roosevelt's policies regarding Germany than Hay had been. Roosevelt continued, however, to conduct personal diplomacy during the conference and believed he had been of great influence in arranging the final settlement and in averting a European war. The Senate approved the Act of Algeciras but attached a resolution declaring that the United States did not thereby depart from its traditional policy of avoiding entanglements in the internal affairs of Europe.

The broad characteristics of American foreign policy during the era under survey are too obvious to need elaborate summary. The United States, whether wisely or not, clearly departed from important elements of its traditional policies. It became a great naval power with a new naval doctrine that was not confined to defensive action; it became an imperial power; it stretched the Monroe Doctrine to include intervention; it abandoned principle for expediency in relation to China, Korea, and Colombia; and one of its most famous leaders dabbled in world politics. None of these things grew from the people or was completely understood by them, and none save the element of power was permanent.

VIII

THE FIRST WORLD WAR

THE TAFT ADMINISTRATION marked the end of one era of American history and foreign policy and formed to some extent a bridge to the next. Unlike Theodore Roosevelt, Taft undertook no large role in world affairs, generally had respect for treaty obligations, and promoted, although without significant success, the principle of arbitration for the settlement of international disputes. At the same time, he had been associated with some of Roosevelt's policies and, not being a strong leader, crumbled when faced with stern opposition from within his own political party. Clearly a new era began—and, as it turned out, ended—with the Administration of Woodrow Wilson, who brought to the Presidency high moral standards, outstanding intellectual competence, steadfastness in the face of opposition, and a determination to chart a new course for the United States. He believed that self-government could be accelerated in American dependent areas, interventionism in Latin America abandoned, respect for treaties restored, and world harmony promoted through freer trade policies, adherence to international law, and the development of international arbitration and conciliation. Perhaps most of all he believed the United States could best serve its own and the world's interests by setting an example of democratic and constitutional government devoted to the freedom, equality of opportunity, and responsibility of the

137

individual. He could not foresee that virtually none of his plans could be fully implemented before a great world war would interrupt or alter them and would lead him to the greatest and most tragic enterprise in world affairs that had yet been undertaken by an American President.

INTERNATIONAL CONCILIATION

President Wilson and his Secretary of State, William Jennings Bryan, believed the United States could make a contribution to world peace through a network of bilateral treaties of conciliation. The principle involved in these treaties was based on the assumption that nations often became involved in hostilities because the facts of disputes were examined on each side from extreme nationalistic and partisan viewpoints, and that great difficulty arose in establishing procedures for settlement once a controversy had reached an impasse. The treaties provided for the creation in each case of an impartial standing commission that could be called upon whenever a dispute between the parties was not settled by the normal diplomatic processes. The commission would determine and make public facts of the controversy and suggest a solution, and the signatories would agree not to engage in hostilities until at least six months after the commission had reported. Although the United States signed about thirty such treaties and ratified about twenty, none was made with Germany. The treaties proved ineffective, therefore, as far as the First World War was concerned, but the principle involved was incorporated into the peace machinery of the League of Nations.

LATIN AMERICA

When Wilson assumed the Presidency, he was anxious to promote a more co-operative and friendly relationship with the nations of Latin America and to remove any fear they might have of further American economic exploitation or territorial acquisition. His policies for Latin America included making amends to Colombia for the Panama affair of the Roosevelt Administration, encouragement of hemispheric trade through lower tariffs, the promotion of political stability and constitutional democracy in

Latin America, and inter-American peace through what was called the Pan-American Pact. Under this proposed agreement, the boundaries of each state would be guaranteed by all the signatories, and each state would agree to control arms shipments abroad and to prevent revolutionary groups from using its territory to stage invasions of other states. In addition, the President favored a policy regarding the recognition of new governments that was designed to encourage constitutionalism and orderly processes of change in governments. This policy had been suggested by Latin-American statesmen and was to the effect that new governments would be recognized if they had come into existence by constitutional means or had been otherwise approved by a majority of the people.

It is not possible to estimate how successful this whole policy would have been if the First World War had not intervened to distract Wilson's attention and to disrupt trade, and if a violent civil conflict had not been in progress in Mexico. The President was unable to secure the approval of the Senate for a treaty of reconciliation with Colombia or general Latin-American approval of the Pan-American Pact. Political chaos in Haiti and virtual chaos and civil war in the Dominican Republic led to American intervention in both areas, and the collapse of orderly government in Mexico led to partial intervention in the affairs of that unfortunate country. It is one of the ironies of the Wilson Administration that a President who probably had less desire than any of his predecessors to interfere in the domestic affairs of Latin-American states intervened in more instances than any previous President. It is possible, and according to the critics of Wilson's policies quite probable, that more competent management of American relations with Haiti and the Dominican Republic would have avoided the need for intervention, and that the occupation of Veracruz in Mexico was a mistake both because it failed to accomplish its purpose of preventing foreign arms from reaching the Mexican government and because it aroused hostility toward the United States both in Mexico and in Latin America.

An extensive revolution in Mexico had occurred during the Taft Administration and a new government under Francisco I. Madero had been recognized by the United States. Just before

Wilson came into office, a rival revolutionary group led by Victoriano Huerta captured Mexico City, murdered the President and Vice President, and established itself in power. Wilson refused to recognize the Huerta government partly because of the violent way in which it had assumed power and partly because two other Mexican revolutionary groups denied the legality of the Huerta regime and were waging war against it. One of these groups, located mostly in southern Mexico, was led by Emiliano Zapata, and a northern group, the Constitutionalists, was under the general leadership of Venustiano Carranza, who had gained the temporary support of three other rebel chieftains, Francisco Villa, Álvaro Obregón, and Pablo González. Wilson's dislike of the bandit Huerta caused him to favor the Carranza movement, although he believed that Villa was the strongest of its several leaders and the one most likely to bring a semblance of peace and order to Mexico. The President's desire to see Huerta removed from office formed one of the reasons for his consent to the occupation of Veracruz. Wilson was mistaken, however, in his estimate of Villa, who was violent in his methods, incompetent in administration, and incapable of loyalty to his erstwhile chief against whom he revolted as soon as Huerta was overthrown by the Constitutionalists in July, 1914. Defeated by Obregón, who remained loyal to Carranza, Villa returned to banditry and in March, 1916, raided the New Mexican border town of Columbus. With the consent of Carranza, Wilson sent a military expedition into Mexico in a futile attempt to capture Villa, but when this purpose was not immediately accomplished, Wilson found that Carranza strongly opposed the continuance of American troops on Mexican soil.

Meanwhile Zapata's forces had been dispersed by González, and thus Carranza was placed in substantial if not complete control of Mexico. There existed, however, strong demands in the United States—on the part of American owners of Mexican property and particularly on the part of the Roman Catholic hierarchy, which denounced the Carranza anti-clerical policies—for general intervention in Mexico against the Carranza regime. Wilson was utterly opposed to general intervention and seized the expedient of calling on a group of Latin-American states to consult on Mexican affairs. This group, consisting of Argentina, Chile,

Brazil, Uruguay, Guatemala, and Bolivia, recommended the recognition *de facto* of Carranza's government, and Wilson accepted this policy in October, 1915, although full recognition was not granted until 1917. During the political campaign of 1916 in the United States, Wilson was denounced by the imperialists for having a weak policy toward Mexico, by the Roman Catholic hierarchy for not intervening to overthrow Carranza, and by others for taking any hand at all in Mexican affairs. By avoiding, however, general intervention in Mexico and by maintaining peace with Carranza, Wilson was relatively free from the Mexican embroilment when the United States entered into war with Germany.

Viewed as a whole, Wilson's Latin-American policy was neither a complete success nor a total failure. It was characterized in some instances by uncertainty and vacillation caused by a lack of knowledge and understanding of conditions in several Latin-American countries and by inadequate management of policy, particularly while Bryan remained as Secretary of State. It failed to realize fully Wilson's hopes of promoting democratic, constitutional, and orderly government in the Caribbean area, and demonstrated that a foreign policy motivated by good intentions and high ideals could not alone confer political stability and moral conduct on nations whose leaders and rulers were unwilling to accept and incapable of receiving such a policy. At the same time, Wilson avoided war with Mexico when there was great demand for it in the United States, demonstrated his desire to make amends to Colombia even though this accomplishment was frustrated by the Senate, and established the precedent—through the attempt to negotiate the Pan-American Pact and through consultation with Latin-American states regarding Mexico—of co-operation between the United States and Latin America in matters of mutual concern. The liabilities of Wilson's Latin-American policy were largely the results of conditions he could not control; the assets of his policy had long-range value.

THE FIRST WORLD WAR AND AMERICAN NEUTRALITY

As soon as the First World War began in August, 1914, President Wilson proclaimed American neutrality, offered the good offices of the United States to effect a peaceful settlement, requested the American people to maintain an impartial attitude toward the belligerents, and set an example in this respect by his own conduct. It is virtually a certainty, however, that from the outset the majority of the American people favored the Allied side. This initial pro-Allied attitude was not the result, therefore, of propaganda, economic interest or influence, political leadership or of any other factor save the traditions of the past and the events that took place at the beginning of the war. American culture had many sources, but its great heritage was English: its language, its basic legal and political institutions, its ideals, and the literature most familiar to the people. To many people England was the mother of parliaments and represented democratic institutions. During the past half century the American and British governments had grown closer together until by 1914 no serious conflict of interest separated them. In contrast with this, Germany since 1871, Germany of the Empire, represented to many people Prussian militarism and had appeared to be, and probably was, the nation most likely to challenge American interests in Latin America and elsewhere and to oppose the American ideal of democracy. In addition, the early events of the war made a strong impression in the United States, an impression adverse to Germany. Among these events was German support of Austrian aggression against Serbia, German violation of Belgian neutrality which Germany was pledged to respect, German bombing of unfortified British North Sea towns, ruthlessness in Belgium, particularly in relation to the university town of Louvain, and the invasion of France although the French Army had been drawn back from the German frontier. There was, however, a substantial minority of the people who were unimpressed with these considerations and defended the acts and policies of the Central Powers.

Whatever may have been the diverse views of the people regarding the respective merits of the belligerents, there was virtually no public dissent from the President's policy of neutrality, although it may not have been universally understood that neutrality was not simply noninvolvement. It was a legal status embracing the rights and duties of neutrals and belligerents as the

United States had so continuously insisted throughout its entire national history. Attempts had been made at the Second Hague Conference of 1907 and at a naval conference in London in 1908 to redefine the rights and duties of neutrals, but neither of the documents produced by these conferences had been universally accepted by the maritime powers and had, therefore, no binding effect on any power. With this in mind, President Wilson announced that the United States would rely on general international law as the basis for its neutral rights and duties, and he established an interdepartmental committee to advise him regarding any problems that might arise between the United States and the belligerents. From then until the United States became engaged in the war, it endeavored strictly to perform its neutral duties and to maintain its neutral rights. But this could not be done without controversy, for pro-Germans did not want neutral rights enforced against the Central Powers and pro-British Americans did not want them enforced against the Allies.

The controversies with the Allies—primarily with Britain—involved the definition of contraband, the doctrine of continuous voyage, the use of the so-called black list, the laying of mines in the high seas, and censorship of the mail. The Allies did not declare a blockade of Germany partly because they could not have enforced it along the German Baltic coast. Instead they progressively extended the contraband list to include all the goods they thought would be significantly useful in the war effort of the Central Powers, and used the doctrine of continuous voyage to keep such goods from reaching them through neutral nations. The United States protested against some phases of these practices, but its position was logically and legally weak, for it had vigorously defended the doctrine of continuous voyage during the Civil War, and international law did not confine contraband to any precise list of goods. The "black list" referred to a list of firms in neutral countries with whom British subjects were forbidden to trade because those firms traded with Britain's enemies. Superficially this might appear to be an infringement of the rights of neutrals, but actually it was not. Any nation had a sovereign right to control its own nationals, and the neutral firms were not interfered with by Britain if they continued to trade with the belligerents. Later the United States used the black-list policy itself and with perfect legal propriety. The United States did not protest the censorship of mail to belligerents or the examination of mail that contained contraband. It protested against interference with what it called "genuine correspondence," but was at a complete loss to explain how this could be discovered without the examination of all correspondence. Its protest, therefore, was irresponsible.

The Second Hague Conference had drafted "provisional rules" regarding the laying of mines in the high seas, and while these rules never became binding on nations they formed the best guide to proper conduct in this respect. The rules provided that the mines should be anchored and constructed so as to become harmless if they broke loose, should not interfere with peaceful navigation, should be kept under surveillance, and should be removed when hostilities ended. Germany began laying mines apparently without observing any of these rules, and some neutral ships were sunk by them, but no American ship. Britain retaliated by placing mines in the southern area of the North Sea, but observed all the above rules, including provisions for the safety of neutral shipping. Neutrals were shown safe routes through the mine fields, and Britain offered to escort neutral ships if requested. The United States could not show that American ships or lives had been lost by Allied mines, that international law had been violated by the Allies, or that lawful commerce had been restrained.

Those Americans who favored Germany, or feared the United States might become involved in the war if it defended its neutral rights, raised other issues. They held that American neutrality was endangered by the travel of Americans on belligerent passenger or merchant ships, that the arming of American merchant ships for defense against submarines was nonneutral, and, most of all, that since German merchantmen could not reach the United States because of British sea power, it was nonneutral for American citizens to lend money or sell goods to the Allies. Regarding American travel on belligerent merchant or passenger ships, the subject could be dismissed without comment, for the United States did not become involved in the war over this issue. It became involved only after American lives had been lost by the sinking of American ships. The issue, however, was irrelevant concerning

American neutrality for another reason. The American policy regarding submarine warfare applied to all belligerents and neutrals alike. This policy upheld the right of belligerents to seize any ship on the high seas carrying contraband and to stop ships for visit and search to determine this fact. What it denied was that merchant or passenger ships could be sunk without determining whether they carried contraband and without making provision for the safety of the passengers and crew. The nationality of the ship made no difference as far as neutral rights and international law were concerned. The United States had the right to arm merchant ships for *defense* against illegal acts on the high seas, and some ships were so armed late in the neutrality period, but that question is also fundamentally irrelevant, for the United States did not become involved in the war until after American lives had been lost by the sinking of *unarmed* American ships.

The third issue, that of lending money and selling goods to the belligerents, was given careful analysis by the United States. The fact was that American citizens were not prohibited by international law or by domestic law from lending money or selling goods of any kind to belligerents, and the President had no authority either to authorize or to prohibit such acts. If Americans sold contraband goods, belligerents could seize them on the high seas or as they passed through blockaded ports. In such matters individuals from any neutral country acted at their own risk. If the United States prevented its citizens from selling goods to one belligerent because it had greater sea power than its opponent, in effect it would have intervened to assist the opponent and would have violated its neutral duty. This was clearly stated by the President and was understood by Congress, which made no move to legislate on the subject.

The problems that arose between the United States and Germany over neutral rights and duties were almost exclusively concerned with submarine warfare. At the beginning of the war, Germany had not planned on using submarines as commerce destroyers, but, after one successful enterprise, decided to do so, and declared the waters surrounding the British Isles a war zone in which all ships would be sunk without discrimination as to their nationality and without making provision for the safety of their passengers or crews. The United States immediately protested against this policy as a violation of international law and an infringement of the rights of neutrals, and declared it would hold Germany to strict accountability for the loss of any American lives and would take whatever steps it deemed necessary for the protection of American life and property. This was the basic American policy from which it never departed, for which it always had the support of Congress and the nation, and in reality was a declaration that unrestricted submarine warfare on American ships on the high seas would be an act of war against the United States. This basic policy was approved in the platforms of both major political parties in the election of 1916 and by the political leaders who opposed the President as well as reaffirmed by the President himself, who made it clear in that campaign that he could not promise to preserve the peace of the nation and at the same time its rights on the seas, for the violation of the latter would not be within his control. He requested the people not to require of him something that was contradictory and impossible.

After a long diplomatic exchange with the United States, Germany temporarily abandoned unrestricted submarine warfare, and until this warfare was renewed early in 1917, the two nations engaged in no serious controversies. During that time some of the controversies mentioned above with the Allies took place, and President Wilson tried in various ways without success to effect a peaceful settlement of the war. He was engaged in such an effort when Germany decided to renew unrestricted submarine warfare. Germany military leaders began in August, 1916, to advocate such renewal. The Chancellor opposed this policy because he knew it would bring the United States into the war, and it was opposed by the German ambassador in Washington as well as by various military and civilian officials attached to the Embassy. They warned the German government and also *directly* warned the military leaders, in a series of remarkable communications, that the United States was being strictly neutral and wanted to remain so, but that the nation was united behind the President's policy on submarine warfare and that its renewal would have "incalculable moral" disadvantage to Germany, would unquestionably bring the United States into the war, and would cause Germany to be defeated. The German High Command did not heed these warnings, believing Germany could win the war in five months after unrestricted submarine warfare had been renewed and before the United States could be a factor in the outcome. They held before the German people their war aims, which included, among other things, indemnities from the Allies sufficient to cover all German and Austrian *war costs,* permanent destruction of the British Navy, control of Poland and Belgium, and various strategic territorial annexations from areas around Germany. Having secured the consent of the Reichstag and the Emperor, the military leaders decided on the renewal of unrestricted submarine warfare beginning February 1, 1917.

The President broke diplomatic relations with Germany on February 3, but in a message to Congress still held the door open for Germany to reconsider its policy, and said he would not be convinced Germany intended to prosecute its ruthless program until an overt act on her part had resulted in the loss of American lives. When this occurred from the sinking of American ships on the high seas during February and March, 1917, the President asked Congress to declare that a state of war existed because Germany had deliberately made war on the United States. In the premises, no other course was open to him.

PEACE PLANS AND THE PRE-ARMISTICE AGREEMENT

Reference has been made to the efforts of President Wilson during the period of American neutrality to assist the belligerents in making a peace settlement, often referred to as a negotiated or as a compromise peace. He tendered the use of American good offices, requested the belligerents to state their war aims, suggested principles on which peace might be based, and, early in 1916, offered to involve the United States in a peace arrangement. His proposal called for a peace conference and a settlement which would provide for the evacuation of invaded areas, the restoration of Belgium, the return of Alsace and Lorraine to France with possible territorial compensation elsewhere to Germany, the acquisition by Russia of an outlet to the sea, and the establishment of a world organization to maintain peace with the United States as a member. He suggested to Britain that if such a conference were held and the Allies accepted the terms of peace while Germany refused, the United States would "probably" become a belligerent on the Allied side. The Allies did not accept the President's proposal or make a formal statement of their reasons for not doing so. Some British leaders apparently felt the Allies should have a positive American commitment, including congressional approval, to this peace program before they should enter upon it. They believed it would be damaging to Allied morale, perhaps fatally damaging, if the Allies proposed peace on the President's terms, Germany rejected them, and the United States refused to enter the war. They wanted the certainty, not just the probability, of American support. Other British leaders may have had different reasons for not acting on Wilson's proposal, or the French government may not have agreed. An examination of German archives that became available after the Second World War indicate that Germany would not have accepted any compromise peace at that time. When the archives of the Allies are opened to examination, they may reveal the reasons for Allied policy in this instance.

After the United States entered the war, the President came to believe that peace could not properly be made until Germany had been defeated and had surrendered, but this did not mean it had to be destroyed or necessarily invaded. Victory for the United States and the Allies, officially known as the Allied and Associated Powers, would be achieved whenever they had secured their war objectives. Wilson had given much thought to the principles on which world peace could be established and the relationship of these to the peace settlement. He had stated some of the principles during the period of American neutrality, but he defined them in greater detail after the United States entered the war and particularly in an address to Congress of January 8, 1918, in which he stated what became known as the Fourteen Points of peace. Earlier he had tried through his representatives in the Senate to secure a resolution from that body approving his peace program, but Senator Henry Cabot Lodge, indicating that he was speaking for the Republican Party, had opposed such a resolution on the theory that Congress should take no part in the formation of foreign policy. It was the President's duty, he said, to formulate policy and the duty of the Congress to consider it later. This was in striking contrast to the attitude of Congress during the Second World War when both houses of Congress were willing to pass resolutions of the kind Wilson advocated.

The German High Command believed they could win the war by a massive offensive during the summer of 1918. The Russian war effort had collapsed after the Bolshevik Revolution, with which Germany had connived, the Italian front against Austria had to be supported by other Allies, submarine warfare was in full swing and causing great damage to Allied shipping, and the American war potential was not yet fully realized. Nevertheless, the German offensive failed, and when it did, the German High Command crumbled in the face of defeat, became panic-stricken, notified the government that the Army was confronted with imminent disaster, and that peace should be made on the best terms possible. What Germany wanted was an armistice, that is, a cease fire, with the Army remaining in place while a peace conference with German participation was held. In such a situation, the Army would have time to strengthen its position, the German negotiators would have the opportunity to intrigue for a division among the Allies, and Germany could renew the war if it chose to do so, perhaps under better circumstances than when the cease fire began.

President Wilson would have no part in such a proposal. He told Germany that it would be obliged to surrender on military terms decided by the Allied military leaders, that Germany would have to establish a responsible government, and that the peace settlement would be made by the Allied and Associated Powers. He agreed, however, as Germany had requested, that the settlement would be made on the basis of the terms of peace he had announced in his address to Congress of January, 1918, and the principles of settlement stated in his subsequent addresses, but he made it clear that these terms and principles would be interpreted by the Allied and Associated Powers. Thus Germany had the option of continuing the war with further loss of life, the certainty of military invasion and occupation, and the absence of any promise concerning the principles of settlement, or of accepting the Wilsonian terms. Germany realized it was greatly to its advantage to accept the latter alternative. The correspondence between Wilson and Germany resulted in a preliminary agreement which became, with a few changes, the Pre-Armistice Agreement.

Having reached an understanding with Germany, Wilson's next step was to secure the acceptance of the agreement by the Allies. They knew of the negotiations, possibly had influenced them in some respects, but were not committed to the draft agreement. There was little room for controversy between the United States and the Allies over the principles of peace, for both Britain and France had stated similar principles as their war objectives. There was a distinction, however, between a statement of principles and a binding multilateral agreement to apply the principles in a peace settlement, and with the taste of victory in their mouths the Allies would have preferred German surrender without legal Allied commitment to the Wilsonian program whatever the moral commitment might be. Wilson virtually told them that the United States would not sacrifice further American lives after its war objectives had been achieved, and the Allied governments did not venture to face their people with a different policy. Wilson accepted at Allied request two changes in the text of the preliminary agreement. One was in effect the substitution of the word "reparation" for "restoration" with regard to German obligations concerning damages to Allied civilian life and property, and the other was to postpone until the peace conference the question of the freedom of the seas. The first of these changes was logical because some kinds of damages to people and property could not in a technical sense be "restored." The other change Wilson accepted with great reluctance because the principle of the freedom of the seas was one of the things the United States had been fighting for. He was willing to agree that the freedom of the seas should not be interpreted to deny the right of blockade under international law, but this did not quite satisfy the British government and Admiralty because questions could arise over the interpretation of the law of blockade. It was a considerable concession, therefore, for Wilson to accept this change. He did so because it was the one issue that threatened to divide the United

States and the Allies, because he was confident of incorporating the principle of the freedom of the seas into the Covenant of the League of Nations, and because it seemed a great achievement to secure complete agreement on all other parts of the peace program.

In view of later events, it seems important to emphasize three significant facts about the Pre-Armistice Agreement. One is that in reality, although not in form, it was a negotiated peace treaty with Germany which provided for German surrender, the military conditions of surrender being given to Germany later in what was improperly called an "armistice." The second is that the peace settlement of Versailles could not be properly called a "dictate" to Germany because Germany had agreed in return for the advantages of escaping invasion to accept a settlement on the basis of the principles stated in the Pre-Armistice Agreement as interpreted by the Allied and Associated Powers. And the third is that the United States, in failing to accept the peace settlement, the Treaty of Versailles, violated its commitments in the Pre-Armistice Agreement both to Germany and to the Allies.

THE PEACE TREATY OF VERSAILLES

Reference has been made to the "principles of peace" as announced by Wilson or the Allies, and to the "terms of peace," a phrase used in the Pre-Armistice Agreement. In his address to Congress of January 8, 1918, the President used the phrase "the programme of the world's peace" in reference to the Fourteen Points of that address. Some confusion at the time and much needless controversy later could have been avoided by a more precise use of the words "principles," "terms," and "program," even though there was no real excuse for misunderstanding. The first five of the Fourteen Points involved several principles of peace rather than terms of a peace settlement with Germany. They involved abandonment of secret treaties, the freedom of the seas save when closed by international action, the removal "as far as possible" of trade barriers, reduction of armaments "consistent with national security," and a settlement of colonial claims with equal attention to the interests of the people concerned and to the "equitable" claims of the controlling governments. To some extent these principles were included in the Covenant of the League of Nations and in that sense were a part of the treaty with Germany, but in any event they were largely prospective. The sixth point referred to Russia, whose condition had changed prior to the Paris conference, and the fourteenth point concerned the establishment of an association of nations. The other seven points were more exactly terms of peace with the Central Powers and can be placed into three divisions: (1) the invaded areas of Belgium, France, Rumania, Serbia, and Montenegro were to be "restored"; (2) the peoples of Austria-Hungary and of the non-Turkish parts of the Ottoman Empire were to be given the opportunity of "autonomous" development; and (3) Poland was to be re-established as an independent state.

In addition to these principles and terms of peace, Wilson referred at various times to other principles of world peace, among them the right of people to self-government. This was nothing more than an affirmation of the basic principle of the Declaration of Independence, which no American statesmen could reject. Wilson commented on this idea many times and with slight variations of phraseology, saying that "governments derive all their just powers from the consent of the governed," and declaring the "right of people everywhere to govern themselves." He took particular care, however, to limit or to clarify this broad principle in its application to the complicated nationalisms of Europe. What he said was that "well-defined national aspirations" should be accorded satisfaction when that could be done "without introducing new or perpetuating old elements of discord . . . that would be likely in time to break the peace of Europe and consequently of the world." He had in mind that the creation of a small state, even if it had well-defined national aspirations, might not be wise unless it was economically viable and politically secure. The principles, therefore, of the removal of trade barriers, the reduction of armaments, the freedom of the seas, and the universal guarantee of boundaries were related to the application of the principle of self-determination.

The most basic Wilsonian principle of world peace, the touchstone of his whole peace program, and the concept on which his statesmanship must primarily be judged at the bar of history, was that a concert of world power was essential for the preservation of peace. This concept was based on the general premise that justice among nations would not exist unless the rights of self-government, independence, territorial integrity, and the opportunity of legitimate peaceful development among weak states were as secure as among powerful states, and that these rights could not be established save through an association of nations whose combined strength was greater than that of any single state or other group of states. He did not hold that all states could be equal in territory, resources, or enterprise, or that the existing situation of states would remain static, or that a given peace settlement would be permanent. He held that the rights of states could be permanent, and that there could be permanent processes of peaceful change. He proposed, therefore, as part of the peace settlement and attached to it, and as an indispensable first step toward the world's peace, the establishment of an association of nations to *guarantee* the "political independence and territorial integrity to great and small states alike." He referred to this as the extension of the *principle* of the Monroe Doctrine to the world, that no nation should be allowed to "extend its polity over any other nation or state." It might appear this principle was later incorporated into the 1928 Pact of Paris, but the difference between that Pact and the Covenant of the League of Nations was fundamental. Under the Pact, nations promised not to use war as an instrument of national policy, but under the Covenant they promised to act against a nation that used war for that purpose.

The Treaty of Versailles and the other treaties that constituted the whole peace settlement cannot be considered here in detail and do not need to be as far as the foreign policy of the United States is concerned. Some of the broad features of the settlement had been accepted in the Pre-Armistice Agreement. Alsace and Lorraine were restored to France and Poland was re-established. The Austro-Hungarian Empire, tottering before the war, had fallen apart before the Peace Conference met and the succession states were at least partially in existence. The conference had the duty of establishing the boundaries of new states along lines of nationality as far as that was possible, or, in terms of the

Wilsonian principle of self-determination, if at all practicable. These boundaries were drawn for the most part by commissions and in a few places left to determination by plebiscites. No territory in Europe was taken from Germany that rightly belonged to it, and no boundary—no matter whether a better one could have been defined—was a basic or determining factor in the causes for the Second World War. The settlement produced, as Herbert Hoover said, the best ethnic arrangement of states Europe had ever experienced. The German colonies and the non-Turkish parts of the Ottoman Empire were placed under mandates subject to the supervision of the League of Nations, and, where suitable, namely with the "A" and "B" classes of mandates, with the understanding they would be afforded opportunities for autonomous development, which eventually materialized. Since the United States did not ratify the Treaty of Versailles, it was not represented on the Mandates Commission which distributed the mandated areas. President Wilson indicated to the Japanese that he would consent to their having a mandate over the German Pacific islands north of the Equator, with the exception of the island of Yap, provided they returned Kiaochow to China. Japan did not accept this proposal, so it cannot be known what position the President would have taken under different circumstances.

The problem of Kiaochow concerned the disposition of an area of that name, in the Chinese province of Shantung, which had been leased by Germany. When the war in Europe started, President Wilson hoped Japan and China would remain neutral, but Japan, with British approval, declared war on Germany and captured Kiaochow and the German Pacific islands north of the Equator. China also declared war on Germany, partly in order to be present at the peace settlement to make sure of recovering Kiaochow. When Japan invaded Kiaochow, a violation of Chinese sovereignty, she declared officially that she did so for the purpose of restoring that area to China. Later, however, Japan made demands on China, the Twenty-One Demands, indicating her desire and intention to dominate the whole of China. The United States reacted to this Japanese *démarche* by declaring, May 11, 1915, that it would not recognize any agreement between Japan and China that impaired American treaty rights in China, Chinese political and territorial integrity, or the open-door policy. The resulting strained relations between the United States and Japan were partially mended by the Lansing-Ishii Agreement of November, 1917, under which Japan appeared to accept the American position, but relations between the two nations were disturbed anew by Japanese activities in Siberia that formed the primary reason for American temporary intervention in that area. Under the circumstances, President Wilson was particularly anxious that the Paris conference should not sanction Japanese control of Kiaochow.

Japan refused to return Kiaochow to China immediately and refused both of Wilson's proposed alternatives: (1) to place the area under the authority of the Allied and Associated Powers, one of whom was Japan, or (2) to stipulate in the treaty of peace that it would be restored. Japan's position was that she had given her word to restore Kiaochow to China, that her word was sufficient and should be respected, and that if it was not, Japan would leave the conference, refuse to join the League of Nations, and do as she pleased with respect to China no matter what the other powers might write into the Treaty of Versailles. Britain, France, and Italy supported Japan. Secretary of State Robert Lansing thought Japan was bluffing and that Wilson should refuse to be coerced, but Wilson believed, as subsequent documentary evidence has shown, that Japan was not bluffing. Thus he was faced with a serious dilemma, for Japan had the advantage. If Japan left the conference and refused to join the League of Nations, that organization would be undermined, and Kiaochow would still remain in Japanese possession unless the United States was willing to undertake alone a war with Japan to effect its restoration. At the same time, if Kiaochow was not restored, justice to China and one of Wilson's principles would be disregarded. With Japan riding high and the Allies with her, Wilson may have felt, in Pindar's phrase, like

> One of the infantry
> Footslogging beside a Lydian chariot.

He had, however, an obvious alternative policy. The United States could accept Japan's word on Kiaochow and secure Japanese membership in the League of Nations with all the restraints that organization would impose on Japan's future relations, not only with Kiaochow but with China as a whole. Justice and principle in this case might be in abeyance for a time but would not be sacrificed. Wilson accepted Japan's word.

This Kiaochow episode is an example, among many that might be chosen, of the way in which the peace settlement was structured on the foundation of the League of Nations, and of the reasons why the League had to be attached to the settlement as an integral part of it. If Wilson or anyone else had supposed, while the peace conference was in session, that the League of Nations would not come into full force with the United States lending it powerful support, the whole peace structure logically should and would have been different.

One of the large problems of the peace settlement was Germany's responsibility, in the words of the Pre-Armistice Agreement, to make compensation for "all damage done to the civilian population of the Allies and their property by the aggression of Germany." Two things are notable here. One is Germany's admission of aggression prior to the Treaty of Versailles, and the other is her agreement to compensate for damages to people as well as to property. As noted earlier, this was a broader obligation than Wilson's prewar and wartime position that Germany should be liable for the "restoration" of invaded areas. The Allies soon realized, however, that Germany could not be expected to make compensation for the full amount of the legal liability she had accepted, even if this liability were calculated in terms only of restoration. For this reason it became necessary for the Allies to decide what Germany could pay and to allot this amount among themselves in proportion to the damage each had sustained. The total amount of damages and, therefore, the legal liability of Germany and the items that might be included in it, were significant to the Allies with respect to percentages of German compensation each would secure, but were of no material importance to Germany. Since the United States requested no compensation at all, and since it was understood that Germany would be required to make compensation on the basis of her capacity to pay rather than on her total liability, Wilson was willing for the Allies to calculate their percentages of compensation in any way that suited them. He would have preferred to have the amount of German liability set by the treaty of peace, but consented to have this referred to a commission under the supposition that the United States would ratify the treaty and would be a member of the commission with veto power over its acts. The amount Germany was eventually required to pay was probably less than it would have cost to restore the invaded areas of France alone, and she managed to avoid paying most of that.

The most important and the most neglected fact about the Treaty of Versailles as far as American foreign policy is concerned is that opposition to it, on the part of those who were most responsible for its defeat in the Senate and were able to bring this about because they were among the most respected figures in public life, was almost wholly confined to Articles One through Twenty-Six, the Covenant of the League of Nations. They did not base their main opposition to the treaty on any boundary settlement, the establishment of any new state in Europe, the mandate system, the disarmament of Germany, or any alleged severity of treatment of Germany either respecting her territory or the damages she was required to pay. This is the central fact and is not invalidated by the minor criticisms of the treaty expressed in order to influence public opinion, or to please certain ethnic groups or special interests. Some critics singled out the Kiaochow provisions because they could be interpreted and represented to the public as a departure by Wilson from principle. The abrasive and dogmatic strictures of English economist John Maynard Keynes on the economic aspects of the treaty, and his irresponsible caricatures of the principal figures of the Paris conference, introduced into the United States by Felix Frankfurter, were widely diffused and often plagiarized in the Senate, but no important political figure advocated the adoption of the proposals of Keynes, which Wilson had opposed partly because he knew the Senate would not accept them. What the Senate and the Harding Administration rejected, therefore, was not the peace settlement; they rejected American participation in a system of world peace.

THE REJECTION OF THE LEAGUE OF NATIONS

Since the controversy in the United States over the Treaty of Versailles was confined primarily to its first section, the Covenant of the League of Nations, the analysis here will be on that issue, although the vote in the Senate was on the treaty as a whole. After a draft of the Covenant had been approved by the Peace Conference in Paris, President Wilson presented this draft for consideration in the United States. Various prominent leaders of both major political parties suggested changes to meet criticisms that had arisen, particularly the absence in the Covenant of any safeguard to the Monroe Doctrine or any provision for a nation to withdraw from the League. The chairman of the Committee on Foreign Relations of the Senate, Henry Cabot Lodge, acting under the advice of Elihu Root, refused to suggest changes, for, as Root said, he would be obliged to approve the Covenant if it were amended in the ways he recommended. Wilson returned to Paris and secured with considerable difficulty all the principal changes in the Covenant that had been advanced in the United States, including those that ex-President Taft declared met all legitimate criticisms of it.

Wilson had reason to believe, therefore, that the amended Covenant would be acceptable to the Senate and to the American people at large. The correctness of this view appears to be above controversy, for it was admitted by those who opposed the League and managed its defeat. It was necessary, therefore, for those who opposed the League, or who saw an opportunity to use the issue for political purposes, to prevent an immediate clear-cut vote on the League in the Senate, to organize partisan opposition to it, to create about it doubts and uncertainties in the minds of the people, and to devise a strategy of action whereby the League could be defeated by indirection. How this was managed and why it was possible cannot be considered in detail here, but the successful device was the attachment by the Senate's Republican majority of conditions to the resolution of advice and consent to the treaty, some of which so fundamentally altered the character of the Covenant as to make the conditions unacceptable to the President. Primary among these conditions was the removal of any American obligation under the Covenant to act against a violator of it, particularly the obligation stated in Article Ten. Thus the Senate was given the opportunity to vote against the League as adopted in Paris with its collective security features intact, and to vote for *a supposititious league,* an altered Covenant, which would, as Senator Warren G. Harding said, leave the United States perfectly free to do as it pleased under any circumstance that might arise.

Wilson was quite willing to accept at all times clarifying amendments, or reservations that amounted to amendments, but the guarantee of action against an aggressor was, in his opinion, so fundamental to the whole peace system, and so basic to the whole structure of the peace settlement, that he was unwilling to accept this kind of change. He felt, as he said on one occasion in France, "under eternal bonds of fidelity" to those who had lost their lives in the war to stand steadfast for a peace system that would justify, as far as that was possible, their sacrifices.

It is essential to note that the Senate was theoretically divided into three groups on the League issue. One group supported the President's stand for *the League* with its essential character unchanged; a second group presumably supported *a league* of the type Harding referred to; and a third group opposed *any league,* but voted for the resolutions advocated by the second group in order to form a majority against *the League.* Since the votes of the third group were necessary in order to secure the reservations advocated by the second group, and the third group had made it clear they would vote against approval of the treaty even with these reservations, legitimate doubt may be cast on the validity of a distinction between the leaders of the second group and those of the third group. All that can be positively known is that none of the three groups had a majority, let alone a two-thirds majority, in the Senate.

President Wilson's first alternative to the defeat of the League in the Senate was to take the issue directly to the people in an extensive tour of the nation. He had already exhausted his physical reserves and knew his health was fragile, but felt constrained to make every personal effort for the League that was humanly possible. Whether he could have been successful in gaining sufficient public support to influence the opponents of the League in

the Senate cannot be known because he became seriously ill before his tour was completed. His second alternative, and that of his
party, was to make the cause of the League clear and primary
in the presidential election of 1920. But here again, as in the
Senate, the League's opponents could thwart this design by con-
fusing the issue. Their strategy, fashioned by Elihu Root, was
quite simple. They placed in the Republican Party platform an
equivocal statement on the League issue which left all factions and
leaders free to advocate what suited them. Their candidate for the
Presidency, Warren G. Harding, spoke with equanimity and contradiction on both sides of the issue: Charles Evans Hughes, Elihu
Root, William H. Taft, Henry L. Stimson, and other prominent
supporters of Harding signed a statement declaring that the party
was bound "by every consideration of good faith" to join a league
essentially the same as *the League* with the exception of the commitment on collective security contained in Article Ten; Herbert
Hoover joined in the above statement and said separately that the
party was pledged to join an association of nations for the preservation of peace, and that the fulfillment of this pledge was the test
of the party's "entire sincerity, integrity, and statesmanship";
while Senator William E. Borah and the group he represented
declared that the party was not obligated to join any league and
would not do so if successful in the election.

The Democratic Party and its candidate for the Presidency,
James M. Cox, advocated outright support for the League without
any substantial change that would alter its fundamental character.
There were many other issues in the election besides that of the
League, and what the people who voted for Harding thought they
were voting for on that issue, in view of the chaos created by
Republican leadership, is purely speculative. Harding was elected
by a large majority and announced after he assumed office that
the election was a mandate against American participation in the
League of Nations. Hughes and Hoover became members of his
Cabinet and Taft was appointed to the Supreme Court, but they
did not refer again to "considerations of good faith" or to the tests
of "sincerity, integrity, and statesmanship" they had talked about
earlier. Secretary of State Hughes negotiated a separate treaty of
peace with Germany under which the United States secured all of

the "rights, privileges, indemnities, reparations or advantages" it would have secured under the Treaty of Versailles but assumed none of the obligations.

This marked the death of an era, and if in this instance an epitaph is appropriate, one could be found in the later speeches of either Wilson or Hoover as preferred. Wilson said the nation had turned its back on its associates in the war, refused to participate in the administration of peace, and had withdrawn into "a sullen and selfish isolation" that was "deeply ignoble because manifestly cowardly and dishonorable." Hoover said the failure of public men to keep their promises to the people was one of the more "destructive forms of dishonor," and that dishonor in public life had a double poison: it poisoned the person involved and "the morals of the whole people."

IX

ISOLATION AND THE NEW
NEUTRALITY

THE TWO DECADES between the two World Wars were covered by the administrations of Presidents Harding, Coolidge, and Hoover, and almost two terms of the administration of Franklin D. Roosevelt. Changing world conditions, new problems, and some diversities of view among the several Presidents produced a lack of complete consistency in foreign policy, but considered as a whole the era was characterized throughout by political isolationism, economic nationalism, progressive military and naval weakness, and the abandonment of American traditional policies of neutrality. The leaders of the people, both in the executive and legislative departments of the government, watched with studied indifference or satisfaction the results of American defection on the vitality of the League of Nations and the ominous growth of powerful and aggressive dictators, contributed by their policies to the economic disorder of the world and of the United States, and calmed the anxieties of the people with panaceas or soothing promises of peace and prosperity.

The height of American isolationism was probably reached in the so-called neutrality legislation of the 1930's, which was a logical development from previous policies as well as a reaction to world affairs, but the principle of isolation was established at the beginning of the period and was continued through a succession of events. It was not until near the end of the era, when the war clouds of Europe and their portent for the United States could no longer be ignored, that changes of policy were initiated.

THE ESTABLISHMENT OF ISOLATIONISM

The Harding Administration set out to reverse the majority of the domestic and foreign policies of the Wilson era. In foreign affairs this reversal included policies regarding Latin America, self-government in dependent areas, tariff and other economic affairs, the military establishment, and the whole area of international co-operation. Some of these matters will be considered separately, but the tone of the Harding Administration was immediately set by the Secretary of State, Charles Evans Hughes, in his attitude toward the League of Nations. President Wilson co-operated with the League as far as he could, and held that the United States had rights regarding the various peace settlements with the Central Powers by virtue of being one of the Allied and Associated Powers. Secretary Hughes did not renounce these rights, but refused to co-operate with the League or any League of Nations agency, such as the Mandates Commission. He discouraged American private citizens from participating in League affairs, and at the outset of his Administration refused to have direct communication with the League. American renunciation of the League and all of its activities could not have been more complete.

France was unable to secure in the peace settlement with Germany the establishment of a buffer state along the Rhine, and was obliged to rely for French security against Germany on the territorial guarantees in the Covenant of the League of Nations and on separate treaties with Britain and the United States under which these two powers promised to assist France in case of attack by Germany. Wilson did not think the separate treaties of guarantee were necessary, but he was virtually obliged to sign the Franco-American treaty in order to secure French approval of changes in the Covenant that he was assured by his advisers would satisfy American objections to it. When the Senate rejected both the Treaty of Versailles and the separate treaty of guarantee, France felt that its security was undermined and began to build as far as it could a system of alliances. Various other states accepted the French view of the effect of American action on the mutual security system of the League, but reacted differently. They secured a resolution in the Assembly of the League that had the effect of lessening their obligations under the guarantee provisions of the Covenant. Although the League remained in existence, in the sense that it retained its name and form, and rendered some services through its various agencies, it had thus been fatally stricken as an institution for world peace. This virtual destruction of the League, as it was intended to be, was the beginning of the steady disintegration of world stability during the next twenty years.

After President Harding declared that the election of 1920 was a mandate against American adherence to the League and this position was accepted by other members of his party, and after the Washington Conference on the limitation of naval armaments, which will be considered later, the majority of American politicians no longer feared the political influence of those who favored the League as much as the influence of those who opposed it. This is shown by the reversal of the Democratic Party on the League issue and the failure of the movement for American adherence to the Permanent Court of International Justice. Various Democratic Party leaders—including Cordell Hull, who later became Secretary of State; former Secretary of the Treasury, Senator Carter Glass; and former Secretary of War, Newton D. Baker —urged the Democratic Party to stand steadfast for the League in the presidential election of 1924. The majority of Democratic leaders, however, opposed this policy. They urged that in view of the action of the Republican Party on the League those who favored American participation in it would vote for the Democratic Party in any event, that some influential groups of the population, particularly those of Irish and German extraction, would be adversely influenced by a pro-League stand, and that the party should concentrate its attention on domestic issues with emphasis on the corruption in government under the Harding Administration. In order to avoid the appearance of a complete reversal on the League issue, they devised a subterfuge, a provision in the party's platform promising a national referendum to decide whether the United States should join the League. No constitutional means existed for such a referendum, and the party leaders were uncertain regarding the method of conducting one.

During the presidential campaign of 1924, the issues of foreign policy were almost as confused as they had been in 1920. While the Republicans completely renounced support of American membership in the League, they denied they were isolationists, claimed support of adherence to the World Court, declared the Washington Conference had made the greatest advance toward world peace that had ever been achieved, promised a new conference to effect further arms limitation, and proclaimed the United States had made and would make greater contributions to world order outside the League than as a member of it. The Democrats had virtually abandoned the League through their referendum proposal, but before the campaign was over, their candidate for the Presidency, John W. Davis, came out strongly for American membership, minimized the Republican claims of international cooperation, and, as far as he could, restored the Democratic Party to the position of Woodrow Wilson. A third party of the day, the Progressive Party, said little about foreign affairs. Its leaders, however, were more isolationists than those of the two major parties. The people, who seemed apathetic to this confusion of leadership, turned out in small numbers to the polls but elected Calvin Coolidge, who had taken practically no part in the campaign.

The Covenant of the League of Nations provided for the establishment of the Permanent Court of International Justice under a separate statute open to the signature of all nations. It was possible, therefore, for the United States to become a member of the Court and to participate in the election of its judges without being connected otherwise with the League. A number of American political leaders who did not favor American membership in the League advocated membership in the Court. This group included the four Presidents who held office during the interwar period, and each of them, with varying emphasis, sought the Senate's approval in one form or another of the statute of the Court, the protocol of signature being in the nature of a multilateral treaty. The isolationists in the Senate were able to prevent American membership in the Court either by direct opposition or by attaching reservations to the resolution of advice and consent that would have required amendments to the statute unacceptable to its members. The final futile effort to secure American membership was made by President Franklin D. Roosevelt in 1935. The failure to accomplish American adherence to the Court was not without a touch of irony, for many of the most prominent Republican supporters of membership had used virtually the same arguments against the League that were used against the Court and had, in effect, prevented in advance American adherence to it. This issue was trivial, however, in its importance for world peace as compared with American rejection of membership in the League of Nations. By 1935 world stability had already been undermined, Japan had invaded China with impunity, Germany had been allowed to violate the Treaty of Versailles, Italy was ready to enter the road of aggression, and the United States was on the eve of its neutrality legislation. Among the complex of factors contributing to all of these events were the various conferences on the limitation of national armaments.

THE LIMITATION OF ARMAMENTS

The limitation of national armaments by mutual agreement among nations was a part of most peace movements, was advocated by President Wilson, and was provided for in the Covenant of the League. It was clear, however, both in Wilson's thought and in the provisions of the League, that the limitation of armaments was justifiable and practicable *only* in connection with the establishment of a mutual security system which would provide greater safety for a nation's sovereignty, independence, and rights than could be achieved unilaterally or through alliances. Wilson argued that if the United States refused to join and to promote the growth of a mutual security system, it had but one logical and safe alternative of policy, namely to construct a powerful naval and military establishment, maintain an adequate reserve of modern military supplies and equipment, establish universal military training, organize a world-wide system of espionage, and delegate to the central government—largely to the executive branch—authority to use the nation's armed forces whenever the nation's interests or security were endangered. This program obviously could not be accomplished without great expense, and Wilson doubted it could be done without undermining American democratic institutions. When, however, it became doubtful that the United States would join the League, Wilson proposed to Congress as the first step toward implementing his logical alternative, a great naval building program, including the construction of capital ships, long-range cruisers and submarines, and aircraft carriers, and substantial improvements in the naval establishments in Hawaii, the Philippines, and Guam. His concern for American security was not confined to the danger of invasion from abroad, but embraced in even greater measure the ability of the United States to safeguard the Monroe Doctrine, to protect American commerce on the seas, to defend its treaty rights throughout the world, and to fulfill its obligations to its dependent areas.

When the Harding Administration decided to remain outside the mutual security system, it was confronted with the stern logic of the Wilsonian alternative. This was opposed, however, by business leaders who disliked the costs involved, by pacifists, and by those who thought a program of such military strength would antagonize Britain and Japan. The Harding Administration devised, therefore, a substitute policy involving the limitation of naval armaments and an agreement regarding the Far East to replace the Anglo-Japanese Alliance.

The policy on naval limitation was based on three related assumptions: (1) that armaments dangerous to American security and world peace were naval armaments; (2) that the significant rivalry in naval armament was in capital ships, large battle cruisers, and aircraft carriers; and (3) that the limitation of naval armament should be based on the principle of "parity" among the naval powers. Acting on these assumptions the United States initiated the conference on naval armaments which began in Washington on November 12, 1921, with Great Britain, Japan, France, Italy, China, Belgium, the Netherlands, Portugal, and the United States in attendance.

Except for a tacit agreement between the United States and Britain that the two nations would accept "equality" in their Battle Fleets (capital ships), the conference met without previous consultation among the several powers. This was contrary to British wishes, but Secretary Hughes wanted the United States to have full credit for initiating the conference and wanted to confront the meeting with a dramatic proposal of naval arms limitation, formulated in great secrecy not only with regard to the other nations but with regard also to the American Congress and people. He proposed the abandonment for ten years of all building programs of capital ships in progress and projected, the scrapping of designated capital ships of the United States, Britain, and Japan, later of Italy and France, and the use of capital ship tonnage as the measure for proportional reduction in auxiliary combat craft. His proposals meant that five principal naval powers would be left with 525,000 tons each of capital ships for the United States and Britain, 315,000 tons for Japan, and 175,000 tons for France and Italy.

Since Britain had already agreed to "equality" with the United States in capital ships, she raised no serious objection to the proposals of Hughes as far as such ships were concerned, but Japan agreed only on condition that one of her new ships, slated for scrapping by Hughes, should be retained, and that no power should be permitted to strengthen its fortifications or naval bases in a designated area of the Pacific, which included the Philippines, Guam, Midway, American Samoa, and the Aleutian Islands. France was distressed at the proposals, first because she was allotted equality with Italy although her strategic position was quite different, and because she felt Britain was neglecting the security of Europe in order to appease the United States and some parts of the British Commonwealth. Hughes was willing, however, to accept the Japanese terms and largely to disregard French objections. In the final agreement, the proposals of Hughes on capital ships were accepted with minor adjustments, the nonfortification condition was adopted, a limitation was placed on the size but not on the number of small cruisers, and a limitation was placed on the total tonnage of aircraft carriers of the United States, Britain, and Japan. No limitation was placed on auxiliary craft, destroyers, and submarines.

In addition to naval arms limitation, the Washington Conference considered a number of other matters including international tensions in the Far East. These resulted primarily from American opposition to Japanese expansionist designs in China and the possibility, owing to the Anglo-Japanese Alliance and the failure of the United States to join the League of Nations, that Britain and the Commonwealth might become involved in a conflict between the United States and Japan. In order to avoid this situation, two treaties were signed at the Washington Conference. Under one of them, the Nine-Power Treaty, the members of the conference, together with several states that adhered to the treaty later, agreed "to respect the sovereignty, the independence, and the territorial and administrative integrity" of China, to refrain from securing special rights, privileges, or spheres of influence in China, and to consult together whenever one party to the treaty felt a situation had arisen that involved its provisions. Under the Four-Power Treaty, the United States, Britain, France, and Japan agreed to respect the rights of each other regarding their possessions in the area of the Pacific Ocean, while Japan and Britain agreed to terminate the Anglo-Japanese Alliance. Neither of these treaties carried provisions for enforcement, and President Harding, in presenting them to the Senate, emphasized that they did not commit the United States either legally or morally to their defense. Nevertheless they incorporated into treaty law obligations concerning China that had hitherto been expressed only in statements of policy or in executive agreements.

It is impossible to assess in all respects the consequences of the Washington Conference because it had long-range as well as immediate influences that became entangled with other events during the complicated interwar period. Secretary Hughes declared the naval treaty "absolutely" ended competition in naval armament, left the relative security of the several powers unimpaired, and made "perhaps the greatest forward step in history" toward the "reign of peace." That the treaty was more important for peace than the League of Nations would have been, as the Secretary implied in his last remark, was his judgment, but the first two parts of his statement were inaccurate. Competition in naval armament was not halted save in capital ships, while the relative security of the United States was seriously weakened, for it not only scrapped a greater quantity of naval tonnage than any other power, but also surrendered the right to strengthen its position in the area of greatest insecurity while it left Japan relatively stronger. Probably even more important, the wide acclaim given to the conference by the Harding Administration strengthened the idea that the limitation of naval armaments was the surest road to world peace, that since harmony allegedly now existed among the great powers, the United States did not need to strengthen its Navy within treaty limits, and that further naval limitation should be effected. As a result, three more naval arms conferences were held, in Geneva in 1927 and in London in 1930 and 1935. The conferences of 1927 and 1935 accomplished little, but under a treaty signed in 1930, Great Britain, Japan, and the United States limited their navies further, including light cruisers, destroyers, and submarines, with Japan securing a higher ratio in cruisers than the Washington ratio in capital ships and equality in submarines. Relatively, therefore, the United States and Britain weakened further their naval strength at a time when world stability was rapidly disintegrating. Although the United States began to strengthen its Navy after Japan denounced the Washington Treaty in 1934, it was not until 1938 that the United States and Britain began fully to realize what they had done or failed to do during the previous sixteen years and hastily started to rebuild their navies, but by that time it was too late to rectify their mistakes in time to prevent the humiliating and costly defeats of 1941 and 1942.

ECONOMIC FOREIGN POLICIES

As in the case of national security, the several American administrations during the interwar era fundamentally rejected Wilsonian foreign economic policies. Wilson believed that one of the basic conditions of world peace was the access of all nations, as far as possible on equal terms, to the trade and raw materials of the world, a principle stated in the Fourteen Points and later incorporated into the Atlantic Charter. After the war, he noted particularly the significance of the creditor situation of the United States, with Europe owing it something near $13 billion as the result of public loans and commercial credits. Since the United States had required no reparations from Germany, no direct connection, based on the economic integrity of nations, existed between reparations and inter-Allied debts. Wilson believed, nevertheless, that reparations, the liquidation of inter-Allied debts, the economic welfare and peace of the world, and American national interests were interwoven, and that it was the duty as well as to the advantage of the United States to facilitate world recovery by assisting in the expansion rather than the contraction of world markets. These economic and world views were not accepted by the Harding Administration, which enacted an Emergency Tariff in May, 1921, and a higher tariff in 1922. A still higher tariff was levied with President Hoover's approval in 1930. These measures of economic nationalism encouraged, or were used to excuse, similar measures by other nations, and Germany in turn used these policies as one of her reasons for not paying reparations.

Germany defaulted in her reparations payments in 1921, and made little attempt until after 1923 to establish a stable currency. After that, owing largely to international agreements known as the Dawes Plan and the Young Plan, some reparations were paid until further payments were abandoned in 1932. According to the chief architect of her shrewd economic management, Hjalmar Schacht, Germany paid about one tenth of her reparations liability of over $32 billion while she borrowed from abroad almost double the amount paid. Meanwhile the United States had scaled down, largely through interest schedules, the amount owed to it by the Allies, but these reduced payments were substantially in default by 1931 when President Hoover suggested a moratorium of one year on the payment of all intergovernmental debts. The following year, a conference at Lausanne virtually agreed to suspend reparation payments and suggested the holding in London of a world economic conference.

By the time the conference met, in June, 1933, Germany was in the hands of Chancellor Hitler and had been secretly rearming with the aid of Russia and in violation of the Treaty of Versailles; Japan had defied the League of Nations, violated the Nine-Power

Treaty, and extended its invasion of China; the world was in the throes of an economic depression; and a futile conference on disarmament was slowly dying in Geneva. Secretary of State Cordell Hull, strongly devoted to freer trade, was hopeful that the conference could achieve international monetary stability as the first step in the expansion of world markets, but his hopes were destined to failure. The members of the conference were agreed that monetary stabilization was desirable, but they were not agreed on how this should be achieved. Within a month before the conference met, President Roosevelt stated that one of its major purposes was "to establish order in place of the present chaos by a stabilization of currencies," and this was the official American policy when the conference convened. While the conference was in session, the President suddenly changed his mind and decided to oppose stabilization, apparently in order to have a free hand in currency regulation as a means of combating the domestic depression. Whether any significant achievement toward world monetary stability could have been made if the United States had provided strong leadership in that direction cannot be known. Economic nationalism ruled the day, and no world statesman had the vision, the intellectual authority, or the necessary will and prestige to lift the conference out of stagnation.

A year later, 1934, Congress passed the Reciprocal Tariff Act, which allowed the President, under limitations, to make bilateral reciprocal trade agreements. Under this and successive extensions of the act, the high tariff policy of the United States was altered. Thereafter the United States could not be accused of being the leader of high protectionism even though the new American policy made no appreciable difference in the flow of world trade. In the same year, Congress had passed the Johnson Act prohibiting loans to foreign nations that were in default on their payments for previous loans. Indirectly this was the first act in the new neutrality legislation that began in 1935.

THE PACT OF PARIS

Among the various ideas for the promotion of world peace that arose as a consequence of the First World War was that of an international antiwar pact. It was argued that wars existed because they were legal under international law and would cease if they were declared illegal by mutual agreement. This theory was not valid in all respects, particularly as it related to nations bound under the Covenant of the League, and at first gained few adherents. Gradually, however, it gained support from people with diverse interests: isolationists who had opposed the League and the World Court, pacifists, and internationalists who thought American adherence to an international agreement against war might be the first step toward further participation in world affairs. Gradually the central idea shifted from a pact to outlaw war, as it was generally referred to, to one in which nations would agree to renounce war as an instrument of national policy and promise to settle their disputes with other nations by peaceful means. President Coolidge and Secretary of State Frank B. Kellogg became interested in the idea after the French Foreign Minister, Aristide Briand, offered to sign an agreement with the United States renouncing recourse to war between the two nations, and after considerable public support had been organized in favor of the French proposal.

Secretary Kellogg suggested to France that the proposed bilateral agreement be extended into a multilateral pact open to the signature of all nations. This was not what Briand wanted, for his purpose had been simply to draw the United States in particular into a chain of French security pacts, and possibly to improve Franco-American relations, which had been strained over the question of Allied debts and reparations. He could not, however, logically reject Kellogg's proposal, and after extended negotiations the two nations agreed, in June, 1928, on a text of a pact for presentation to other nations. The principal powers reacted favorably, but wanted to make sure that the pact as drawn did not interfere with their obligations under other treaties, such as the Covenant of the League, or limit their rights of self-defense as determined by themselves. Since neither of these items was mentioned in the pact, various nations took special pains in their official statements concerning their acceptance of it to make clear that the protection of whatever they considered to be their vital interests were measures of self-defense. No nation, however, was more explicit in this regard than Secretary Kellogg himself, who declared that the right of self-defense was "inherent in every

sovereign state" and was "implicit in every treaty." "Every nation," he said, *"alone* is competent to decide whether *circumstances* require recourse to war in self-defense [italics supplied]."
The most ardent supporter of the pact in the Senate, William E.
Borah, stressed the same points of interpretation as the Secretary
of State, and placed equal emphasis on the absence of any obligation of a signatory of the pact to enforce its provisions. In short,
the nations agreed under the pact not to undertake self-declared
aggressive war. The pact, signed in August, 1928, contained
nothing not already in the Covenant of the League, in various
European treaties, or in agreements among Pan-American states,
and prohibited nothing sanctioned by international law.

The significance, therefore, of the Pact of Paris in American
foreign policy was the attitude of the people concerning it. President Coolidge declared there was "every reason to suppose" that
the existence of such an agreement in 1914 would have prevented
the war, and that it held "greater hope for peaceful relations than
was ever before given to the world." Secretary Kellogg and other
influential men made similar statements, and these sentiments
were echoed generally in the press. A few senators and others
tried to warn the nation how unrealistic it was to rely on the pact
as an instrument of peace and how dangerous it was to suppose
that American security could safely rest on pious words alone.
But these warnings were not what the people wanted to hear. The
pact was approved in the Senate by a vote of 85 to 1, was adhered
to by all the principal powers of the world, and by all sovereign
states but three. The leaders of the American people, having convinced them that war was no longer possible, and that the Pact of
Paris "paved the way," as President Hoover said, to greater limitation of armament, were not disturbed when the United States
weakened further its naval power at the London Conference of
1930. They were less well prepared for the Japanese invasion of
China a little more than two years after the pact went into effect.

THE FAR EAST

The Japanese excuse for invading northeastern China, Manchuria, on the night of September 18, 1931, was to protect the

Japanese South Manchuria Railway from bandits whom the Japanese claimed had destroyed a portion of the railway's track a few miles north of Mukden. This so-called Mukden Incident was manufactured by officers of the headquarters staff of the Japanese Kwantung Army, which quickly occupied Mukden, rapidly spread out into surrounding areas, and met with only disorganized resistance from the troops of Marshall Chang Hsueh-liang, governor of the Mukden area. To what extent, if any, the civil government of Japan was involved in the action of the Army cannot be determined. The Foreign Minister, Kijuro Shidehara, and the Prime Minister, Reijiro Wakatsuki, testified later that they protested against the action of the military. If so, their protests were either *pro forma* or weak and in either case wholly ineffective. The moment for the invasion was well chosen. Russia was occupied with internal problems, and probably had an understanding anyway with Japan over their respective interests in Manchuria. The United States and Europe were enmeshed in economic difficulties, while China was not fully united under the leadership of Chiang Kai-shek. Progress in this direction was being made and Chiang's ministers were preparing to negotiate with Japan over any difficulties between the two nations. If China became united and strong, and willing to settle amicably any legitimate Japanese grievance, and if the great powers became less preoccupied elsewhere, the Japanese opportunity for successful adventure in China might be lost.

By coincidence the Council of the League of Nations was scheduled to meet in Geneva the day following the Mukden Incident, and as soon as the news of it reached the Council, it was assured by the Japanese delegate, Kenkichi Yoshizawa, that any occupation of Chinese territory by Japan was police action and would be strictly temporary. By September 21, however, the astute Chinese delegate, Dr. Alfred S. K. Sze, knew of the continuing advance of the Japanese forces and requested the Council to act under Article Eleven of the Covenant, which declared that any war or threat of war was of concern to the whole League and that the League was obligated to take "effectual" action to safeguard the peace of nations. China requested the sending of a commission of inquiry to Manchuria and the issuance of a demand for the immediate withdrawal of Japanese troops. The Japanese delegate assured the Council that no investigation was necessary, that the Japanese troops were already being withdrawn, and that any difficulty between China and Japan could be settled by direct negotiations. Katsuji Debuchi, the Japanese ambassador in Washington, made similar positive statements to Secretary of State Henry L. Stimson, and added that the exercise of any pressure on Japan through the League or otherwise would weaken the government and strengthen the activist elements in the Army. Each day, however, brought fresh news that the Japanese Army was continuing its advance.

The principal members of the League were willing to do as much as, but no more than, the United States would do in restraining Japan, even though they had obligations to China under the Covenant which the United States did not have. Their great difficulty in co-ordinating their action with the United States was the impossibility of discovering what it intended. Secretary Stimson could not make up his mind whether to co-operate fully with the League if it led the way, to co-operate with it only if it acted on his advice, to act independently, or to do nothing at all. He did all these things at different times and frequently followed two policies at once. At first he advised the League not to act as China requested because he trusted the word of Ambassador Debuchi. Later, having found out he had been misled, he advised the League, in a remarkable document, not to "relax its vigilance and in no way fail to assert all the pressure and authority within its competence" in regulating the actions of Japan and China, and promised the United States would "endeavor to reinforce" what the League did. But when the League acted strongly and issued virtually an ultimatum to Japan to withdraw its troops from China, he disapproved such action and let the League know the United States would not endeavor to reinforce what it had done, and that the United States would do nothing at all in the way of sanctions against Japan. The League immediately and ignominiously backed down, saving face as much as it could by deciding to send an investigating commission to the Far East.

From the beginning of the episode, Secretary Stimson seemed to think the Pact of Paris should be the instrument of policy concerning Japan, and the League powers were willing to accept this view if it brought the United States into co-operation with them. The pact, however, was the least useful of any international agreement for such a purpose, for the United States as well as other nations had explicitly stated that the pact did not exclude war in self-defense, and that what fact or circumstance constituted self-defense was within the competence alone of each nation. The Secretary, nevertheless, decided on issuing a statement, generally known as the Hoover-Stimson Doctrine of nonrecognition, based partly on the pact. The doctrine stated that the United States would not recognize any situation *de facto,* or any agreement between Japan and China which impaired the treaty rights of the United States or its citizens in China, or any situation or agreement contrary to the Pact of Paris. As far as American treaty rights were concerned, the principle of the doctrine had been asserted by Secretary William Jennings Bryan in 1915. Although the nonrecognition doctrine was approved by the League, it was not accepted by all signatories of the League or of the Pact of Paris. The Japanese puppet state of Manchukuo, carved out of northeast China, was recognized during the 1930's by the Vatican, El Salvador, the Dominican Republic, Italy, Spain, Germany, Poland, Russia, Hungary, and Slovakia. By the time the doctrine was issued, Japan knew the United States did not intend to defend by force its rights in China. In effect, the United States asserted rights and at the same time granted Japan immunity in violating them. The moral and legal position of the United States in asserting its rights was valid; its willingness to sustain them was lacking. Japan continued its conquest of China as far as the Great Wall, then, needing time to consolidate its conquests, made a truce with China in May, 1933, temporarily ending hostilities.

Probably no simple explanation exists for the confusion, indecision, and weakness of American foreign policy during this period of the Sino-Japanese affair. As noted, the Secretary of State moved forward and back without advancing toward the restraint of Japan. President Hoover, although not a pacifist, believed world peace could be promoted better through disarmament than through sanctions against an aggressor. The American people had been led willingly to believe the nation was secure in its isolation and military weakness, and that its world interests could not be attained through collective international action. The members of the League were unwilling to abide by their obligations under the Covenant.

The election of Franklin D. Roosevelt to the Presidency in 1932 brought no immediate or significant change in American foreign policy. Regarding the Far East, the President-elect announced that his Administration would continue the nonrecognition policy of Secretary Stimson. This does not mean that no changes in foreign policy occurred during the next few years. The United States began slowly to improve its naval strength, adopted the Reciprocal Tariff Act, which could have been used to expand Japanese-American trade, offered to "consult" with European or other nations regarding world affairs, and supported the establishment of laws granting the President discretionary power to embargo the sale of arms abroad under certain circumstances. This latter policy would have enabled the President to co-operate to a degree with other nations in the use of sanctions against an aggressor. As will be noted later, Congress refused to grant the discretionary power and instead enacted in 1935 the first mandatory neutrality law.

Meanwhile, important events took place in China and Japan during the truce, which lasted with only minor violations until 1937. China tried to achieve political unity within its unoccupied area, to hold in check Chinese Communists, and to implement a program of social and economic reform. This program met with sufficient success to alarm the more aggressive elements among the military and civilian rulers of Japan, the more so because of the rising influence of a "moderate" element in the Japanese government which was sensitive at least to world opinion and out of sympathy with the trend of Japanese affairs. At the same time, the Chinese people were growing restless under the inactivity of the government against the Japanese invaders. As a result in China, the government made a quasi-agreement with the Communists that permitted greater effort against Japan, while in Japan various moderate leaders were assassinated in February, 1936, and the government passed more completely under the control of the military. Japan signed the Anti-Comintern Pact with Germany, renewed the war against China in July, 1937, and proclaimed a blockade of the China coast to all Chinese shipping.

The renewal of the war by Japan, indiscriminate bombing of Chinese cities, and the loss of some American lives, increased American sympathy for China and led to a growing boycott in the United States of Japanese goods. Anti-Japanese sentiment was one of the factors that caused President Roosevelt to refrain from declaring that war existed in China since this would have obliged him to embargo the sale of arms to both belligerents under the neutrality laws. He prohibited, however, the carrying of arms to China on government-owned ships and notified the owners of private ships that they would carry arms to China at their own risks. He advised all Americans to leave China, and indicated no disposition to support American treaty rights in China, not only with respect to trade but also regarding the gradual closing of the open door in areas under Japanese control. China appealed again to the League of Nations, which responded by passing anti-Japanese resolutions and calling for a conference under the Nine-Power Treaty.

For a little while, primarily in October, 1937, it appeared possible that the moribund League might rekindle its feeble spark of life and with the aid of the United States take some action in support of China. Belgium agreed to invite the Nine-Power Treaty states, along with several others, to a conference in Brussels in November. President Roosevelt had made a speech on October 5, in which he said harsh things about nations that violated their treaty obligations and international law. He suggested that peace-loving nations should unite and join in a "quarantine" against world lawlessness. Two days later *The New York Times* published a letter from ex-Secretary of State Stimson denouncing Japanese aggression and expressing the hope that the President's address indicated a "rebirth of American courage" in facing and carrying through its responsibilities. The French and British governments informed the United States they would support sanctions against Japan if the United States would enter into a pact of solidarity with them. With Germany and Japan in an alliance, which Italy joined just as the conference opened, they did not intend to risk war with Japan unless they had greater assurances than in 1931 of American support.

The conference was a complete fiasco, and for China and the principle of collective security, a disaster. Germany and Japan refused to attend, the latter saying she was acting in China only in self-defense. Italy attended as the open defender of Japan. Great Britain and France would do nothing beyond what the United States would do, and the remaining states would do nothing at all. The American delegate entered the conference empty-handed, with nothing to propose save a reaffirmation of the Nine-Power Treaty, and China, whose hopes for assistance had been high, was left stranded. The League, the Nine-Power Treaty, and the principle of collective security were discredited. Japan was triumphant. It pushed its conquest of China, and on December 12 attacked and sank the United States gunboat *Panay,* and disabled several American merchant vessels, all stationed in the Yangtze River near Nanking. The United States secured an apology and an indemnity for the *Panay,* but did not replace it. A little before this event, in August, 1937, Secretary Hull had stated that the United States did not intend to abandon its nationals or its interests in China. In March, 1938, he repeated this statement and declared that if a nation waived its rights and abandoned anywhere its nationals in the face of threatened violence—and thereby failed to perform its obligations—it encouraged violation of its rights everywhere. The United States, he said, should not withdraw from the Far East as some Americans proposed, not primarily because of economic considerations or because of long-established cultural and other relations with China, but because of its more fundamental interest in promoting and preserving "law, order, morality, and justice as the unshakable bases of civilized international relations." The United States, he continued, might turn its back on its past, abandon the things that had made it a great nation, and fail through fear or unwillingness to safeguard its interests abroad, but if it did so the sphere of its international relations would "shrink and shrivel" until it would stand alone and would find that isolation was a fruitful source of insecurity. It was a powerful statement, upholding the highest standards of national and international conduct, but it proposed no program; it was empty of action.

THE NEW NEUTRALITY

The influences that produced the isolationist sentiment among the American people during the interwar period and the neutrality legislation were deep in the whole history of the era and reached back into strong traditions of the nation. While these traditions were based partly on a knowledge of American history and partly on the lack of such knowledge, there was, nevertheless, a historical foundation for the belief that foreign entanglements were a danger to American prosperity and security. Among the more immediate influences, however, that produced the desire for noninvolvement in world affairs were the repudiation by European nations of their debts to the United States, the failure— no matter what the cause—of collective security, the isolationist agitation of ultranationalistic patriotic societies, the attitudes of some minority groups with strong emotional ties to their "fatherlands," the considerable acceptance of pacifist doctrines that surrender to violence was preferable to war, and wishful thinking that declarations such as the Pact of Paris and disarmament would produce peace.

These factors in the formation of public opinion were interwoven and connected also with still other important influences. The successful agitation against the League of Nations, which embraced all isolationist arguments, trapped those who had engaged in it. Thereafter they were unable to oppose national policies which were the logical consequences of their former assertions, even though time and events had shown them false. Equally influential were the successful efforts of the Revisionists, who attempted to show that the United States had declared war on Germany, not for the reasons alleged by President Wilson, but at the instance of munitions makers and bankers who had vested interests in Allied success. One of the chief instruments of this activity was a Senate investigating committee under the direction of Senator Gerald P. Nye. The committee promised two sensational disclosures a day, one for the morning and the other for the afternoon papers, and many of them responded with large headlines concerning these prospective disclosures without giving equal attention to subsequent failures of the committee to provide evidence. History was distorted by the committee and the press with irresponsibility and without regard for the defamation of character either of the living or the dead. The Revisionists included also those who denounced the Treaty of Versailles as unjust to the degree of saying that Germany was justified in violating it and in establishing the Nazi dictatorship for the purpose. All the while, during the 1920's and through the middle 1930's, the most responsible political leaders of the nation either supported or succumbed to the isolationist influences. They delighted, as Winston Churchill said of British leaders during the same era, in "smooth-sounding phrases," desired "popularity and electoral success," avoided the unpleasant problems of the world, and although without evil intent contributed to the miseries that awaited it.

The neutrality legislation which the Congress began in 1935 reached its most complete form in the act of 1937. This act provided that if the President found a state of war to exist, it would be illegal for American citizens to sell, among other items, war materials to the belligerents, to buy or sell within the United States their bonds or securities, or to travel on their ships. Goods other than those prohibited could be sold to belligerents provided the title to them was transferred prior to transportation abroad. Under the theory of the act, the United States was not interested in distinguishing between aggressors and their victims, and could avoid involvement in foreign wars by surrendering its neutral rights. The act applied to civil wars under certain conditions— the Spanish Civil War being the objective—but did not apply to Latin America. Indirectly the neutrality laws placed a premium on planned aggression with the stockpiling of munitions, and gave advantage to nations that could purchase goods in the United States without credit and protect their coasts against blockade. They were enacted with bipartisan support in Congress and were probably approved by a large majority of the people.

LATIN AMERICA

Cordial relations between the United States and Latin America tended to decline after the First World War and reached a low ebb toward the end of the 1920's. Broadly speaking, the Latin-American states were dissatisfied with the high protectionist policies of the United States, its continued military occupation of some areas, and its dominating influence in Pan-American conferences. Relations between the United States and Mexico were strained because of Mexican expropriation of American property. Some of these problems had been adjusted prior to 1933. An agreement, although abortive, for the settlement of American claims against Mexico had been reached, American troops had been withdrawn from the Dominican Republic and arrangements had been made for the removal of troops from Haiti and Nicaragua, and the United States had proclaimed that it no longer adhered to the so-called Roosevelt Corollary to the Monroe Doctrine. Herbert Hoover visited Latin America as President-elect and in various ways throughout his Administration established better relations between that area and the United States. He was unwilling, however, to modify his high protectionist policies or to renounce the rights of intervention under the general principles of international law. Secretary of State Cordell Hull was an ardent champion of closer Latin-American ties with the United States, and at the Pan-American Conference in Montevideo in 1933, set the stage for improved inter-American relations by his attitude of cordiality and his announcement of the reciprocal trade policy. Also, the United States soon revised its treaties with Cuba and Panama giving up its treaty rights of intervention in those countries. It was not until 1936, however, that it was willing to surrender completely its rights of intervention under international law.

By that time the United States had become seriously concerned over the revival by Chancellor Hitler of a German idea that Germans living anywhere constituted a part of the German Empire. German interests in Latin America were being actively promoted through the establishment of branches of the Nazi Party, Hitler Youth movements, labor, educational, and other organizations, military missions, economic and trade agreements, and widespread propaganda aimed particularly against the United States. The United States was alarmed also over the growth in South America of German airlines. As one means of counteracting further German penetration and influence, the United States was instrumental in calling a special inter-American conference at Buenos Aires in

December, 1936. The United States wanted to warn the Latin-American states against possible German subversion, to promote greater inter-American "solidarity" in the face of mounting European tensions, and to create by treaty a permanent standing committee which could promptly unify the action of the several states if the peace of the hemisphere were endangered. In order to achieve these purposes the United States government accepted a declaration under which the signatories renounced the right to intervene in the domestic or foreign affairs of each other "directly or indirectly for whatever reason." A permanent co-ordinating committee was not established at Buenos Aires, but was effectively created at the Pan-American Conference in Lima in 1938. At that conference the members proclaimed their willingness to act together in case their security was endangered, to co-ordinate "their respective wills" through consultation, and to call a meeting of their foreign ministers whenever needed for this purpose. This statement was in the form of a declaration and was legally less binding than a treaty or a formal agreement. It provided the way, however, after the beginning of the Second World War, for the United States to call meetings of the foreign ministers, whose resolutions the United States considered as legal sanctions. In no other areas of the world was American diplomacy, during the decade prior to 1940, more astute or more productive than in Latin America.

THE UNITED STATES AND EUROPE ON THE EVE OF THE SECOND WORLD WAR

It appeared certain by midsummer, 1935, that Italy was building up an excuse to invade Ethiopia. Ethiopia appealed to the League of Nations to intervene and to effect a settlement of any difficulty she had with Italy through arbitration, and to the United States to examine what means existed of securing observance of the Pact of Paris. Replying to the latter appeal, Secretary Hull referred to the obligations of nations under the pact, but admitted indirectly that the United States had no suggestions concerning its enforcement. Alarmed over the approaching war between Italy and Ethiopia, Congress, in October, 1935, hurriedly enacted the First Neutrality Act making it mandatory on the President, if he found a state of war to exist, to prohibit the sale of arms, munitions, and implements of war to the belligerents. When Italy invaded Ethiopia, the League was aroused enough to declare Italy an aggressor and to impose a variety of economic sanctions against her. These might have been of serious consequence to Italy over a period of years but did not exclude the sale to Italy of items she needed for the conquest of Ethiopia, accomplished by May, 1936. What effect if any the American neutrality policy had on the failure of the League to impose drastic sanctions against Italy, and on the haste of its members to acquiesce in Italy's aggression, cannot be determined. The mild sanctions against Italy were not applied by all members of the League and the governments of Great Britain and France, at odds over policies concerning Germany for her violations of the Treaty of Versailles, worked secretly to appease Italy while they pretended to fulfill their obligations under the Covenant. In the midst of such confusion, Germany had occupied the Rhineland in further violation of the Treaty of Versailles.

From 1936 the tragic drama of Europe, along with its counterpart in Asia, moved with mounting portents of doom to its conclusion. France and Britain, followed by the United States, maintained the pretense that Europe was being neutral in the Spanish Civil War although they knew that Italy, Germany, and Russia were taking part. The Brussels Conference of 1937 played out its futile role, and by the dawn of 1938 the League of Nations, the Pact of Paris, the Nine-Power Treaty, the idea of peace by disarmament, a long list of interwar peace treaties and movements, and the nonrecognition doctrine had passed into "the limbo of departed shades." In March, 1938, Germany absorbed Austria, and a year later the remainder of Czechoslovakia not acquired through the "Munich Appeasement" of the previous September, an area whose independence she had promised to respect. Five months later, in August, 1939, Germany and the Soviet Union made an alliance and were ready, as the Russian Foreign Minister, Vyacheslav Molotov, phrased it, "with one swift stroke" to destroy Poland, "that ugly duckling of the Treaty of Versailles."

During the critical year 1938 and the more critical months prior

to the German invasion of Poland in 1939, the United States government watched world events with growing concern, divided
counsels, and uncertainty of action. President Roosevelt was unwilling to promote a stronger policy than nonrecognition, or to
approve openly appeasement of Germany, Italy, and Japan, yet
he favored at times "practical adjustments" that would have been
appeasement under a different name. Like all appeasement ideas,
this attitude assumed the existence of limited ambitions of the
aggressors and a greater respect on their part for new commitments than they had shown for those of the past. He was jolted
somewhat by the Munich Agreement of September, 1938, which
he did not publicly denounce, and by Japan's announcement in
November, 1938, of the Greater East Asia Co-Prosperity Sphere,
which left no doubt of Japan's intention of closing the open door
in China. He was moved to recommend to Congress an increase
in the armed forces and an amendment of the Neutrality Act permitting the sale of arms and implements of war to belligerents
on a cash-and-carry basis. This movement failed, but neither the
President nor the Secretary of State provided strong leadership
in its behalf.

The President was not content either to keep his hands out of
European affairs or firmly to thrust them in. Instead he proposed,
on April 15, 1939, that Germany and Italy promise not to attack
any of the independent states of Europe and the Middle East,
and that discussions among the various states should be held looking toward the settlement of their problems. The United States
would be willing to take part in the discussion regarding armaments and trade but not concerning political problems. It is difficult to assess the reasons for or the effect of this proposal. It indirectly denounced Italy and Germany as aggressors, appealed to
them to abandon their evil ways, apparently opened the way for
some appeasement, possibly encouraged free states to resist further aggression, but offered no support to them if they did. Both
Italy and Germany rejected the proposal. Italy had recently invaded Albania, and Germany had already taken the first steps in
preparation for the invasion of Poland. President Roosevelt was
well informed about the imminence of war in Europe, believed
the United States in its own interests should be in a position to aid

Great Britain and France, and made one more attempt, during May and June, to secure modification of the Neutrality Act, this time with greater leadership than earlier, but without success. In a conference with leaders of the Senate, Senator William E. Borah told the Secretary of State that war in Europe was unlikely, and that he had better information on the subject than was contained in State Department files, which he refused to examine. The unparalleled arrogance of this statement, matched only by its misinformation, could be said to mark the height of American isolationism.

X

WAR AND PEACE: THE SECOND
CHANCE, 1939–1945

THE CONTROVERSY in the United States over foreign policy, particularly between the outbreak of the Second World War in Europe and the passage of the Lend-Lease Act of March, 1941, has often been called the "Great Debate" because it resulted in the virtual abandonment of the basic foreign policy of isolation that the United States had been following for twenty years and initiated a revolution in policy that ended in the signing of the United Nations Charter in 1945. This "debate" was in reality an intensified continuation of the discussion over foreign policy that had existed since 1920. World events provided many diverse *issues* over which the discussion ranged, but the fundamental *principles* involved remained the same. On one side were those who believed that the welfare and security of the United States were inescapably connected with events elsewhere in the world and that the United States had the necessity of helping shape these events in the direction of world order. On the other side were those who believed that the nation could pursue "an independent course." It is convenient to speak of the first group as "internationalists" and the second as "isolationists" or "nationalists." It is clear, however, that these terms cannot always be applied with accuracy to opinion on a particular issue, that neither group had a formal organization throughout the era, that the line separating them was often indistinct, and that in some cases the two groups might agree on a policy, the distinction between them being their reasons for agreement and their objectives. It is clear also that one group was not necessarily more realistic than the other, more patriotic, or more devoted to the national interest. They simply made differing assessments of the national interest and held diverse views on what policy could best advance it. Although these two groups existed and debated issues of foreign policy with mounting tension between 1939 and 1941, in the end events rather than logical arguments determined American policies, the principal events being Germany's conquest in Europe, the creation of the Axis alliance of Germany, Italy, and Japan, the attack on Pearl Harbor, and the creation of the atomic bomb.

SAFEGUARDING THE HEMISPHERE

Two days after Britain and France declared war on Germany following German invasion of Poland, President Roosevelt proclaimed American neutrality, and almost immediately turned to problems of hemispheric solidarity and security. A meeting of the foreign ministers of the American republics was held in Panama, September–October, 1939, the objectives of which were threefold: (1) to keep the several nations at peace and neutral in the war, (2) to keep the war as distant from the hemisphere as possible, and (3) to take protective measures against economic dislocations resulting from the war. The most unusual act of the meeting, and the least effective, was the Declaration of Panama. This established in the oceans around the republics an alleged neutrality zone about three hundred miles wide, within which all warlike activities were to be proscribed. Extravagant claims were made by some newspapers and commentators regarding the propriety and legality of such a zone, but the United States did not officially claim it was sanctioned by international law, made no attempt to enforce it, and eventually abandoned it. Great Britain and France were willing to conform to the declaration if Germany would keep its warships out of the proscribed area, but Germany would not accept this limitation unless the Allies would likewise keep their merchant ships out of it, a policy they would not accept. The United States appeared to have two main purposes in supporting the declaration. One was to provide the color of an excuse for patrolling the zone and indirectly assisting the Allies by reporting on standard radio waves the location of German ships, and the other was to create the impression of inter-American co-operation in maintaining neutrality.

By July, 1940, German victories in Europe and the threatened invasion of Britain created the possibility that Germany might attempt to establish its authority over those possessions in the Western Hemisphere belonging to the powers that had been overrun by German armies. In addition, Latin-American trade with Europe was being severely curtailed as a result of both Allied and German policies. Latin America was willing, therefore, to take stronger measures to safeguard the hemisphere and sought greater inter-American economic collaboration. At the Second Meeting of Foreign Ministers of the American republics at Havana, July, 1940, a convention was proposed, the Act of Havana, providing that if possessions in the Americas of non-American states should be in danger of becoming the "subject of barter of territory or change of sovereignty," the American republics collectively, or in an emergency any one of them individually, could assume control of the territories and administer them provisionally until they were restored to their previous condition or elected to become independent. The United States ratified the convention, and later Congress authorized the President to act in accordance with it. Neither the convention nor the act of Congress had standing in international law, but no occasion arose for the action contemplated. At the Havana meeting, the foreign ministers also made a Declaration of Reciprocal Assistance in which they stated that an act of a non-American state against the independence of an American state should be considered as an act of aggression against all signatories of the declaration. It was widely held that the Act of Havana along with the Act of Panama and the Declaration of the Reciprocal Assistance "multilateralized" the Monroe Doctrine. Although the United States diligently promoted such ideas, its progressive steps to abandon neutrality were all taken without consultation with the American republics.

The United States adopted a number of measures to strengthen the economic ties of the hemisphere. It extended to Latin America aid under the Lend-Lease Act as soon as it was adopted, purchased strategic materials for stockpiling in the United States, and otherwise assisted Latin-American economy in order to counteract subversive Axis influences. In addition, the United States sent cultural and military missions to Latin America and arranged for the lease of strategic areas, particularly for the defense of the Panama Canal. Meanwhile, in August, 1940, the United States and Canada established a Permanent Joint Board of Defense with authority to "consider in the broad sense the defense of the north-half of the Western Hemisphere," and in April, 1941, President Roosevelt and the Prime Minister of Canada issued the Hyde Park Declaration. The two leaders announced that they had considered how their two nations could co-ordinate their economic resources so as to promote their mutual defense. Also, under an exchange of notes, an "interpretation" of the Rush-Bagot Agreement of 1817 was effected whereby Canada and the United States could build and arm on the Great Lakes naval vessels intended for use elsewhere.

THE GREAT DEBATE AND THE COLLAPSE OF NEUTRALITY

The swiftness of German and Russian victories in the Polish campaign aroused President Roosevelt to make another attempt to secure the repeal of the arms embargo. The President and Secretary Hull would have preferred the outright repeal of the entire neutrality legislation, but judged the temper of Congress to be opposed to this and were unwilling at the moment to provide strong leadership in that direction. Instead they limited their request to the repeal of the arms embargo alone, and based their argument more on the inconsistencies of the Neutrality Act than on the high ground of American rights under international law, or openly on the desire to aid the Allies. They proposed also to restore to the basic act the cash-and-carry provisions, which had expired, and to retain all of its other isolationist features, including the prohibition on American ships being armed or entering war zones as proclaimed by the President and the prohibition of Americans traveling on belligerent ships.

The isolationists in Congress and in the country marshaled their forces to oppose any change in the Neutrality Act except to strengthen it and, in support of their position, reviewed all the isolationist arguments that had been devised during the past twenty years. This time, however, the isolationists met with much greater organized opposition, both from those who opposed the principle of the Neutrality Act and from those who wanted it revised in a way that would aid the Allies but avoid, they thought, the danger of becoming involved in the war actively on their side. As a result, Congress passed the repeal legislation which went into effect on November 4, 1939. No matter to what extent the new act retained isolationist features or to what degree it was defended as a measure for keeping the United States out of the war, it was in fact, and was understood and intended to be, a means of assisting the Allies, for they rather than Germany were able to bring ships to American shores, and the cash-and-carry section favored the Allies since at the moment they did not need American credits. The act, in thus recognizing that the cause of the Allies was of importance to the United States, was the first breach in the isolationist barrier.

What ideas Chancellor Hitler had, during the first stages of the European war, about future German-American relations is not entirely clear, but no doubt exists concerning German policy toward the United States as long as the conquest of Europe remained incomplete. It was to do whatever was possible to keep the United States neutral. This meant taking particular care not to sink by mistake an American merchant ship outside the "war zones," the avoidance of controversy over American patrols on the high seas under the Act of Panama, refraining from interference with European colonial areas in the Western Hemisphere, and playing down the importance of the repeal of the arms embargo. In addition, Germany let loose a barrage of propaganda aimed at assisting the influence of American isolationists, pacifists, anti-British, anti-Semites, and Fascists. Germany held that her principal objective was to destroy the oppressive Treaty of Versailles, to create a United States of Europe, to redress the balance between "the haves and the have-nots," to punish Great Britain for starting the war, and, after the break with the Soviet Union, to resist Communism. She declared her support of the Monroe Doctrine, denied any intention of conflict with the United States, and tried to turn American thoughts toward Japanese aggression in the Far East. Later, in September, 1940, she promoted the Tripartite Pact with Italy and Japan in the hope that the fear of a two-ocean war would divert the United States from giving further assistance to Britain. The effect of this propaganda in the United States is purely speculative, but it seems likely that the growing hostility toward Germany tended to discredit the influence of those whose arguments echoed Germany.

After the repeal of the arms embargo, events in Europe probably had more influence on American foreign policy than arguments. In April, 1940, Germany occupied Denmark without armed resistance, forced Sweden into compliance with her demands, and invaded Norway, and in May she overran Luxembourg, the Netherlands, and Belgium, whose fate was sealed by her surrender and the tragic but heroic evacuation of the British Army from Dunkirk during the last days of the month and the first few days of June. During June also, Germany forced France to its knees in an "armistice," while Italy, sensing the ultimate triumph of Germany, declared war on the Allies. Spain, like Italy, wanted to share the spoils of German victory. She occupied the International Zone of Tangier, threatened to attack Gibraltar, and offered to join the Axis alliance, but she set her price higher than Germany was willing to pay. Before the year was over, Russia had absorbed Lithuania, Estonia, and Latvia, Germany was in virtual control of Rumania, Italy had invaded Greece and Egypt, and Hungary and Rumania had joined the Tripartite Pact.

After the fall of Belgium and France, Britain stood alone, met the German onslaught from the air and on the seas, and fought Italy in Greece and Africa, powerfully aided by American assistance in the materials of war. President Roosevelt virtually opened American arsenals to Britain, supplied war materials out of current production, and stretched the neutrality laws as far as he legally could if not beyond, his most famous act being the so-called destroyer-bases agreement of September, 1940. This was in response to Britain's appeal for help in meeting the German submarine menace. In an executive agreement, the President traded fifty United States destroyers in return for the right to establish military bases for a period of ninety-nine years on six British possessions in the Caribbean area. Britain added as a gift the same rights in Bermuda and Newfoundland. The President's legal authority to trade or sell a part of the American Navy without specific authorization of Congress was more than doubtful, but he feared delays if not rejection by Congress if he sought its approval. Later merchant ships were sold to Britain, and in December the President announced what was already a fact—that the United States was the "arsenal of democracy."

The full force, however, of American aid to Britain was not reached until after the passage of the Lend-Lease Act of March 11, 1941. Prime Minister Churchill had informed the President late in 1940 that British financial resources for the purchase of war materials in the United States were about exhausted. The President's reaction was the introduction into Congress in January, 1941, of the Lend-Lease Act, which had been prepared by the Treasury. The act was remarkable for the extent of authority granted to the President and for its oblique but unmistakable abandonment of American neutrality. Subject to a few restrictions, it authorized the President to assist the government of any nation whose defense the President deemed "vital to the defense of the United States," "to sell, transfer title, exchange, lend, lease, or otherwise dispose of," any defense article to such a government, and to repair, outfit, or recondition defense articles, and to communicate to such a government defense information. The conditions under which this aid could be given were those the President deemed "satisfactory." The act did not authorize the use of the Navy for convoy, but neither did it prohibit this.

In his State of the Union message to Congress of January 6, 1941, which was preparatory to the introduction four days later of the lend-lease measure, the President all but requested a declaration of war on the Axis powers. He said the nation was in peril from Axis aggression and could not afford for its own security to permit these powers to dictate peace in the world. If they considered American aid to those who resisted them an act of war, it was a risk the United States should take, for, he said, "the Nation's hands must not be tied when the Nation's life is in danger." He proclaimed American support of the "four essential freedoms," the freedoms of speech and of religion, and the freedoms from want and fear. The President's message and the Lend-Lease Act produced the last important phase of the bitter Great Debate on foreign policy. The act was opposed by many prominent people, often in extravagant terms, and for a diversity of reasons, but mostly because of its alleged unconstitutional delegation of power to the President and its warlike implications. The spokesmen for the Administration and other proponents of the measure did not deny it might lead to war, but emphasized the danger to the United States if the aggressors should be victorious, and declared that the purpose of the act was to keep the war as far from American shores as possible. In the end the Senate passed the act by a majority of 60 to 31, and the final vote in the House was 317 to 71.

From the passage of the Lend-Lease Act until the beginning of the "shooting war" in the Atlantic, the President—and, near the end of the period, Congress—took one measure after another in the gradual movement toward complete American participation in the war against Germany. In April, 1941, the President, under an agreement with the ambassador from Denmark, assumed the protection of Greenland and soon established military bases there, and in July relieved the British of the occupation of Iceland. These areas were declared within the Western Hemisphere and under the aegis of the Monroe Doctrine. The President planned to seize the Azores as a protection of the hemisphere if Germany moved through Portugal and Spain—an event that did not take place—and in November, in an agreement with the Netherlands government in exile, occupied Dutch Guiana. After the occupation of Iceland, the Atlantic Fleet was ordered to protect American and Icelandic shipping against hostile attack by "escorting, covering, and patrolling," or by "destroying hostile forces" that threatened such shipping.

Gradually the "neutrality patrol," theoretically under the Act of Panama, and the convoy patrol connected with shipping to Iceland, was extended until by late summer or early fall the United States was protecting both American and Allied shipping over the entire western half of the Atlantic. Acting under its established policy, Germany still avoided conflict with the United States, but the situation was bound to produce a clash. The first serious episode occurred on September 4, when the U.S.S. *Greer,* a destroyer en route to Iceland, made contact with a German submarine, notified a British patrol plane, and after keeping contact with the submarine was fired on by it and dropped depth charges in return. Neither ship was damaged, but this was the real beginning of the "shooting war." During the following month, the U.S.S. *Kearny* was attacked and damaged, and the U.S.S. *Reuben James* was sunk. On its part, Congress repealed most of the remainder of the neutrality laws by permitting defensive arming of American merchant ships and abolishing the former war zones on the high seas that they had formerly been forbidden to enter.

The statement made by the President's critics that he "slicked" the United States into the war without the consent or knowledge of the Congress, is too extreme. In passing the Lend-Lease Act, Congress was well informed by the law's opponents of its possible consequences, made no protest over the occupation of Greenland and Iceland, passed measures for the war preparation of the United States, appropriated funds for lend-lease activities, and repealed important segments of the neutrality laws. In addition, the President stated publicly after his orders concerning the protection of the sea lanes to Iceland that further defense measures would be taken. Yet it is true that the full extent of American naval activities in the Atlantic were kept secret as well as the degree of British-American Army and Navy staff planning for co-operation in case the United States entered the war. Perhaps it could be said that although Congress and the American people wanted to avoid war with Germany and Japan—and that although some of them objected strongly when lend-lease was extended to Russia after her break with Germany—they knew about, and the majority approved, the major steps which inevitably led to that result both in the Pacific and the Atlantic areas. The issue of keeping secret the convoy activity of the Navy was sharply debated by the President's principal advisers. Some thought it should be made public as a means of strengthening the morale of the Allies in letting them know American aid would reach their shores. Others favored publicity because they feared public resentment against the Administration when the Navy's activity became known, or because they thought secrecy in this matter was inconsistent with American constitutional government. Nevertheless secrecy was maintained, and in this as well as in other acts and statements of the President the record may show he was lacking in candor. It does not show that the American people were deceived about the direction of American policy.

One of the significant steps in Anglo-American co-operation during 1941 was the meeting between President Roosevelt and Prime Minister Churchill and their principal political and military advisers at Argentia, Newfoundland, in mid-August. Due to illness, Secretary Hull was not present. The conference ranged over a wide variety of subjects: the military aspects—including co-ordination of procurement and supply—aid to Russia, and possible strategy under various situations that could arise. Since the United States was still neutral, the President could not enter into specific military commitments. He agreed, however, to American escort of British as well as American merchant ships as far as Iceland. The British wanted the President to take a stronger stand against the advancement of Japan toward Southeast Asia, but the President believed that war with Japan might still be averted and, if not, should be postponed as long as possible. On the political side, Roosevelt and Churchill agreed on a "joint declaration," commonly known as the Atlantic Charter, which stated the "common principles in the national policies" of their two nations on which they based "their hopes for a better future for the world." The principles were highly reminiscent of Wilson's principles of peace as stated in the Fourteen Points and in other addresses. Omitting technical details that would require elaboration, the principles affirmed opposition to aggression; support of self-determination, the freedom of the seas, and economic co-operation among nations and their equal right of access to world trade and raw materials; reduction of armaments under proper conditions; and the establishment "of a permanent system of general security."

The phrasing was sometimes oblique, partly because the President did not want to create controversy in the United States and partly because the Prime Minister did not want to commit Britain too specifically on issues that involved the Empire and Common-wealth. Nevertheless the principles of the charter were incorporated into the Declaration by United Nations of January, 1942, and inasmuch as they stated conditions that should be applied to all nations, victors and vanquished alike, they constituted indirectly a statement of principles on which a peace settlement should be made. It could be argued, therefore, that the United Nations might well have offered to the Axis powers a peace settlement based on these principles rather than a demand for unconditional surrender.

During most of the period between the fall of France and the Japanese attack on Pearl Harbor, the United States, in general collaboration with Britain, had extensive diplomatic relations with the government of unoccupied France—the Vichy government—and throughout the period with Spain. The policies of the United States toward these governments came under sharp and protracted criticism, but Secretary Hull defended them with unusual asperity. In maintaining diplomatic relations with the two governments, the United States was able, the Secretary claimed, to restrain them from making further concessions to Germany, to negotiate more easily with French representatives in Africa, and to promote continued Spanish "neutrality." The critics of the policies doubted the validity of these claims and held in addition that the moral position of the United States was sacrificed to a doubtful expediency.

THE FAR EAST

American relations with Japan progressively deteriorated after 1937 and were marked by tortuous diplomacy and complete frustration. In the seemingly endless exchange of repetitious notes between the two nations and in the almost continuous diplomatic negotiations, two facts stand out and render all other events relatively insignificant even though they would be important parts of a detailed study. The first is that friendly co-operative relations between the United States and Japan could have been restored at any time after 1931 if Japan had been willing to abide by its voluntary treaty obligations, particularly under the Nine-Power Treaty concerning China, the Four-Power Treaty concerning the Pacific area, and the Pact of Paris. At no time was the Japanese government willing to do this. As the danger of war with the United States became imminent, some Japanese naval officers opposed war because they believed Japan would be defeated and a number of elder statesmen thought the Japanese policies of aggression were not justified, but these people were not in control of the government. Secretary Hull stated and restated the principles of peace, those of the several treaties, and his last statement was not essentially different from his first. The way to peace was always open to Japan.

The second important fact is that the United States was unwilling to recognize the conquests of Japan or to surrender the treaty rights of the United States in the areas of Japanese aggression. Its policies in respect to these matters were weak, for it did nothing to support them by force, but they were never abandoned. American economic acts regarding Japan, notably in 1940 and 1941, were taken, not primarily because the American government thought they would force Japan to reverse its course, but because the Congress and the American people were unwilling to assist Japan directly or indirectly in its conquests. The Japanese-American commercial treaty was abrogated in 1939, and in 1940 American trade with Japan in such important items as petroleum, aviation gasoline, and high-grade scrap steel were put under a license system, but some trade with Japan continued until July, 1941, when Japanese assets in the United States were frozen and all normal trade was ended. Similar action was taken by Britain, India, Burma, and the Netherlands Indies. The severe phases, however, of these economic policies were not taken until after Japan had signed the Tripartite Pact of September, 1940, and the so-called Neutrality Pact of April, 1941, with the Soviet Union. It has been noted, nevertheless, that some restrictive economic measures were taken by the United States against Japan before these pacts were signed and may have been a factor in Japan's decision to sign them, and that the more restrictive measures, together with the unwillingness of the United States to recognize

Japanese conquests, provided Japan with an excuse for war. Some critics of American policies toward Japan would go even further and suggest that Japan, cut off from other supplies of petroleum, was *forced* to move into the oil-rich areas of Southeast Asia. If this argument has merit, it is based on the assumption that the victim of aggression rather than the aggressor is responsible for any conflict between them.

One of the many important events leading to war between the United States and Japan was the latter's agreement to the Tripartite Pact of September 27, 1940. Although the United States was not mentioned by name, the pact was directed against it. Under the agreement, Italy and Germany recognized Japan's leadership in establishing a "new order in Greater East Asia," while Japan recognized the leadership of Germany and Italy in Europe. The three powers pledged economic, political, and military assistance to each other if one were attacked by a "third power" not engaged at that time in war either in Europe or China. Shortly thereafter, Japan made its Neutrality Pact with Russia, moved more vigorously to complete the conquest of China, and prepared with greater urgency to advance into Southeast Asia. Its ideas of conquest were expansive and embraced—as decided in a secret agreement among its principal leaders, including the Premier, Prince Konoye—the domination or annexation, in addition to China, of the former German islands under Japanese mandate, Indochina, Thailand, Malaya, Burma, the East Indies, Borneo, Australia, New Zealand, and India, and further unspecified areas when conditions warranted.

It was noted earlier that the way to peace was always open to Japan. The same comment could be made with reference to the United States, for all that was required for peace was for it to acquiesce in the efforts by the Axis powers to control the remainder of the world. Since the United States believed this road to peace would lead only to its own destruction, war with Japan as well as with Germany was virtually certain after the signing of the Tripartite Pact. The objectives, however, of the United States and the Axis, in the roads they took, were not the same. The United States had recently provided for the independence of the Philippines, had championed the freedom and integrity of China, had offered Japan—and continued to offer—extensive co-operation in meeting its legitimate economic needs.

The story of Japanese-American relations during 1941 is somewhat confused, however, by statements made after the war by the American ambassador to Japan, Joseph C. Grew, placing a large share of the blame for the war on the United States. The ambassador could not make up his mind, or could not keep it made up, whether Japan was determined on its course of aggression or was willing to abandon this completely and return to peaceful ways. In December, 1940, he told President Roosevelt that Japan was "openly and unashamedly one of the predatory nations," and that neither Premier Konoye nor any other Japanese leader could reverse her policy, which would not be changed unless "insuperable obstacles" were placed in the way. By August, 1941, he had somehow convinced himself that Japan wanted peace, would be willing to withdraw her armies from China and elsewhere, renounce the Tripartite Pact, and agree to all the conditions of peace the United States desired. This could be effected, he thought, through a secret meeting between President Roosevelt and Premier Konoye. The President did not refuse such a meeting, but wanted to make sure on the basis of preliminary agreements and substantial evidence that the meeting would be successful, a condition that could not be arranged.

The hard fact was that Prince Konoye had no power to control Japanese military leaders who were determined on further conquests, and did not intend himself, if a meeting had been held, to offer more than a token withdrawal of Japanese forces from China and Indochina, into which they had moved. The Japanese ambassador to the United States, Admiral Kichisaburo Nomura, warned his government that the United States believed Japan was insincere in talking about peace and asked to be relieved of his post because he disliked being placed in a hypocritical position. Konoye resigned in October, 1941, and was replaced by the more militant General Hideki Tojo, but decision on war had already virtually been made at an Imperial Conference the previous month, even though the final decision was not made until early in December. The Emperor, who had been hesitant about war, consented to it after he had been assured of Japanese success. Through intercepted Japanese messages, the United States knew war was imminent, and Secretary Hull warned the President and American military leaders that Japan might strike at any place in the Pacific at any time. The military commanders in the Pacific posts were alerted, but were unprepared when the attack came on December 7, 1941. This action by Japan brought unity to the United States in its opposition to the Axis powers, and made it unnecessary to decide whether the United States would declare war on Japan if she moved against the British and Dutch in the Pacific, temporarily bypassing American possessions.

WARTIME DIPLOMACY

American wartime diplomacy was complicated by the lack of clear distinction between diplomacy as such concerning political matters and decisions of military policy, the latter frequently being made without consideration of their political implications or their possible effects on postwar foreign policy. As far as it existed, diplomacy was largely conducted by President Roosevelt in "summit conferences" in which he acted more as Commander in Chief of the armed forces of the United States than as the political head of the nation who needed to share agreements with other branches of the government. One important effort of diplomacy was to create and maintain a harmonious "grand alliance" between the United States, Britain, Russia, and China. Such an alliance was never fully achieved and was always tenuous as far as it existed at all. Russia refused to enter the war against Japan until Germany was defeated (and, as it turned out, Japan also), constantly demanded greater Allied effort in Europe, sought Allied acceptance of her postwar political and territorial ambitions, and constantly suspected British and American promises not to make a separate peace with Germany and Italy. Chiang Kai-shek urged Britain and the United States to give a larger share of their attention and war effort toward the defeat of Japan, but had to accept their determination to give primacy to the war in Europe. China was used as a pawn rather than a partner in the "alliance." Britain and the United States were often at odds over military strategy, but managed on the whole to achieve unity. Political problems were partly subordinated to military needs, but mostly they were postponed until the end of the war when the necessity of facing them ended the fiction of the grand alliance.

The beginning of wartime diplomacy was the conference in Washington, under the code name "Arcadia," between Prime Minister Churchill and President Roosevelt late in December, 1941. In addition to military planning, including reaffirmation of the decision made earlier to concentrate their main efforts against Germany, the two leaders drafted the declaration by United Nations, to which twenty-six nations subscribed immediately and twenty other nations adhered before the end of the war. Since not all the United Nations were at war with the same members of the Axis alliance, the declaration had to make allowance for that situation. The signatories subscribed to the principles of the Atlantic Charter, pledged their full resources against the members of the Axis alliance with whom they were at war, and promised not to make a separate armistice or peace with their enemies. Soon after the Arcadia meeting, the President announced the terms under which aid would be given to other nations under the Lend-Lease Act. He indicated that the benefits the United States would accept in return for aid would depend not only on the use of such aid during the war but also on the postwar policies of the various recipients in establishing stable exchange rates, eliminating discriminatory treatment in international commerce, and removing barriers to trade.

Having set in motion co-operative arrangements with its European and Far Eastern allies, the United States arranged a meeting of the foreign ministers of the American republics in Rio de Janeiro beginning on January 15, 1942. By that time the nine Central American and island republics of the Caribbean had declared war on the principal Axis nations; Mexico, Venezuela, and Colombia had broken diplomatic relations with them; and all the rest of the American republics, had granted nonbelligerent status to the United States and had reaffirmed their faith in the principle of hemispheric solidarity. The United States was not anxious for other Latin-American nations to declare war on the Axis because it was not prepared to give them substantial military aid. It hoped the foreign ministers would unanimously agree to a resolution calling on all the republics to break relations with Axis nations in order to secure the removal from the Americas of their diplomats and other agents who might engage in subversive activities. Argentina and Chile were not willing to agree, the former because of pro-Axis sentiment in her government, and the latter primarily because she felt unable to defend her long Pacific coastline. The ministers reaffirmed, however, that an act of aggression on an American state by a non-American state was an act of aggression against all of them, and "recommended" breaking diplomatic relations with Japan, Germany, and Italy, "since Japan had attacked and the other two had declared war on an American country."

As referred to earlier, much of the wartime diplomacy was conducted at "summit" or "near-summit" conferences. In addition to their first wartime conference (Arcadia), President Roosevelt met with Prime Minister Churchill nine times, with Josef Stalin twice, and once with Chiang Kai-shek. The British Foreign Minister, Anthony Eden, came to the United States, Secretary Hull journeyed to Moscow, and the President's special adviser and envoy, Harry Hopkins, made various trips to Great Britain and Russia. After Roosevelt's death, President Harry S. Truman met with Churchill and his successor, Clement Attlee, and with Stalin at Potsdam in July–August, 1945. At these various conferences, and through the exchange of letters and other communications, the main lines of foreign policy of the three principal Allies were hammered out and the attitudes toward each other revealed. Stalin made it clear long before the Yalta Conference of February, 1945, that Russia wanted a preponderance of power in Manchuria, the annexation of some areas adjoining Russia, control over a ring of states contiguous to Russia, influence in the eastern Mediterranean, the breakup of Germany, and large indemnities from Germany and her allies. Although Stalin recognized that the invasion of Africa in November, 1942, and of Italy in 1943, drained to some extent German power away from Russia, he constantly demanded the initiation of a "second front" against Germany in western France, and openly accused the United States and Britain of intending to violate their agreement not to make a separate peace. Russia fought Germany with undiminished fury, and knew what it wanted and intended to have when the war was over, and cared for nothing else.

The attitude of Britain and the United States toward Russia was a combination of co-operation, suspicion, and appeasement. Churchill worried about the position in Europe and the world that Russia might seek to occupy after the war, was gravely concerned over British interests in the eastern Mediterranean area, wanted to establish a second front in eastern Europe in order to be in occupation of that area when the war ended, and was willing to reach an understanding with Russia in which their postwar spheres of influence would be agreed upon at a time when Russia needed British and American aid. The United States would not agree to either of the latter two proposals, and Britain had to be content with American willingness to undertake the African campaign of 1942, constancy in giving priority to the war in Europe, and its massive build-up for the Western Front assault. Churchill had no part in the agreement between Roosevelt and Stalin concerning China, was always suspicious of Stalin's good faith in keeping his promises, and within a month after the Yalta Conference was aware that he and the President might, as he said, have "underwritten a fraudulent prospectus" when they accepted the Yalta arrangement regarding Poland under which Russia promised to hold free elections to determine Poland's permanent government and agreed that her western boundary would be settled later by a peace conference.

The attitude of President Roosevelt toward Stalin is difficult to fathom with certainty. He appeared to believe that Stalin could be relied upon to keep his promises concerning postwar foreign policy. In an address to the Supreme Soviet in Moscow, December 6, 1941, Stalin declared that the war against Germany was one "of liberation of enslaved people," and that the Soviet Union had no intention to seize territory, to impose its will on others or to interfere in their domestic affairs which they should be allowed to arrange with "absolute freedom." The President seemed to accept this as representative of Russian policy and to believe that Britain rather than Russia would be the stumbling block to postwar unity in the "grand alliance." In an address to Congress after his return from Yalta, the President said that on every point of discussion at

Yalta "unanimous agreement was achieved." The Allies, he said, were nearer unity on peace aims than ever before and were agreed that liberated peoples should solve their problems under democratic processes with free elections. There would be, he continued, no more "unilateral action and exclusive alliances and spheres of influence and balances of power," or other expedients for peace that had failed in the past. The President must have remembered that Russia did not keep its promises under the Litvinoff agreement of 1933, that at Yalta Russia demanded and was accorded by the President a sphere of influence in China, and that many of the "unanimous" agreements at Yalta were to postpone decisions because agreement could not be reached. It required extraordinary optimism to suppose that the Soviet Union would promote elsewhere democratic institutions that were denied her own people. Various theories have been advanced to explain American policies and President Roosevelt's attitude toward Russia. He may have been impressed with an idea, quite commonly held in the United States, that Russia should be appeased in order to demonstrate the absence of Western hostility and thus secure her friendship and co-operation, or with military advice that Russian aid in the war against Japan should be a primary consideration. It is possible also that the President was supremely confident of his ability to deal with Russia whenever conflicts in policy could no longer be postponed. It is equally likely, however, that the explanation is more complicated. The United States supplied Russia with about $11 billion worth of lend-lease materials before the war was over, and the American people had been led to believe the "grand alliance" was a reality, an assumption on which the structure of the United Nations was later based. It was easier to indulge in wishful thinking than to meet head-on the hard realities of Russian policy.

At the end of the Casablanca Conference of January, 1943, between Roosevelt and Churchill, the President announced the decision to compel the "unconditional surrender" of the Axis powers. This policy was approved by Churchill but was opposed by Secretary Hull, who thought it would "solidify Axis resistance into one of desperation," and might prolong the war. He thought surrender terms should be flexible, allowing for different policies as the situation of a particular nation warranted. It seems probable that Roosevelt and Churchill were still trying to allay presumed Russian fears that they would make a separate peace, and the President apparently wanted to avoid the kind of criticism that had been made against Wilson by Republican Party leaders for not demanding unconditional surrender of Germany in 1918. Although the policy caused much discussion, its significance could be easily exaggerated. It was not used in a strict sense in the surrender of any Axis nation but Germany, and no conclusive evidence exists to show it prolonged the war. It may have done so, however, and may have contributed to the muddled management of the surrender of Italy, but no positive conclusion concerning its wisdom or its effect on the war seems possible.

The feeling in the United States of hostility toward Germany grew as the war continued, and there was little inclination, such as had existed during the First World War, to make a distinction between the responsibilities of the German government and the German people. General agreement existed in the United States and among the Allies that Germany should be occupied, disarmed, "demilitarized" and "de-Nazified," her most responsible leaders tried as war criminals, some of her industrial war potential eliminated, and an indemnity required. The idea of dividing Germany into two or more separate states was seriously advocated and not wholly abandoned until after the Potsdam Conference. President Roosevelt and his principal advisers all favored harsh measures against Germany but differed on the degree of harshness, Secretary Hull arguing that policies should not be such as to create a lasting spirit of revenge in Germany or to make her an economic liability on Europe and the United States. On some of these matters agreement in detail was never reached among the Allies, and this failure provided the beginning of the so-called cold war.

By the time of the Yalta Conference in 1945, the three principal Allies had decided to divide Germany into three zones of occupation, the United States having the southwestern area, Great Britain the northwestern, and the Soviet Union the remainder. While each zone would be controlled separately by the occupying powers, their policies were to be co-ordinated by a council of the supreme military commanders of the several zones, with headquarters in Berlin. Russia acquiesced in France being given a zone carved out of the areas allotted to Britain and the United States and membership on the Control Council. Berlin, located well within the Russian zone, was to be a separate area, controlled jointly by the four powers. A European Advisory Commission with representatives of Britain, the United States, and the Soviet Union had been created in 1943 to make plans and co-ordinate policies concerning, among others, the surrender, occupation, and control of Germany. The American representative, Ambassador to Britain John G. Winant, suggested to the United States that detailed provisions should be made regarding routes of access of the Western Allies to Berlin by highway, rail, and air. This suggestion was rejected by the War Department with the comment that the matter would be arranged by the military commanders after Germany had surrendered. No specific agreement, however, was ever made on the subject. The commission made plans also for the occupation and control of Germany, but these, too, were disregarded, and when the war ended, instructions concerning American occupation policy were hastily drawn in the War Department. They outlined the general policies to be followed, but left the details of how they would be executed to the military government. The indemnity or reparations to be required of Germany was considered at the Yalta Conference and a "basis for discussion" was agreed upon, but this subject as well as others was referred to a council of foreign ministers, who made little progress toward an agreement prior to the Potsdam Conference. By that time Russia was already removing "war booty" and other German property from her zone of occupation. No agreement was reached at Potsdam on the amount of reparations that should be required of Germany or on the items of property that should be considered as such. Britain and the United States agreed to deliver to Russia a portion of the industrial equipment they took from their zones, and Russia was to deliver to the two Western powers a portion of the foodstuffs she took from her zone. This chaotic situation soon became a contributor to the cold war.

None of the wartime conferences where foreign policy was considered produced as much postwar controversy as the Yalta (Crimea) Conference of February, 1945. Some of the acts of this conference have already been considered and others will be considered later in their proper context. The critics of American policy have alleged that President Roosevelt made, *ad hoc,* personal decisions without consulting his advisers at the conference or without basing them on previous consideration by the Department of State, and that many of these decisions were highly favorable to Russian interests and unfortunate for the interests of the West. Others have held that most major decisions at Yalta were justifiable and that the failure of the Soviet Union to abide by the agreements was the principal reason for later dissatisfaction with them. It is true that most of the problems at Yalta had been considered by the United States prior to the conference and that the number of decisions made by the President without consultation has been exaggerated. Yet it cannot be denied that many important agreements, such as the holding of free elections in Poland and in other so-called liberated areas and the promises of the Soviet Union regarding China, depended for their fulfillment on Russian good faith, and that in other areas, where agreement could not be reached, the differences among the three powers were glossed over by referring the problems to commissions or to other bodies. Churchill wanted the United States and Britain to agree on major postwar policies before the conference met and then to confront Russia with a firm and united position while the two Western Allies still possessed great military strength in Europe. Roosevelt would not agree to this, partly because the war in Europe as well as in the Far East had not yet been won, and possibly also because of his attitude toward Britain and Russia that has been mentioned earlier. It cannot be determined now what the results would have been if Churchill's ideas had prevailed.

Meanwhile, since December, 1941, the United States had been waging war against Japan in the Pacific with mounting power and fury and growing success, but with distressing cost in lives. By July, 1945, Japan's Navy had been largely destroyed and Japan was sustaining severe attacks from the air. The United States estimated, however, that Japan had an army of about five million men, with two million on her home islands and the remainder distributed in her occupied areas of China, Korea, the Philippines, Southeast Asia, and the East Indies. Japan had also some navy left for defense and a stockpile of about five thousand dive bombers. American military leaders believed Japan's defeat would require another year of war at the cost of a million Allied casualties and a greater number of Japanese. This was the general situation when President Truman was obliged to decide whether to use the atomic bomb in the hope of bringing the war to a speedy end with the least possible cost in human lives.

Since the development of the atomic bomb was a closely guarded secret, there was no public discussion in the United States regarding the wisdom or morality of its use in the war. These matters were considered by the President and by his principal scientific, military, and political advisers who recommended its use; later its use became the subject of sharp debate. Some of the atomic scientists who had contributed to the development of the bomb thought the use of such a destructive weapon would create a moral issue different from the one caused by the use of a large number of less destructive weapons even though the resulting loss of life might be the same. These people advocated giving Japan full information about the new weapon or the demonstration of its power in some isolated area with Japanese officials being given the opportunity of observing its destructive force. Those who opposed these suggestions held that the relative destructiveness of a weapon did not involve a moral issue, and that the main reason for using the bomb was to shorten the war and thus to avoid greater loss of life than would follow from the failure to use it. They held, in addition, that although they believed the bomb could be detonated when dropped from an airplane, they had no absolute assurance of this. The United States had only two bombs. If Japan were invited to observe a demonstration of the bomb's destructiveness, and the demonstration were a failure, the result, it was urged, would be to strengthen Japanese resistance with the consequent loss of a greater number of lives.

Whatever may have been the merits of these considerations, the decision was made to use the bomb, but not until Japan had been given the opportunity to surrender under specific terms and a warning of the wrath to come. The terms, outlined in the Potsdam Declaration, were sent to Japan on July 26, 1945, and specified that Japan would be deprived of her conquests, occupied and disarmed, and that her "war criminals" would be tried and her war potential destroyed. They stated also with equal emphasis that Japanese soldiers would be "permitted to return to their homes with the opportunity to lead peaceful and productive lives," that "freedom of speech, of religion, and of thought, as well as respect for the fundamental human rights" would be established, and that occupation would end as soon as these objectives were accomplished. Japan was warned that if she did not surrender, military might would be unleashed against her "immeasurably greater" than was used against Germany, and the result would be Japan's "utter devastation" and "destruction."

When Japan refused to surrender, the first atomic bomb was dropped August 6, 1945, on a military administrative and staging center, Hiroshima, and a few days later, August 9, the second bomb was dropped on a war industry center, Nagasaki. Between these two events, Russia declared war on Japan as she had promised to do at Yalta, but in violation of her Neutrality Pact with Japan of 1941, and invaded Manchuria. These developments completely discredited the Japanese military leaders who had promised the Emperor success, and after a brief exchange of notes with the United States, which implied that the Emperor would not be considered a war criminal, he brought about the surrender of Japan on August 14, 1945.

THE UNITED NATIONS

During the interwar period it had become politically expedient in the United States to discredit the League of Nations, and it had been considered intellectually sophisticated to support Revisionist views of American entrance into the First World War. After the outbreak of the Second World War in Europe, American sentiment began to change, but President Roosevelt was still very cautious about referring in the Atlantic Charter to a new league of nations. With the entrance of the United States into the war, opinion changed more rapidly. By July, 1942, in a statement regarding American war objectives, Secretary of State Hull included the creation of an international agency to keep the peace, and in the Moscow Declaration of 1943 the principal Allies promised to create a "general international organization" for "the maintenance of international peace and security." In September, 1943, the House of Representatives had passed a resolution favoring the participation of the United States in establishing "international machinery with power adequate to establish and to maintain a just and lasting peace," and a little later the Senate declared the United States should join in establishing an "international authority with power to prevent aggression and to preserve the peace of the world."

Plans for an international organization, formulated separately by the United States, the Soviet Union, Great Britain, and China, were co-ordinated at discussions involving the four powers in Washington (Dumbarton Oaks Estate) during the late summer and fall of 1944, were further perfected at Yalta, and completed at a conference of all the United Nations at San Francisco, which ended on June 26, 1945. Most Latin-American states were dissatisfied with the draft Charter of the organization as drawn at Washington and Yalta without their participation, and virtually obliged the United States to call a meeting of Pan-American states at Mexico City prior to the San Francisco Conference. At this meeting the Act of Chapultepec was adopted, which declared that an act of aggression against an American state was an act of aggression against all, and recommended the creation of an inter-American mutual security system. The United States was morally obligated, therefore, to secure provisions in the United Nations Charter permitting regional security arrangements and was bound to unite as soon as possible with the Latin-American states in creating such an arrangement for the Americas.

In many ways the Charter of the United Nations created an international organization similar to the League of Nations, but in one notable respect it was entirely different. Under the Covenant of the League, each member was obligated to assist all other members in preserving their territory and independence against external aggression. Members of the League might disregard their obligations, as they did, but this did not affect the fact that the League as an international organization was a mutual security system. A considerable number of small states persistently attempted at the San Francisco Conference to secure a similar guarantee against aggression in the United Nations Charter, but the United States, along with the other so-called great powers, absolutely refused to undertake such a guarantee. Under the Charter, the primary responsibility for world peace and security was placed in the Security Council of eleven members, five of whom were permanent members: the United States, Great Britain, China, France, and the Soviet Union. No decision to act against an aggressor, or any other substantive decision, could be taken without the "concurring votes" of all five permanent members. The General Assembly, composed of all members of the United Nations, could *recommend* such action but *only* to the Security Council. Since no permanent member of the Council would be expected to vote against itself as an aggressor or against its satellite or other state whose aggression it supported, the field of action by the United Nations with respect to national security was limited indeed. The Charter did not deprive nations of the "inherent right of self-defense," but this is a right which the United States under its Constitution can neither limit nor surrender by treaty.

After the outbreak of the Korean War, when it became clear, if it had not been obvious earlier, that great-power unanimity was a fiction, the General Assembly passed Resolutions on Uniting for Peace, November 3, 1950. Under these resolutions it was decided that whenever the Security Council failed, because of lack of unanimity, to exercise its primary responsibility for the maintenance of peace and security, the Assembly could make appropriate recommendations directly to its members for the use of collective measures to maintain or restore peace. The resolutions did not change the Charter, which could be amended only with the consent of the permanent members, and any action passed under them had no binding force, as will be noted when the Korean War is considered.

XI

THE FADING AFTERGLOW OF
VICTORY, 1945–1950

THE PERIOD between the end of the Second World War and the outbreak of the war in Korea was marked most notably by the breakdown of co-operation between the Western Allies and the Soviet Union and the beginnings of the cold war and "bipolar diplomacy." The Soviet Union seized the three small Baltic nations which Germany had occupied and secured control over Bulgaria, Albania, Hungary, Rumania, Poland, Yugoslavia, Czechoslovakia, and to a large extent Finland. She obstructed a peace treaty with Austria, caused the virtual breakup of Germany, resulting in the creation of the West German Federal Republic and the East German Democratic Republic, and initiated a crisis over Berlin. Russian pressures on Greece and Turkey led to the Truman Doctrine and American economic and military assistance to those areas, and the fears of Communist advance into western Europe, together with European economic weakness, promoted the Marshall Plan and eventually the North Atlantic Treaty Organization. Meanwhile, co-operation with Russia broke down in Japan and Korea, the Chinese Communists overran mainland China, and the Middle East was thrown into confusion over the creation of Israel. Only in the Western Hemisphere, where a mutual security system was developed, did American policy run a relatively smooth course.

ECONOMIC REHABILITATION

American postwar economic planning was based on the assumption of the continuance of the "grand alliance," the same assumption that determined its political planning. This meant cooperation among the Allies for world peace and prosperity, the promotion of international trade through the reduction of trade barriers and import quotas, the establishment of stable currencies and exchange rates, the curtailment of expenditures for armaments, and the promotion of mutual assistance in economic reconstruction and development. To this end, various international agencies were established, among others the Food and Agriculture Organization for improving the production and distribution of agricultural products, the International Monetary Fund to aid in facilitating exchange stability, and the International Bank for Reconstruction and Development to provide needed capital where it might not otherwise be available. The United States adhered also to the General Agreement on Tariffs and Trade designed to reduce trade discrimination.

The United States realized, however, that in addition to the prospect of world economic recovery through the normal efforts of states and the aid of the international agencies, the vast wartime destruction of property and dislocation of industry would necessitate emergency measures of reconstruction and rehabilitation. This idea had been a part of the lend-lease policy, which had been designed to avoid the problems of war debts that had occurred at the end of the First World War. The United States had undertaken while the war was still in progress to provide relief for warstricken populations as soon as they could be reached. Since greater effort along this line was needed, the United States largely financed the United Nations Relief and Rehabilitation Administration (UNRRA) which spent about $4 billion to restore wartorn areas to something like normal conditions—providing food, maintaining health, re-establishing communications and public utilities, and promoting agriculture.

Additional measures proved to be necessary partly because of disharmony between the Western Allies and the Soviet Union and partly because the effects of war devastation had been underestimated. Great Britain had exhausted her external assets, increased her foreign liabilities, and diminished her gold reserves. Her industries were in need of repair and modernization, her foreign markets had almost disappeared, and her lack of raw material for industry was acute. The United States came to her assistance by granting her a loan of $3,700,000,000 to be paid back over an extended period at a low interest rate. British internal economic and social policies together with inflation in the United States, which increased the cost of American goods purchased by Britain, reduced the value of the loan in terms of British economic recovery. Soon Britain as well as other European states needed further American aid.

Meanwhile the United States became involved in the Middle East. During the latter part of 1945 and throughout 1946, while the United States was still trying to accommodate its differences with Russia over Germany, Russia not only consolidated her authority in Poland, and in other European states occupied by her armies, and established close ties with Yugoslavia and Albania, but sought also to expand her influence over Iran, Turkey, and Greece, to secure trusteeship over Tripolitania, and to establish a base in the Dodecanese islands of the Aegean Sea. During the war Russian, British, and American troops had been stationed in Iran with the understanding they would be withdrawn as soon as the war ended. British and American forces had been withdrawn prior to March 2, 1946, the date on which Russian forces were scheduled to leave. Russia, however, retained and increased her military strength in Iran and took other measures apparently designed to make that state a Russian satellite. When Great Britain and the United States made strong representations to Russia that implied the sending of aid to Iran, Russia removed her troops. Russian demands on Turkey, beginning in June, 1945, included requests for territorial cessions in eastern Turkey, joint control with Turkey of the Turkish Straits and the right to establish military bases along the straits, and a commercial treaty similar to those between Russia and her Balkan satellites. The United States

was willing to support a new arrangement concerning the Straits
but not on Russian terms, and Turkey was unwilling to accept any
of the Russian demands. Again the United States acted, this time
more firmly than in Iran, and not only rejected the Russian proposal concerning the Straits but sent the battleship *Missouri* to
Istanbul, outwardly on a friendly mission but clearly as an indication of strength.

American support of Iran and Turkey was not the result of a
broad reorientation of policy in the Middle East. Rather it was a
reaction to specific instances of Russian policy and was in line
with American opposition to Russian trusteeship over Tripolitania.
A more general consideration of policy was induced by the situation in Greece and by the decline of British power to fulfill her
accustomed role in Middle Eastern affairs. Greece had been invaded by Italy and Germany, had been left scourged and desolate
when the German forces withdrew, and had been further disturbed
by an attempt of Greek Communists to seize control of the government. For a time the Greek government was able to hold the
Communists in check with the aid of Britain, but they renewed
guerrilla warfare in 1946 with assistance from Albania, Yugoslavia, and Bulgaria. This was the situation in February, 1947,
when Britain informed the United States she could no longer
provide substantial assistance to Greece and Turkey. Early in
March, the Greek government made an urgent appeal for American assistance. The United States was obliged, therefore, to consider in more than a piecemeal fashion its interest in Communist
expansion in the Middle East.

On March 12, 1947, President Truman requested Congress to
provide economic assistance to Greece and Turkey and to authorize him to send military as well as civilian personnel in order
to aid those countries in the task of reconstruction. In his address
to Congress, the President announced principles that have become known as the Truman Doctrine. He said that one of the primary objectives of American foreign policy was the creation of
conditions in which the United States and other nations would be
able to "work out a way of life free from coercion," and that this
objective could not be realized unless the United States was willing
"to help free peoples to maintain their free institutions and their

national integrity against aggressive movements that seek to impose upon them totalitarian regimes." "I believe," the President said, "that it must be the policy of the United States to support free peoples who are resisting attempted subjugation by armed minorities or by outside pressures." Congress debated the issue for about two months and enacted a measure, signed by the President on May 22, 1947, which provided assistance for Greece and Turkey substantially in the form of the President's request.

By this time it had become evident to various American leaders, and particularly to the Under Secretary of State for Economic Affairs, William L. Clayton, that western Europe was on the verge of political and economic disintegration. As a result, the United States offered to assist Europe, excepting Spain but including Russia and her satellites, through an integrated European Recovery Program wherein mutual self-help would be supported by large-scale American aid, commonly called the Marshall Plan. In broad outline the plan proposed that each participating nation would survey its economic situation, decide what it needed most for recovery, and estimate what it could contribute to the co-operative program. These findings would be submitted to a central committee which would formulate an integrated program for consideration by the United States. Russia sent delegates to a conference in Paris called to consider the proposal, but withdrew as soon as she discovered she could neither delay the plan nor alter its co-operative character. Russia's reasons for her decision are speculative. She may not have wanted to expose her economic situation to foreign observation, may have thought she would be obliged to contribute too large a share to the common effort, or may have feared the effect of economic co-operation on her whole authoritarian system.

Sixteen European nations eagerly accepted the American offer, and Congress provided an interim aid program of about half a billion dollars while it considered the larger aid enterprise which anticipated an expenditure of probably $17 billion. The favorable action of Congress in June, 1948, was spurred by the Communist coup in Czechoslovakia. This European aid program was enormously successful and did not need modification until after the Korean War. The United States spent about $42 billion in lend-lease assistance and about $23 billion for the relief and re-construction of Europe prior to 1950.

TREATIES WITH GERMAN SATELLITE STATES

Although the wartime Allies failed to make a general peace treaty with Germany or Japan, or a state treaty, as it was called, with Austria because that country was not considered an Axis satellite, treaties were made by February, 1947, with the remaining five Axis members: Italy, Bulgaria, Hungary, Rumania, and Finland. The treaty with Italy was the most extensive because it involved boundary settlements with Yugoslavia and France, colonial possessions, and Italy's relations with Albania and Ethiopia in addition to domestic affairs. Broadly speaking, the treaties deprived the several states of colonial and conquered areas if such existed, required them to surrender war criminals for trial, restricted their future military potential, and exacted war reparations amounting to a total of $1,330,000,000—$900,000,000 being allotted to the Soviet Union.

ALLIED CONFLICTS OVER GERMANY AND EASTERN EUROPE

It is not strictly accurate to refer to the breakdown of Allied unity over policies concerning postwar Germany because unity on many matters never actually existed. Such unity as existed gradually deteriorated from the time of the Potsdam Conference of 1945 until the breakup of the Control Council for Germany and the Russian blockade of Berlin in 1948. This development was characterized by apparent agreement on general policies but disagreement on their interpretation and fulfillment, and by tortuous and fruitless diplomatic maneuvering. American wartime discussions concerning policy toward Germany revealed sharp diversities of opinion within the government, and since President Roosevelt did not resolve these differences, the war ended without a well-defined American position. Emphasis during these discussions was placed on the trial of war criminals and the determination to prevent Germany from again endangering the peace of the world. Various plans among the Allies for the dismemberment of Germany were considered but largely abandoned before the end of the war. Specific agreement was reached concerning the four Allied zones of occupation, the establishment of a Control Council composed of the military commanders of the occupied zones, the administration of Berlin as a separate area under the joint control of the four powers, and the policy of considering Germany as an economic unit.

Prior to the conference at Potsdam, the United States had agreed to some transfer of German minorities from neighboring states *provided* such transfer was selective, orderly, and under international supervision. For the purposes of defining the zones of occupation, Germany was to be restricted to her 1937 boundaries, but no agreement was ever reached on the final boundaries, that matter being left for determination by a peace conference which could not be arranged. Reparations in the form of capital goods were to be taken from Germany, and some general arrangements for this were agreed upon, but the United States did not agree that reparations could be taken from current production until German exports were sufficient to pay for essential imports. Industrial equipment was to be supplied to Russia from the British and American zones and Russia was to transfer to their zones food and other materials from her zone. No agreement was ever reached on the total amount of reparations or on the exact distinction between reparations and "war booty." By the spring of 1946 the general agreement to treat Germany as an economic unit had broken down. The United States and Great Britain were supplying food to their zones while Russia was removing current production from her zone. The Control Council had reached agreements on some matters but not on such important things as labor organizations, nation-wide political parties, central economic administration, foreign and internal trade, currency, land reform, and education.

Secretary of State James F. Byrnes thought that possibly Russian attitudes and unilateral acts concerning reparations, Russia's refusal to treat Germany as an economic unit, her removal of German peoples from her areas of control, her arbitrary position concerning Polish boundaries, and her violations of agreements regarding political affairs in eastern Europe were due, at least in a large measure, to her fear of a German renaissance as a great power and the suspicion that the Western Allies were in sympathy with this development. He proposed, therefore, as early as September, 1945, the signing of a four-power pact between the Soviet Union, the United States, Great Britain, and France guaranteeing the demilitarization of Germany for a period of twenty-five years. The Russian Foreign Minister agreed to consider the matter. Byrnes prepared a draft of such a treaty, secured general approval of it from Britain and France and from prominent leaders in the American Senate, and pursued the matter with Russia in February and April, 1946. Russia suggested the treaty should run for forty years and Byrnes accepted this proposal. After George C. Marshall succeeded Byrnes as Secretary of State, he let Russia know that the United States was still willing to sign such a treaty, and the idea was not abandoned by the United States until after a meeting of the Allied foreign ministers in Moscow in April, 1947. Russian rejection of the treaty was by indirection, in suggesting trivial changes, in introducing irrelevant matters, and in what Secretary Marshall called the "diplomacy of exhaustion." The policy of Russia was to use the prospect that she might agree to such a treaty in return for concessions from the Western Allies concerning Germany and eastern Europe which they could not accept.

The Russian attitude toward this treaty provided further evidence that Russia did not intend to co-operate with the Western Allies under the terms of the Yalta and Potsdam agreements. Sensing this fact, Secretary Byrnes announced in September, 1946, that the United States did not intend for Germany to be either a pawn between Russia and the Western Allies or a partner, and that it favored a decentralized federal goverment for all of Germany and an increase in the level of German industrial production to keep her from being a further economic drain on the occupying powers. Since these policies could not be implemented throughout Germany, they were gradually put into effect in the Western zones of occupation, and the Soviet Union retaliated by leaving the Control Council in March, 1948, and by establishing a blockade of Berlin in June of the same year.

The blockade was made possible because Berlin was completely surrounded by the Russian zone of occupation, and it produced a crisis partly because the Western Allies had permitted their military strength to decline while Russia had not, and partly because the Western powers were caught without plans concerning what to do in case of a blockade although its possibility had been foreseen. Some people in the United States favored withdrawal from Berlin rather than risk a war with Russia, while others, including General Lucius D. Clay, the American military commander in Berlin, favored the strong policy of sending an armored convoy into Berlin because they believed a weak policy was fundamentally unwise in dealing with Russia. They thought the blockade was being used by Russia as a test of Western unity and determination rather than a threat of war. Neither of these two clear-cut policies was adopted by the United States; instead it decided to make a diplomatic protest against the legality of the blockade and to supply Berlin by air with food, fuel, and other supplies while diplomatic means of settling the issue were attempted.

The United States held that its rights, and the rights of the other Western Allies, to free access to Berlin were derived from its position as one of the four occupying powers of Germany and therefore from rights inherent in many international agreements concerning the occupation, and most notably from the withdrawal of American military forces from positions well within the Russian zone of occupation as previously agreed upon, a withdrawal that was made with the *understanding* that free access to Berlin by rail, road, and air would be arranged. This understanding was never put into a written formal agreement, but the United States held it had been tacitly confirmed in various ways and had been sanctioned by usage. Wearisome negotiations between the United States and the Soviet Union over Berlin dragged on through the remainder of 1948 and until May, 1949, when the blockade was lifted. Meanwhile Berlin had been supplied by air, its people had shown remarkable unity and stability during the crisis, and the United States had increased its determination to strengthen its military potential at home and through alliances abroad. Russia was obviously unwilling to risk war by attacking the airlift to Berlin and presumably lifted the blockade because it was proving to be detrimental to Russian prestige. The American government hailed the episode as a victory for American policy, but it left undetermined, much more than it had been earlier, the right of ground access to Berlin, and equally undecided whether the stronger policy would not have settled this matter as well as saved the lives of Americans lost through accidents during the airlift.

The Berlin crisis was only one illustration of the fact that American foreign policy between 1947 and 1950 was a mixture of boldness and timidity derived from divided counsels in the government and from its inability to formulate policies for various areas of the world that were inherently consistent. The Russian attempts to expand Communist influence in Greece and Turkey were met by the firm policy of the Truman Doctrine, but in China the United States advocated co-operation between the Nationalist government and the Chinese Communists. At the same time that the United States was adopting strong measures to strengthen stability in the Middle East by aiding Iran and Turkey, it alienated the Arab world and reduced its influence in the area, as will be noted later, by its policies concerning Palestine.

Formation of a consistent American policy was further inhibited by the contradiction between the government's statements and its actions regarding the United Nations. It continued to declare that the United Nations was the cornerstone of its whole foreign policy and to foster the belief among the people that the organization was one on which the United States could rely for world peace. The validity of this belief was already undermined by American experiences in the United Nations, and it had been disregarded in practice by American unilateral action under the Truman Doctrine and by the organization of a separate security system for the Western Hemisphere. The wisdom of American policies and their possible justification are not under examination here, for they may be defended in consideration of the context of the times, but they lacked coherence on the foundation of basic principles.

This lack of clarity of policy was illustrated also by the anomalous character of the North Atlantic Treaty Organization (NATO) and the diversity of opinion in the United States concerning what it meant and how it should be implemented. The idea of the alliance was a logical development of the policy of uniting western Europe against Communist penetration, and was supported by those who believed that regional security systems were either good in themselves or in some way would strengthen the United Nations. A European mutual defense agreement known as the Brussels Pact had been signed in 1948. The signatories of this pact—Britain, Belgium, France, the Netherlands, and Luxembourg—agreed to give all possible military and other aid to any of them that "should be the object of an armed attack in Europe."

The United States believed this pact should be expanded and took the leadership in negotiating the North Atlantic Treaty, which was signed in April, 1949. The original members of the alliance included the signatories of the Brussels Pact and in addition the United States, Canada, Denmark, Iceland, Italy, Norway, and Portugal. The Irish Republic and Sweden were urged to adhere to the treaty but declined. Later, after 1950, Greece, Turkey, and the Federal Republic of West Germany were included in the agreement. The treaty provided that an "armed attack" against one or more of its signatories would be considered as an attack against them all, and that each would take "such action as it deems necessary, including the use of armed force, to restore and maintain the security of the North Atlantic area." This area was specified to include the territory of any signatory in Europe or North America, the Algerian departments of France, islands under the jurisdiction of any signatory in the North Atlantic area north of the Tropic of Cancer, and the vessels or aircraft in that area of any signatory. The treaty established a council to consider the implementation of the agreement, provided that other European nations could be admitted to signature by unanimous agreement, and permitted denunciation of the treaty by any party to it after twenty years and upon a year's notice. Obviously the treaty area had to be redefined when Greece and Turkey were admitted to membership, and presumably Algeria ceased to be within the treaty area when it became independent in 1962.

Prior to the negotiation of the treaty, the State Department had secured a Senate resolution approving American association "by constitutional process" with such regional and collective arrangements as were based on "effective self-help and mutual aid" and affected American security. This appeared to sanction an agreement such as the North Atlantic Treaty, but when the treaty was presented to the Senate for approval, many difficult questions arose. It was not clear whether the treaty implied an obligation on the part of the United States to provide continuous economic and military assistance to western Europe, or what the constitutional procedures would be regarding treaty commitments. The relation of the treaty to the Charter of the United Nations was also obscure. Secretary of State Dean Acheson thought the treaty was related primarily to the provisions of the Charter concerning collective self-defense, others insisted it was more properly a regional agreement, and still others thought that, although it mentioned the Charter, it was essentially a separate matter justified under general international law.

Of these and other matters of uncertainty, the constitutional issue was the most vital. Would an armed attack within the treaty area on any signatory *automatically* commit the United States to war the same as if the attack were on the territory of the United States, and did the treaty expand the constitutional powers of the President? Secretary Acheson thought both parts of this question should be answered in the negative since the United States would be obligated to do only what it deemed necessary, and since the treaty stipulated that its provisions would be carried out by the signatories in accordance with their constitutional processes. But the questions lingered and were not answered, for the treaty provided that an attack against one signatory was an attack against them all. If this meant that such an attack would be the *same* as an attack against the territory of the United States, did not the President have not only the power but also the duty to act whenever he decided American defense was involved, without waiting for a declaration of war and therefore within constitutional processes? This appeared to be the interpretation of the treaty by the Committee on Foreign Relations of the Senate and may have been implicit in American defense strategy regarding instantaneous retaliation against an attack on the United States or a treaty member. Under this interpretation, it would be clear that the treaty profoundly altered the American constitutional system.

A further constitutional question involved the right of the Executive to send troops abroad to implement the treaty in the absence of direct congressional authorization. This was also the object of diverse interpretations. Congress undoubtedly had the constitutional authority to decide what troops if any should be sent abroad, perhaps the sole authority, and also to define American obligations under the North Atlantic Treaty, but no clarifying legislation was enacted.

THE MIDDLE EAST

Prior to the First World War, American interests in the Middle East were confined largely to trade and to various missionary, educational, and philanthropic enterprises. The United States did not participate after the war in the imperialistic activities of France and Great Britain for the spoils of the Ottoman Empire, but used its influence while President Wilson was in office to promote the principle of self-determination for the peoples of the area. As a result, a strong sentiment of friendship existed for the United States among the Arab people. The development during the interwar period of American interest in Middle Eastern petroleum gave the United States a larger national interest in the area. During the Second World War, Turkey remained neutral, and the Middle East was of strategic importance to the Allies in numerous ways. After the war, the United States took strong measures already noted to protect the independence of Turkey and assisted in securing the withdrawal of Russian forces from a part of Iran. It became involved, however, in the problem of Palestine and developed policies that changed its position in the Middle East and had consequences elsewhere.

The problem of Palestine grew out of the Zionist movement, which had roots in Judaism and became political in the late nineteenth century and an international issue during and following the First World War. This movement virtually defies brief analysis because Zionism meant different things to different people at different times and could not be equated with Judaism, nor was it confined to Jewish people or embraced by all of them. As early as 1892 a Zionist meeting in Basel declared the purpose of Zion-

Middle East

ism was to establish a Jewish "national home in Palestine." Some
Zionists interpreted this to mean the creation of a Jewish national
state, some thought it meant the establishment of semiautonomous
Jewish communities, and others believed it meant simply securing
for the Jewish minority in Palestine equal rights with all others in
the population. This difficulty over the meaning of the word
"Zionism" and the interpretation of the term Jewish "national
home in Palestine" is of critical historical importance because the
word and the term were used by various American Presidents,
the United States Congress, the British government, and various

Jewish and other leaders without precision of definition. Even after the Second World War, when Zionism more clearly had come to mean the creation of a Jewish national state, many Zionists favored this only if it could be done without force and violence.

A significant landmark in the Zionist movement was a declaration of the British government in 1917, known as the Balfour Declaration, which was later incorporated into the provisions for the British mandate for Palestine and consented to in a treaty between the United States and Britain regarding American rights in Palestine derived from an earlier American treaty with the Ottoman Empire. The declaration stated that Britain favored the establishment in Palestine of a national home for the Jewish people, but with the clear understanding that "nothing should be done which might prejudice the civil and religious rights of existing non-Jewish communities in Palestine." The terms of the mandate provided that Britain should facilitate Jewish immigration to Palestine "while ensuring that the rights and position of other sections of the population" were not "prejudiced." The Arab population in Palestine, and in the Middle East generally, bitterly opposed the idea of a Jewish state in Palestine or any significant Jewish immigration to the area and were alarmed over the possible meaning of the Balfour Declaration. The British government assured them in 1918 that it supported Jewish immigration only to the extent it was consistent with the economic and political rights of the Arabs in Palestine, and that it supported the basic principle of self-determination for the area. During the period of her mandate, Britain supported Jewish immigration to Palestine against constant Arab opposition, which finally broke into an open rebellion that was not suppressed until Britain promised in 1939 to restrain further immigration without Arab consent. It seems clear that the terms of the Balfour Declaration and of the mandate and the promises Britain made to Zionist and Arab leaders were inherently contradictory.

After 1939, and particularly during and after the Second World War, Zionist leaders who were determined to create a Jewish state in Palestine turned against the British government, promoted illegal immigration into Palestine, prepared for the use of force against the Arabs, and sought assistance for their cause in the United States, where Jewish immigration to Palestine had become interwoven with sympathy for the tragic plight of Jewish people under German rule. President Roosevelt, however, assured King Ibn Saud of Arabia, both orally and in writing, that he would take no action regarding Palestine "which might prove hostile to the Arab people." This policy was consistent with the later statement of President Truman in October, 1945, that the United States would not approve territorial changes in any friendly part of the world unless they accorded "with the freely expressed wishes of the people concerned." The Arab population of Palestine at the beginning of the British mandate was about ten times greater than the Jewish population, and in 1945 it was about double the Jewish population.

After the end of the Second World War, Zionist leaders in the United States and elsewhere continued their demand for removal of the restrictions on Jewish immigration to Palestine and made clear their intention of creating there a Jewish state. Various leaders of both major political parties in the United States competed with each other in proclaiming support for the Zionist movement, and President Truman publicly urged the British to resume the admission of Jewish immigrants to Palestine, but he did not offer to assume British responsibilities for such a policy. Weakened by its long struggle against the Axis powers, weary of dealing with Jewish terrorists in Palestine, and discouraged by American pressure for policies it could not adopt without arousing further Arab hostility and violating its promises to them, the British government announced it would terminate its mandate and turn the problem of Palestine over to the United Nations. The Assembly of the United Nations passed a resolution in November, 1947, which recommended the partition of Palestine into separate Jewish and Arab states, defined their boundaries, provided for their economic unity, and proposed that Jerusalem be a separate area under the control of the United Nations. This action of the Assembly was bitterly opposed by Arab leaders, who held that Palestine should be accorded the right of self-determination, and was not taken until the United States had exerted strong pressures in the Assembly in its favor. This policy was opposed in the Departments of State and Defense, but President Truman assumed personal responsibility for it and overrode all opposition.

The Assembly had no power to implement its resolution and the Security Council would assume none. Arab leaders rejected the recommendation of the Assembly altogether, and the Zionist leaders accepted only that part providing for the establishment of a Jewish state. As soon as Britain relinquished her mandate, the State of Israel was proclaimed, the United States immediately recognized it, and the new state prepared to defend itself by force against Arab opposition. War in Palestine followed until a truce was arranged through United Nations efforts, but not until Israel had expanded her boundaries beyond those indicated by the partition resolution and almost all of the Arab population of Palestine under the control of Israel had become refugees. The Arab states of the Middle East looked upon Israel as a state created and imposed on the Middle East by Western powers, particularly by the United States, whom they considered primarily responsible. The United States was confronted with dilemmas no matter what policy it adopted thereafter regarding Arab-Israeli relations. It had violated its own principles of self-determination in supporting the partition of Palestine against the will of the majority of its inhabitants, and had acted on the assumption that the resolution of the General Assembly was a legal sanction for partition, but was unwilling to enforce against Israel the parts of the resolution Israel would not accept. The Arab states did not want the Palestinian refugees and Israel would not permit them to return to their homes in Israel. The United States looked in vain for a solvent Middle Eastern policy.

EASTERN ASIA

1. *Southeast Asia.*   Prior to the Second World War, Southeast Asia consisted of one independent state, Thailand, and five dependent areas: French Indochina; British Burma, Malaya, and Borneo; Dutch Indonesia; and the Philippines. Japan swiftly overran the area and occupied most of it for over three years. The Thai government offered only token resistance to Japan, made a

treaty of alliance with it, and declared war on Great Britain and the United States. The Thai minister in Washington notified Secretary of State Cordell Hull of the declaration of war, but said he was keeping the declaration in his pocket because he was convinced it did not represent the Thai people. The United States accepted this view, did not declare war on Thailand, co-operated with a Free Thai Movement, and re-established friendly relations with the Thai government after the war.

The United States was critical of French rule in Indochina and urged that Indochina should not be restored to France but placed under United Nations trusteeship. The United States consented, however, to the return of French rule over the area with the understanding it would be granted independence within a reasonable time.

Queen Wilhelmina of the Netherlands stated during the war that the Netherlands East Indies would be given commonwealth status, and the United States exercised very little influence in Indonesian affairs until the problem of its independence was presented to the United Nations.

A strong nationalistic movement had existed in Burma prior to the war, and the Japanese, whose invasion of Burma was not resisted, declared Burma independent in 1943. Burma soon became disenchanted, however, with nominal independence under Japanese control although it did not welcome a return to British rule. The United States had announced that it wanted to be consulted about all postwar arrangements in Southeast Asia, but it took no significant part in the re-establishment of Britain's authority over her former dependencies.

By an act of Congress passed in 1934, the United States had promised independence to the Philippines on July 4, 1946. During the war, some people in the United States thought the date for independence should be postponed on account of political and economic dislocations in the Philippines, but Congress reaffirmed its pledge in a joint resolution of June, 1944, a presidential election was held in the islands in April, 1946, and full independence was granted on the date set. In the remainder of Southeast Asia, movements for independence progressed more slowly, but with minor exceptions the whole area became independent before 1960.

2. *Korea.* The principal Allies agreed during the Second World War that Korea should become free and independent, and the Russian and American military planners at the Potsdam Conference arranged that Russian forces would remove Japanese troops from Korea north of the 38th parallel, while the American forces were assigned the same task for the area south of that line. The commanders of these forces were to co-operate for the establishment of a freely elected Korean government. When this co-operation immediately failed, the United States, Britain, and Russia agreed—with the later concurrence of China—to establish an American-Russian Joint Commission to carry out the basic policy for Korea. No progress was made by this commission either toward political or economic co-operation, and after two years of futile effort to achieve co-operation the United States submitted the Korean problem to the United Nations. The Assembly of the United Nations established a Temporary Commission on Korea with the "right to travel, observe, and consult" throughout the whole area. The Russians refused to grant these rights within their zone of control and established there a pro-Communist military and political authority. The United States co-operated fully with the commission and under its observation held free elections which resulted in the establishment of a government recognized by the Assembly of the United Nations as the Government of the Republic of Korea and the only legal government in Korea. The United States terminated its Korean military government on January 1, 1949, and soon withdrew its military forces save for a few troops whose assistance was requested by the Korean government for training purposes.

3. *Japan.* The initial postwar Japanese policy of the United States was similar to its policy regarding Germany. In Japan, however, the United States was the sole occupying power, and although it was supposed to be guided by an inter-Allied Far Eastern Commission, it was authorized to act independently if the commission failed to agree. Differences of policy existed within the commission, not only between the Soviet Union and the United States, but also between the United States and other members. No significant controversy arose over the restriction of Japan to its home islands, the trial of war criminals, the elimination of the

Japanese military potential, or the efforts of the United States to reconstruct Japan's economic and social systems in line with democratic ideals. The nations that had been overrun by Japan, however—Korea, China, and the Philippines in particular—expected substantial reparations from Japan and were fearful of any policy that might permit her to become again a menace to their security. During the early part of the occupation, American policy was consistent with these views, for the United States assumed cooperation with Russia, the existence of a strong and unified China, and the economic viability of an eastern Asia independent of Japan. By about 1947, however, the United States began to realize that its policies in Japan needed to be reappraised. The increase of population in Japan, wartime destruction of her property, the loss of her vast empire, and American "reforms" had so reduced her economic production that she was a liability to the United States. In addition, the deterioration of American-Russian relations in Korea as well as in Europe and events in China contributed to the American decision to shorten the period of occupation and to assist Japan in becoming self-sufficient. This policy virtually eliminated the possibility that Japan would be obliged to pay substantial reparations and created the necessity for her to develop an armed force sufficient to maintain internal order. This change of policy was on the point of completion at the beginning of the Korean War.

4. *China.* The tangled web of American postwar policy toward China will probably never be unraveled. It produced the most acrimonious debate on foreign policy in the United States after the Second World War, became deeply involved in domestic politics and in ideological conflicts, and resulted in one of the outstanding failures of American policy in the nation's history. The Communist movement in China was about a decade old when Japan invaded China in 1931, and from then until the success of the Communists on the mainland of China in 1949, the leader of the Kuomintang Party—the Nationalist government—Chiang Kai-shek, was as apprehensive of Communism as he was of Japanese domination of China. By 1937, when Japan renewed the conquest of China, the Communists had been confined to a relatively small area around Yenan, but the exigencies of the war

against Japan produced a kind of truce between the Nationalist and Communist elements which had a precarious existence until the end of the war when it appeared likely that the Communists would be suppressed.

This prospect became involved, however, with Russian designs on Manchuria and with American policy. At the Cairo Conference of November, 1943, Roosevelt and Churchill promised Chiang Kai-shek that China would have restored to it all the territories seized by Japan, specifically including Manchuria, Formosa, and the Pescadores Islands. At the Yalta Conference, however, the two Western leaders promised Stalin that the port of Dairen would be internationalized with the "pre-eminent interests" of Russia safeguarded, that Russia would have a lease on Port Arthur as a naval base, and that the Chinese-Eastern and the South-Manchurian railroads would be jointly operated by Russia and China with Russian "pre-eminent interests" also safeguarded. Roosevelt undertook to secure the concurrence of Chiang Kai-shek to the agreement, and Stalin expressed a willingness to recognize the Nationalist government, to make a treaty of alliance with it, and to assist China in becoming economically prosperous. The agreement with Russia concerning Manchuria was to be "unqualifiedly fulfilled" nevertheless. This was a secret agreement which infringed on the sovereignty of China in Manchuria and to that degree violated the Cairo Declaration. After President Truman assumed office, Russia made it clear that she would not enter the war against Japan unless China agreed to the Yalta provisions regarding Manchuria. Under pressure from the United States, China accepted what she could not prevent and made a treaty with Russia substantially confirming the Yalta agreement.

While the United States undertook to see that China fulfilled American promises to Russia regarding Manchuria, it did not undertake to see that Russia fulfilled its promises to China. Russia denuded Manchuria of industrial equipment under the guise of taking Japanese war booty, delayed the departure of her troops until the Chinese Communists had infiltrated much of the area and had acquired Japanese military supplies, and possibly gave the Communists military assistance. China was confronted, therefore, with broken Russian promises and a strengthened Communist army.

The United States had several clear-cut alternatives of policy: (1) it could abandon the Nationalist government to its own resources as the Western Allies abandoned Poland and eastern Europe; (2) it could support, as it had done in Greece, the Nationalist government with whatever economic and military aid was necessary in its struggle with the Communists; or (3) it could assume that the Communists were indigenous agrarian reformers who should not be opposed. It adopted none of these policies consistently. It gave some military and economic aid to the Nationalists, and then at a critical moment in their struggle against the Communists, withheld aid in order to bring about a truce and the establishment of a coalition government including the Communists. The Communists consolidated their forces, broke the truce when they were ready, gradually defeated the Nationalists, and by 1949 gained control of mainland China. To what extent these developments were the result of Russian policies in Manchuria, American policies, possible military mistakes of the Nationalists, or of many other factors in the domestic situation in China cannot be determined. The State Department published a selected collection of diplomatic documents purporting to show that the Nationalists were wholly responsible for their defeat and the United States wholly blameless.

5. *Micronesia.*   The disposition of the Pacific islands formerly mandated to Japan under the League of Nations, and captured by the United States with so much loss of life, was naturally of American concern at the end of the war. The United States had declared that it sought "no aggrandizement, territorial or other," but it was not willing for the islands to become again a danger to American security. It was prepared to place them under United Nations trusteeship with itself as the administrating authority, provided the trust territory would be designated a strategic area. This would permit the United States to establish in the territory naval, military, and air bases and fortifications. The Security Council approved an arrangement with the United States to this effect, and Congress sanctioned the agreement by joint resolution and established the Territory of the Pacific Islands.

LATIN AMERICA

After some delay the United States fulfilled its promise to the Latin-American states at the conferences of 1945 in Mexico City and San Francisco to co-operate with them in establishing a regional security system. The first step in this direction was the signing of the Inter-American Treaty of Reciprocal Assistance in 1947 (Pact of Rio), the second was the creation of the Organization of American States in 1948, and the third was the signing of the American Treaty of Pacific Settlement in the same year. The first of these treaties, unlike the United Nations Charter, was a mutual security agreement. The signatories agreed that "an armed attack by any state against an American state shall be considered as an armed attack against all the American states," and each signatory undertook "to assist in meeting the attack." The region in which this agreement applied was defined in the treaty and substantially was the Western Hemisphere. The treaty provided also that if the "integrity of the territory or the sovereignty or political independence of any American state should be affected by an aggression that is not an armed attack or by any extra-continental or intra-continental conflict, or by any other fact or situation that might endanger the peace of America," an assembly of the Organization of American States, awkwardly called the Organ of Consultation, could take action by a two-thirds vote. The decisions of this body were binding on all members with respect to economic and diplomatic sanctions, but no state was required to use its armed forces without its consent. The new American system created by these and other agreements contained all the necessary elements of international co-operation, assistance, and defense.

XII

A DECADE OF FRUSTRATION, 1950–1960

THE DECADE of the 1950's may properly be called an era of frustration in American foreign relations, not because the United States failed to make heroic efforts and great sacrifices in the interest of world peace, or necessarily because its foreign policies were inept, for they were successful in some instances and may have been the best possible even when they failed. It was a decade of frustration because the fundamental problems of world order were no nearer solution at the end of the period than at the beginning. The Korean War ended in stalemate, Communism expanded in Southeast Asia and Latin America, tensions in Europe mounted, confusion grew in the Middle East, competition in the production of destructive weapons increased, neutralist nations multiplied, and American alliances, based theoretically on the principles of self-help and mutual assistance, appeared to develop more in the direction of demands for greater American aid than in their mutual assistance aspects. Yet the decade was not retrogressive. Western Europe, Japan, the United States, and some other areas made significant economic progress, the old colonialism almost disappeared, Communism was not greatly extended, and a nuclear war was avoided. Because of their nature a few of these topics will be held over for consideration in the next chapter.

237

THE KOREAN WAR

By the beginning of 1950, the American government had fully accommodated itself to the Communist victory on the mainland of China and was prepared to accept the further success of the Communists in overthrowing the Nationalist forces of Chiang Kai-shek on Formosa. President Truman announced early in January that no military aid or even military advice would be afforded the Nationalists. A few days later Secretary of State Dean Acheson made a broad policy statement concerning eastern Asia. He said the United States was committed to the defense of Japan and the Philippines, the "defensive perimeter" being along the Aleutians to Japan, and thence to the Ryukyus and the Philippines. It was "hardly sensible or necessary," he continued, to guarantee other areas in the Pacific against attack, and if an attack should come, they would have to rely for their security first on themselves and second on the "commitments of the entire civilized world under the Charter of the United Nations" which, he declared, had "not proved a weak reed to lean on" by any people who were determined to protect their independence from outside aggression. Later in the statement, the Secretary said the United States had a "direct responsibility" and a "direct opportunity to act" in Japan and that the "same thing to a lesser degree" was true in Korea.

This statement left the policy of the United States regarding the defense of Korea in confusion. Korea was clearly placed outside the American defensive perimeter but inside the protection of the United Nations. The United States had demonstrated, however, by the Truman Doctrine and by the creation of the North Atlantic Alliance, that it regarded the United Nations as a weak reed indeed for the defense of free nations in Europe. How it could be a stronger reed in Asia was not disclosed, nor was American responsibility for Korea clear if it was the same as in Japan but "to a lesser degree." Prior to the Secretary's statement, the Department of Defense had been requested to make an appraisal of the importance of the defense of Korea in relation to American security obligations in the Pacific, and had replied that from a purely military point of view its protection was not essential but might be very desirable from the political point of view. The

United States was giving Korea economic and military aid and assisting in the training of a Korean army, but the latter was far more in the nature of a mobile police force than a military establishment capable of sustaining an attack from North Korea, where Russia had built a strong military machine. While the United States had an army of occupation in Japan, it did not have there a significant number of combat-ready troops to send to Korea.

When the Russian-trained and -armed North Korean Army launched a massive assault against the Republic of Korea all along the 38th parallel on the morning of June 25, 1950, the United States government was caught without a previously formulated policy to deal with the problem, although it had ample warning that such a situation might arise. General Albert C. Wedemeyer had informed President Truman in 1947 that sizable elements of North Koreans were operating with the Chinese Communists forces, "possibly to acquire battle conditioning," and that Russian-trained North Koreans would be a threat to, and probably would attack, South Korea if American troops were withdrawn. Just prior to the attack, American intelligence services had reported that North Korean troops were being massed along the 38th parallel and that civilians were being removed from the area. It seems beyond doubt that American policy, both military and political, concerning the Korean War was formulated initially on the basis of crisis and thereafter piecemeal in consideration of changing military situations in Korea and developing political influences in the United States and the world. Policy formed in this manner, whether justified or not, could scarcely avoid being one of shifting expediency.

As soon as President Truman was convinced the attack on the Republic of Korea was not a feint to mask a Russian or Russia-inspired attack of greater moment elsewhere, he was apparently convinced that American leadership should be exerted to bring about strong action by the United Nations against North Korea, and that the fate of the United Nations as an international security agency was at stake. He considered the situation in Korea as analogous to that in China in 1931 when the League of Nations failed to suppress Japanese aggression. The fact that the two situations as well as the two legal systems—those of the Charter and the Covenant—were not analogous does not need to be considered here. The important question was how the United Nations could legally act in the Korean case since the Security Council was the sole organ of the United Nations with authority to act against aggression, but could not act in accordance with the provisions of the Charter because Russia at that time was absenting herself from the Security Council.

The Charter provided that on all substantive questions, those other than procedural, the Council could take action on the affirmative vote of seven members, including the affirmative vote of all permanent members. An ingenious argument was advanced at the time of the Korean crisis and was employed later, an argument that although the "naked words" of the Charter required for legal action the concurring votes of all permanent members, these words could be interpreted to mean the concurring votes of "all permanent members who participated in the voting." This was contested by those who believed that, in the interpretation of legal documents, particularly those of such enormous importance as the Charter of the United Nations and the Constitution of the United States, the "naked words" of the document, where their meaning was clear and beyond dispute, were the only words that could be considered without peril to the foundations of legal and constitutional government and, in the case of the Charter, without danger to future national interests of the United States. Consistent with this view, international co-operation in the Korean War should have been sought outside the Charter or theoretically under the Charter's provisions for the establishment of separate arrangements for collective self-defense as was done in the North Atlantic Alliance. Whatever may have been the merits of these conflicting views, the United States government accepted the idea that the Security Council could act in a legal way regarding the aggression of North Korea without the concurring vote of Russia.

Acting under the leadership of the United States, the Security Council passed a resolution on June 25 calling on North Korea to withdraw its forces to the 38th parallel and upon all members of the United Nations to assist in the execution of this resolution, and when North Korea did not comply, recommended on June 27 that members of the United Nations furnish "such assistance to the

Republic of Korea as may be necessary to repel the armed attack and to restore international peace and security in the area." Shortly thereafter, the Council recommended that members of the United Nations responding to these resolutions place their military forces under the unified command of the United States, that the United States designate a commander of such forces, and that the United Nations flag could be used along with those of participating nations. President Truman quickly designated General Douglas MacArthur as Commander in Chief of the forces in Korea. Such were the resolutions of the United Nations Security Council under which the United States assumed that the war against North Korea was a United Nations war and was under *United Nations* authority.

A domestic counterpart to this legal problem was the source of the President's power to commit the armed forces of the United States to a major military engagement—in every way a war—without a declaration of war by the Congress. The President deemed he had this right, and the State Department issued a memorandum sustaining the presidential view. It held that the President's authority was derived from his position as Commander in Chief of the armed forces of the United States, his duty to defend the United States against invasion and to see that its laws were executed, to perform his responsibility for the maintenance of peace, to protect the foreign policy of the United States, and to implement the resolutions of the Security Council of the United Nations. The memorandum was diffuse and did not state which of the reasons given was relevant to the Korean case or what American historical precedent, if any, was analogous to it. Some members of the Congress believed the President infringed on the constitutional authority of Congress to decide on war and peace, but the great majority of them approved the President's action whether or not they granted his authority to act, and Congress indirectly sustained his policy through subsequent legislation, leaving the important constitutional question in abeyance.

The first thrust of the North Korean invasion almost succeeded in overrunning the whole of South Korea. The American and Korean forces managed, however, to maintain a foothold in Korea, gradually strengthened their position, eventually executed a brilliant military maneuver in establishing a new front behind the North Korean lines, and by the end of September had driven the invading forces back to the 38th parallel. This raised the question of whether the United States and its allies should advance into North Korea for the purpose of suppressing the Communists and establishing a free and unified Korea under a government of its own choosing. A free and united Korea had been the postwar policy of the United States, and the resolution of the Security Council of June 27, 1950, had called on the members of the United Nations "to restore international peace and security to the area." The resolution did not define the word "restore" or designate the "area," but the United States decided to seek additional sanction from the United Nations for carrying the war into North Korea for the purpose stated. This "sanction" was provided by a resolution of the General Assembly of the United Nations of October 7, 1950. The General Assembly rather than the Security Council was used in this instance because Russia had decided to resume its representation at the Council and was in a position to obstruct any action by that body. The Resolutions on Uniting for Peace, referred to in an earlier chapter, were not enacted by the Assembly until November 3, 1950, but the principle on which they were based was the same as that on which the October 7 resolution was passed, namely, that the Assembly could make recommendations on security matters directly to its members whenever the Security Council could not act because of the lack of unanimity.

Within about a month after this decision was made, in the words of the General Assembly, "to ensure conditions of stability *throughout* Korea [italics supplied]," the American and allied forces had shattered North Korean resistance and had advanced almost to the Chinese-North Korean border. The military situation was suddenly changed by the intervention of Communist China, whose forces entered Korea, launched a powerful offensive, and drove the American and allied troops not only back to the 38th parallel, but beyond. Gradually, however, the Chinese were driven in turn back to the 38th parallel. During the period from November, 1950, until about June, 1951, confusion reigned supreme over American policy concerning the Korean War. American political leaders said they could not formulate policy until the military situation was clarified, and the military leaders said they could not plan military strategy until political objectives were determined. Various leaders made statements contradicting each other and themselves. Spurred by resolutions passed in the Congress that the United Nations should declare the Chinese Communists aggressors, the government sponsored such a resolution in the General Assembly and one was passed on February 1, 1951.

Consistent with this resolution, as well as with the resolution of the Assembly of October 7, 1950, General MacArthur favored a strong policy against the Chinese Communists, including attacks on their staging areas north of the Chinese-Korean border. This policy was rejected by the President, who removed MacArthur from command of the American and allied forces. In reporting this action to the nation in April, 1951, President Truman said that the United States believed the best chance of stopping the Communist plan of conquest "without general war was to meet the attack in Korea and defeat it there." In June, Secretary Acheson said that the United States "condemned aggression of any kind," rejected "appeasement of any kind," and believed that aggression could best be brought to an end by "continuing the punishing defeat of the Chinese in Korea." These statements seem to admit only one interpretation: while MacArthur's forward policy of attacking the Chinese Communists inside China would be rejected, the war in Korea would be continued until the Communists there had been defeated and Korea could be united under a government of its own selection. In the same month, however, that Secretary Acheson made his statement, June, 1951, the United States accepted a Russian proposal to negotiate an armistice. Negotiations began in July, 1951, and lasted two years while a war of attrition continued in Korea resulting in the additional loss of about nine thousand American lives. During this time the Chinese Communists built up their military strength in Korea and carried on a campaign of propaganda and vilification against the United States. The armistice negotiations were brought to a conclusion after President Eisenhower had assumed office and apparently had threatened to abandon the war of attrition for a more aggressive policy. The "armistice" agreement was not a peace settlement. It was an uneasy truce leaving Korea divided, the military lines being generally but not exactly along the 38th parallel.

A Korean policy that began with apparent determination, proceeded into confusion, and ended in stalemate was the product of many factors, some of which the United States could neither control nor influence. At the beginning of the conflict, the Truman Administration believed that Communist China would not intervene in the war if assurances were given that American and allied objectives were wholly confined to the unification of Korea. It seemed safe to proceed with this unification, which obviously could not be accomplished without a military defeat of the Korean Communists. When the Communist Chinese entered the war and the possible danger arose that Russia might come to their assistance, American policy faltered and American statements of policy became conflicting. Rightly or wrongly, the United States was primarily concerned with the possibility of Soviet aggression in Europe and was unwilling to become involved, or to take the risk of becoming involved, in an expanded conflict in Asia. The United States had reason, however, to be appalled at the disunity of the non-Communist world. Of the fifty-nine members of the United Nations in 1950, only fifteen besides the United States gave military aid to the Republic of Korea, and their combined assistance amounted to about 10 percent of the United Nations effort, the remaining 90 percent being supplied by the United States. About thirty-four thousand Americans lost their lives in the Korean War, more than half as many as were killed in the First World War. The non-Communist nations of Europe were preoccupied with their own affairs, the Arab world nursed its grievances against the United States for having promoted the creation of Israel, India and some other neutralists opposed the action of the General Assembly on the unification of Korea and seemed to support the position of Communist China as much as the position of the United States, France was deeply involved in Indochina, and all of Latin America save Colombia looked on at a safe distance. The Republic of Korea defended its independence with heroism and sacrifice, but neither its efforts nor those of the United States inspired the non-Communist world to regard Communist aggression in Asia as a serious menace to themselves. The United Nations was not just a weak reed; it was no reed at all. Under these conditions the American government was willing to bring the Korean War to an end and to assume that the United States and the United Nations had achieved their objectives.

NEW EAST ASIAN ALIGNMENTS

An American proposal in 1947 that a peace treaty with Japan be considered at a conference of the nations most concerned with Far Eastern affairs came to nothing because of Russian opposition, and no significant progress toward a treaty was made prior to the Korean War. Subsequently the United States decided to appoint a presidential commission to negotiate separately with Japan and the other nations and to effect a treaty settlement with or without the concurrence of Russia. The commission was headed by John Foster Dulles, and the negotiations were conducted on the basis of a "peace of reconciliation" under which Japan would be accorded full sovereignty without being subjected to further punishment or discrimination. After about a year of intensive discussions of various drafts of a treaty, a final agreement was reached and signed by forty-nine nations, including Japan and the United States, on September 8, 1951. The entire peace settlement, however, as distinct from the Japanese peace treaty, included a series of treaties, agreements, and declarations of policy by Japan without which the peace treaty could not have been concluded. In these arrangements the United States took care to insure that Japan would make a treaty with Nationalist China, would permit the United States to maintain military bases in Japan for as long as the United States desired, and would agree to a treaty satisfactory to the United States concerning the high seas fisheries of the North Pacific area.

As far as East Asia nations were concerned, aside from the Communists, the main hindrances to a Japanese treaty arose from the fear that Japan might become again a danger to their independence and from their desire for reparations. On the latter point, the United States took the strong position that Japan, deprived of her former empire and with a growing population, could not become self-sufficient and pay substantial reparations. Under the treaty, Japan "recognized" that she *should* pay reparations for damages caused by her during the war, but she was *required* only to negotiate on the matter with those powers "whose present territories" she had occupied. The Philippines, New Zealand, and Australia were reconciled to the peace treaty by the willingness of the United States to conclude with them security treaties. The mutual security treaty with the Philippines and the security treaty with New Zealand and Australia had virtually the same provisions. Each party recognized that an armed attack in the Pacific area against any of the other parties would be a danger to its own peace and safety, and declared "it would act to meet the common danger in accordance with its constitutional processes." The same provisions were incorporated into a mutual defense treaty with the Republic of Korea in 1953, and in this treaty, as well as in a separate security treaty between the United States and Japan, the United States secured the right to establish military bases in or about the area. All these security treaties except the one with Japan were to remain in force indefinitely, but could be terminated by any party on a year's notice. The treaty with Japan could not be terminated unilaterally by Japan.

At the end of the Second World War, the United States had been reluctant to see France re-establish her authority in Indochina but had acquiesced with the understanding that France would soon provide for the actual or substantial independence for the area. France moved slowly in this direction, but by 1954 she had agreed to the division of Indochina into three independent states: Vietnam, Cambodia, and Laos. A group of Communists in Vietnam resisted the government of that state and established a rival government which was recognized and aided by Communist China. The question arose whether the United States would provide military forces in the aid of France and Vietnam. For a time, early in 1954, the United States seriously considered this possibility, but decided against it even though Communist troops also invaded Laos. The reasons for this decision were numerous. France was weary of the war in Indochina, and the United States was unwilling to undertake, virtually alone as in Korea, the burden of meeting the Communist advance in Southeast Asia. As a result,

France signed an armistice with the Communists which left them in control of the northern part of Vietnam, Vietminh.

These events led the United States to promote the establishment of a Southeast Asian Alliance, known as the Manila Pact, with France, Britain, Australia, New Zealand, the Philippines, Pakistan, and Thailand, creating the Southeast Asian Treaty Organization. The treaty, signed in September, 1954, contained the same provisions regarding an armed attack on any of the parties that were included in the security treaties mentioned above, but the United States limited its commitment under the treaty to an armed attack by Communists aggressors. In a protocol to the treaty its signatories extended their protection to Cambodia, Laos, and the territory under the jurisdiction of Vietnam. Although this alliance resembled to some extent the North Atlantic Alliance, it lacked geographical unity since India, Burma, Ceylon, and Indonesia refused to become members. It lacked also, as did all the East Asian security treaties, the specific statement contained in the North Atlantic Treaty that an attack on one party would "be considered an attack against them all," and it did not contemplate the establishment of a joint military force. For these reasons, this alliance, as well as all the other Asian security treaties, was considered to be similar to the Monroe Doctrine in that it stated an intent and a policy rather than made a specific pledge.

The last in the chain of East Asian security treaties was the treaty with the Republic of China. As soon as the Korean War started, the United States shifted its policy regarding the defense of Formosa, which hitherto had been placed outside the American "defense perimeter," and ordered the Navy to defend it against Communist invasion. After the Korean armistice was signed, however, Communist China reaffirmed her intention to invade Formosa and began shelling the islands of Quemoy and Matsu, which were close to the mainland but under the control of the Nationalist Chinese government. The United States signed a mutual defense treaty with the Republic of China in December, 1954, containing the same provisions concerning an armed attack on either party that were included in the other East Asian treaties. The treaty area, as far as China was concerned, included only Formosa and the Pescadores, but Congress authorized the President to use the armed forces of the United States not only to defend the treaty area but also "such related positions and territories" of the area "then in friendly hands" as he judged appropriate in assuring the defense of Formosa and the Pescadores. This unusual delegation of authority was requested by President Eisenhower because he wanted to avoid any controversy over the constitutional right of Congress to declare war. He announced that he would not use his delegated power in such a way as to bring on a general war.

THE MIDDLE EAST

At the end of the Second World War, Russia sought to extend her influence in the Middle East. As noted earlier, she supported a Communist regime in a portion of Iran, attempted to exercise control over the Turkish Straits, aided the Communist movement in Greece, and tried to secure authority over one of Italy's North African colonies. The United States reacted strongly to these Russian moves by a show of strength in supporting the governments of Iran, Turkey, and Greece. In 1951 it tried to promote a Middle East military command under which the military strength of the area would be unified against Russian pressures. This proved impossible because the countries of the area were more concerned about internal dissensions and conflicts than about the common danger of Communist expansion. When John Foster Dulles became Secretary of State, he thought a regional alliance similar to the North Atlantic Alliance might be created in the Middle East which would buttress a "northern tier" of Middle Eastern states along the border of the Soviet Union and would extend the line of Russian "containment" from the Atlantic to India. By the end of 1955, Turkey, Iran, Pakistan, Iraq, and Great Britain had formed a defensive agreement known as the Baghdad Pact, but the remaining states of the Middle East did not become members, partly because of the reasons that defeated the movement for a unified military command, and partly because the United States decided to remain outside the formal agreement. The United States sent representatives to meetings of the council of the pact nations and made military assistance agreements with them, but the pact lacked inherent strength from the beginning and may have tended to divide rather than unite the nations of the area. Iraq withdrew from the pact in 1959, leaving no Arab state within it, and its name was changed to the Central Treaty Organization (CENTO), but whatever effectiveness it had in the containment of Communism continued to be the sum of American military aid to Turkey, Iran, and Pakistan.

The policy of the United States in the Middle East was complicated by its responsibilities for the existence of Israel. The Arab states would not join a mutual defense agreement that included Israel for they did not recognize her legitimate existence or accept as permanent residents the Palestinian Arab refugees. Arab-Israeli hostility was further intensified by the policy of Israel in promoting world-wide Jewish immigration, which to the Arab states meant an eventual movement toward Israel's expansion. The United Nations made no progress in reducing Arab-Israeli tensions because it was unable to implement either its earlier resolutions or new ones. In the interest of peace in the Middle East, the United States, France, and Great Britain declared, in a tripartite statement of May 25, 1950, that they would not permit the violation of frontiers or of armistice lines by either Israel or the Arab states, that they were unalterably opposed "to the use of force or the threat of force between any of the states in the area," and that in supplying the various states with arms for internal security and legitimate self-defense, they noted the assurance given to them by the several states not to undertake acts of aggression against any other state. This tripartite statement did not prevent raids and counterraids across armistice lines, and when Egypt failed to secure from the three Western powers the amount of arms she requested, she secured arms from Communist countries, denounced the Baghdad Pact, and recognized the government of Communist China.

These events came at a time when the United States was collaborating with Egypt for the construction of a dam across the Upper Nile, the Aswan High Dam, designed to provide electricity for industrial development and irrigation for about two million acres of land. When the United States suddenly withdrew from this project, Egypt responded by nationalizing the Suez Canal, in exact terms by seizing the Compagnie Universelle du Canal Maritime de

Suez, in July, 1956. Neither the United States nor Egypt defended its policy with candor. Egypt was looking for an excuse to seize the canal anyway, and while the United States gave technical excuses for its action, its reasons were primarily political. Some Congressmen objected to any aid to Egypt and the government wanted to indicate its displeasure at Egypt's international conduct. The seizure produced fruitless negotiations between Egypt on the one side, and the United States, France, Britain, the United Nations, and the principal "canal users" on the other, and was one cause for the invasion of Egypt by Britain and France on October 30, 1956, an action that followed by one day the invasion of Egypt by Israel.

Israel's decision to invade Egypt was the product of a number of causes, among which were her desire to destroy Egypt's growing military strength and her determination to secure by force the use denied to her by Egypt of the Suez Canal and the Gulf of Aqaba. France was in collusion with Israel and aided her invasion partly because of the canal seizure, but more particularly because she hoped to overthrow the Egyptian government, which had been giving aid and encouragement to Arab rebels in Algeria. Great Britain's reasons for collaborating with France are more obscure. Her avowed reasons—to stop the Israeli-Egyptian war and to safeguard the Suez Canal—are difficult if not impossible to accept. None of the three nations consulted the United States before they invaded Egypt, although they knew the United States would oppose such a policy because President Eisenhower had reaffirmed in November, 1955, the tripartite statement of May, 1950, under which the United States was obligated to "take action, both within and outside the United Nations" if the frontiers or armistice lines of the Middle Eastern states were violated. Some people in the United States thought the government should disregard its obligations under the tripartite statement since France and Britain had disregarded theirs, but the United States took a strong position that whatever may have been the grievances of the three nations against Egypt, the use of force and violence was not the proper means for obtaining redress.

Britain soon decided to withdraw her troops from Egypt under pressure of strong opposition to her policy at home and in the

Commonwealth, the hostility of the United States, and the threat of aid to Egypt from the Soviet Union and Communist China. Although the United States quickly countered the threat from Russia, which came after the American policy was clear, this only increased American influence on Britain. France reluctantly followed the British decision, but Israel refused to withdraw her troops until she had secured a measure of her objectives. Her use of the Gulf of Aqaba was assured, and a seven-nation volunteer police force under United Nations auspices was established to guard the Israeli-Egyptian armistice lines.

The whole episode was distressing from the American point of view. It demonstrated the weakness of the Baghdad Pact to prevent the Communists from spreading their influence south of the northern tier of Middle Eastern states, the continued instability of these states, and the failure of the members of the North Atlantic Alliance to act together in matters of common concern. In an attempt to counteract Russian influence in the area and possibly to promote greater stability, President Eisenhower formulated what became known as the Eisenhower Doctrine and requested from Congress a resolution, similar to the one concerning Formosa, giving him the authority to use the armed forces of the United States to protect the territorial integrity and political independence of any Middle Eastern state if it requested aid against "overt armed aggression from any nation controlled by international communism." Congress responded slowly to this request, but eventually passed a joint resolution stating that the independence and integrity of the nations of the Middle East were vital to American national interest and that the United States was prepared to use its armed forces to assist any nation in the area to meet armed aggression from a Communist-controlled country. The resolution did not specifically delegate authority to the President.

During 1958, what little stability existed in the Middle East seemed on the edge of disintegration through the growth of revolutionary movements in Iraq, Jordan, and Lebanon. With economic aid from the United States and military assistance from Great Britain, the government of Jordan survived, and the sending of American troops to Lebanon on the request of that government enabled it to effect peaceful change. Although a violent revolution occurred in Iraq, the new government succumbed neither to Communist penetration nor Egyptian control, but it withdrew from the Baghdad Pact leaving no Arab state in that alliance.

As the decade of the 1950's ended, no permanent settlement of any major Middle Eastern problem was in view. Turkey, Iran, and Pakistan depended on the United States for support and sought additional aid. The Palestinian Arab refugee problem was as far from solution as it had ever been, and the United States continued to supply about 70 percent of Western contributions to refugee support. Disunity and instability characterized the Middle East, but the Communists did not appear to have made permanent advance in the area either by aggression, economic penetration, or subversion.

THE HUNGARIAN REVOLUTION

The invasion of Egypt by Israel, Great Britain, and France coincided in time, October–November, 1956, with the ruthless Russian suppression of a revolutionary movement in Hungary. This nation had been closely held within the Russian orbit, but her people had become increasingly restless under Communist rule, and a reform movement which had little organization and did not begin as a full-fledged revolution, spread with astonishing rapidity and vitality during October, 1956, and resulted in the establishment of a government under the leadership of Imre Nagy. Since this government lasted but a short time, the revolution being completely crushed by November 14, it is impossible to know how fully it represented the Hungarian people or what its policies would have been over a longer period of time. What is certain is that it represented an independent Hungary, disassociated from a Soviet alliance and with an initial desire to be neutral between the Soviet Union and non-Communist nations. Whether there was any connection between the origins of the Russian decision to invade Hungary and the decisions to invade Egypt cannot be known, but it is at least arguable that the actions of Britain and France in Egypt and the preoccupation of the United States with the Egyptian crisis influenced American and European action in the Hungarian episode.

It may be that Russia would have moved against Hungary in any event because a successful independence movement there would probably have had serious repercussions in other areas of Russian control, particularly in Rumania, Poland, and Czechoslovakia. Nevertheless, Russia did not move with overwhelming force into Hungary until after Israel had invaded Egypt and France and Britain had become involved in that enterprise. Consistent with its policies, pronouncements, and commitments in the Middle East, the United States had no alternative but to oppose the invasions of Egypt. Thus the three Western allies were in no position to provide assistance to Hungary, and any moral condemnation of Russia by Britain and France was vitiated by their own conduct.

It could be said that the United States exerted equal efforts through the United Nations in behalf of Egypt and Hungary. Nothing could be done in either case through the Security Council since Russia took the side of Egypt and posed as a friend of all the Arab states, and in both cases the General Assembly called on the invading nations to withdraw their armed forces. It would not be accurate to assume, however, that the United States exerted equal influence in both cases. The nations that invaded Egypt were vulnerable to American economic pressure, and widespread belief existed that the United States intended to use such pressure even though an influential group in the Congress opposed any sanction against Israel. No action of any kind was contemplated against Russia, probably because none would have been effective save armed intervention. Communist China and Yugoslavia announced their support of Russia. British subjects who favored their government's policy in Egypt thought the United States had a double standard.

WESTERN EUROPE

The Korean War stimulated the American government to build greater strength among the North Atlantic Alliance nations to meet the Communist threat. It urged these nations to establish a centralized command over an integrated military establishment, to release Italy from the military restrictions imposed by the treaty of peace, and to include troops from the West German Federal Republic in the unified effort. The proposed German rearmament met with opposition from within Germany, aroused the fears of France, was opposed by many people in the United States, and was agreed to by the Department of Defense only on condition that the German forces would be integrated with and would not be superior to the combined European defense establishment. The approval by Congress of sending American troops to Europe, as far as anyone could foresee on a permanent basis, required all the influence of President Truman and the persuasiveness and great prestige of Generals Eisenhower and Marshall, and even then the approval was indirect.

The Senate enacted a resolution, April 4, 1951, supporting the co-operation of the United States in the defensive efforts of the North Atlantic Alliance and approving the sending of four divisions of ground forces to Europe for this purpose. The resolution stated, however, that Congress should be consulted about sending troops abroad, that before sending such troops the Joint Chiefs of Staff should be able to assure the Department of Defense that the European members of the alliance were giving "full, realistic force and effect" to the provisions of the treaty of alliance regarding "continuous and effective self-help and mutual aid." While this was intended only as a concurrent resolution, not having the force of a legislative act, it did not achieve even that much dignity since the House did not act on it. It represented, therefore, only an expression of opinion by those who voted for it. The President's authority for sending troops abroad was as hazy as was his authority for entering upon the Korean War. Nevertheless, by 1960 the United States had about five divisions of ground forces under the combined European command, more than a fourth of the combined forces. In addition to providing these troops, the United States established air bases in Europe, North Africa, and the Middle East. Under various mutual defense assistance programs, it provided also direct military aid to the nations of the alliance, "defense support," and general economic assistance.

The position of Spain in European defense strategy was a special problem for American foreign policy. At both the Potsdam and San Francisco conferences of 1945, the United States had agreed that the pro-Axis Spanish government of General Francisco Franco should not be admitted to the United Nations or any of its agencies. The United States, Britain, and France issued a statement in March, 1946, expressing the hope that the Spanish people would overthrow the Franco regime and offering to recognize and give economic assistance to a revolutionary movement that would accomplish this objective. In the same year, the General Assembly of the United Nations declared that the Franco government was Fascist in character, and that Franco was a "guilty party with Hitler and Mussolini in the conspiracy" against the nations later forming the United Nations, and recommended that these nations withdraw their ambassadors and ministers from Spain.

Notwithstanding American approval of these statements and actions, the policy of the United States toward Spain underwent a gradual change, the beginning of which could be observed as early as 1948. It is impossible, however, to be certain about the relative force of the various factors that influenced this change. Influential lay and clerical leaders of the Roman Catholic Church in the United States opposed the anti-Franco policy from its beginning. Some agricultural interests favored giving credits to Spain for the purchase of American agricultural products, and the Defense Department advocated the inclusion of Spain in the European defense system. These influences were observed in the Congress, and their effect was enhanced by the Korean War. In November, 1950, the General Assembly, with American support, removed its diplomatic ban against Spain, and although President Truman announced it would be a "long, long time" before he would appoint an ambassador to Spain, he appointed one the following month.

Consistent with its new policy, the United States granted immediate economic aid to Spain, and in 1953 concluded with her a defense agreement, an economic aid agreement, and a mutual defense assistance agreement. During the next several years, the United States constructed in Spain air bases, a naval base, and various installations connected with these establishments. American economic aid in various forms and American expenditures in Spain amounted to at least a billion and a half dollars by 1960. Many people in the United States doubted the validity of the military reasons for the policy shift toward Spain, but whether the reasons were valid or not, the shift was as sharp as in any postwar American policy.

YUGOSLAVIA

The relations between the United States and the Federal Republic of Yugoslavia, under the presidency of Josip Broz—Marshal Tito—were often referred to in the United States as an example of pure expediency, and, in that sense, similar to American relations with Spain. Tito was a leader of one of the many movements resisting the control of Yugoslavia by Germany and other Axis powers during the Second World War. Being an avowed Communist before the war, he opposed the anti-Communist resistance movement led by Draja Mikhailovitch during the period of the Russo-German alliance. After the break between the Soviet Union and Germany, Tito opposed and fought with equal vigor the Mikhailovitch group and the Axis invaders. This violent internal strife in Yugoslavia produced problems for the Western Allies, who made contact with both resistance groups. Gradually, Tito gained greater military strength than Mikhailovitch and, with Russian support, was recognized by the Allies at the time of the Teheran Conference as the principal anti-Axis leader in Yugoslavia. He was given further recognition at the Yalta Conference, having satisfied the United States that he intended to establish a "democratic" government in Yugoslavia. As soon as the war ended, he removed whatever democratic elements existed in his provisional government and made Yugoslavia a member of the Russian Communist orbit.

The Communist regime of Tito, however, was more indigenous than the Communist governments in the Russian satellite areas of Europe, and Tito was personally ambitious to play a leading role in the Communist movements in Greece and Albania. Gradually, therefore, a rift grew between Tito and the Soviet government under Joseph Stalin and developed into an open break in 1948.

In this situation the United States decided to assist Yugoslavia under the policy of supporting any nation that resisted Soviet pressures. The policy of assisting Yugoslavia, which was started under the Truman Administration, was followed by the Eisenhower Administration, and was continued under the Kennedy Administration. By midsummer of 1962, the United States had given around $2 billion in economic and military assistance to Yugoslavia.

This policy was never popular with Congress, nor probably among the American people, since neither Tito nor the United States government tried to disguise the fact that the Tito regime was both totalitarian and Communistic. It was frankly a policy of expediency, or among its more severe critics, of Machiavellism. Tito proclaimed he was "neutral" between the United States and Russia, but he often seemed to lean more toward Communist interests, whether in Russia or elsewhere, than toward the interests of the United States and the West. If American policy was based partly on the hope that other Communist satellites of the Soviet Union, observing Yugoslavia and American assistance to her, would develop nationalistic movements, this hope was not realized. Possible exceptions might be made in relation to Albania and Hungary. The Albanian "ideological" break with Russia had origins in the decade of the 1950's but was publicly manifest in 1960 and particularly in 1961. This "defection" was less a movement toward independence or neutralism than toward closer ties with Communist China, a maneuver within the Communist bloc and an outgrowth of Albanian economic and political vulnerability. The Hungarian Revolution of 1956 might have become a real threat to Communist solidarity, but, as already noted, the United States made no move to support it except through resolutions in the United Nations.

LATIN AMERICA

Latin America continued to be confronted with economic and political problems arising from a rapidly growing population, comparative decrease in food production and industrial development, currency inflation, social and political unrest, virulent nationalism, and in many cases political instability. The broad policy of the United States toward the area was to promote inter-American co-operation, to provide as much economic assistance as was possible in view of the greater needs for American aid elsewhere, and to avoid intervention in the domestic affairs of Latin-American states. During the decade of the 1950's the United States extended aid in various forms amounting to over a billion and a half dollars, and more aid would have been available from both private and public sources if Latin America had been willing to create the conditions of economic and political stability that would have attracted such aid. It was not the policy of the United States to "support" Latin-American dictators, as was claimed by some elements of both the Latin-American and the American population, or to extend military instead of general economic assistance. The United States followed a policy of recognizing *de facto* Latin-American governments in view of its general policy of non-intervention. The United States made military assistance agreements with eighteen Latin-American states in order to promote hemispheric defense, to enable them to resist Communist subversion, and to counteract their procurement of military aid from Communist nations. American military aid amounted to less than five percent of Latin-American expenditures for military purposes.

Communist penetration of Latin America was an American concern. The Communist pattern of action was to identify itself with nationalism, with every element of unrest and aspiration in a particular country, and with opposition to "Yankee imperialism." The Communists found a "soft spot" for their activities in Guatemala, gradually penetrated the government, and secured virtually complete control of the nation during the presidency of Jacobo Arbenz Guzmán. Disturbed over this development, and fearing that some form of intervention in Guatemala might become essential for the security of the United States and the hemisphere, the United States secured a resolution at the Tenth Inter-American Conference of American States at Caracas, in March, 1954, condemning the "international communist movement" as constituting intervention in American affairs, and declaring the intention of the American states to take necessary measures to protect their independence against such intervention. No direct action, however, was taken at the conference regarding the Communist regime in Guatemala.

A critical situation developed when Guatemala began to secure arms from Communist sources and to threaten the independence of neighboring states, particularly Nicaragua and Honduras. At their request the United States furnished military supplies to these states, and probably assisted one of them, Honduras, in aiding a military organization, under the leadership of a Guatemalan exile, which invaded Guatemala and overthrew the Arbenz regime. Before this was accomplished, the United States called a meeting of the foreign ministers of the Latin-American states to consider the Guatemalan situation under the terms of the Caracas resolution, but the swiftness with which the Communists in Guatemala were overthrown made this meeting unnecessary. Later it was affirmed, and not officially denied in the United States, that the United States Central Intelligence Agency had managed the invasion of Guatemala, but the exact involvement of this organization has not been revealed. The major problems, however, of Latin-American economic and political instability remained, and the United States was soon confronted with a new center of Communist penetration in Cuba.

XIII

THE CONTINUING CRISIS

THE UNITED STATES has experienced a number of critical times when its national security has seemed to be seriously endangered. Until after the Second World War, each danger to its security was met and removed, sometimes through peaceful means and at other times at great sacrifice of life and treasure. But after the Second World War and the failure of the dream of the "grand alliance," the United States found itself in a continuing crisis. This derived from many causes, the most outstanding being the desire of Communist nations to spread their system of life and government throughout the world, the development of destructive weapons greater than mankind had known before, and the failure of the non-Communist world to form a united force against Communism. There may have been some support in the United States for a "preventive war" against the Communist nations, but this was not advocated by the government or seriously considered by the great majority of the people. The continuing crisis, it was believed, had to be met through attempts to secure greater unity and strength among non-Communist nations, through all possible peaceful means, and through resistance by force to the spread of aggressive Communism whenever it seemed clear that the independence and security of the nation were at stake. As the United States moved into the decade of the 1960's, its foreign problems assumed, therefore, an ever-increasing significance.

ATTEMPTS TO LIMIT AND CONTROL ARMAMENTS

One of the major objectives of the United States in the Second World War was the creation of postwar conditions of world peace and security that would permit the reduction of national armaments. Statements to this effect were made in the Atlantic Charter and in the Moscow Declaration of 1943, and the Security Council of the United Nations was given the responsibility of making plans for "the regulation of armaments." As soon, however, as the United States developed the atomic weapon, it considered how this new destructive force could be controlled in the interest of world peace. It believed the atomic bomb was the "absolute weapon" against which there would be no adequate defense. It proposed, therefore, the establishment of an international agency that would be given complete control of all factors in the production and use of atomic energy. This would mean international control of the production of atomic materials, of scientific research in the field of nuclear physics, and of the processing and use of atomic matter. The agency would have unlimited authority of inspection within nations, and penalties would be provided for the disregard of its regulations. Once this agency was established and had become effective, the United States would destroy its atomic weapons, turn over to the agency its atomic materials and its knowledge of atomic science. This plan is commonly known as the Baruch Plan because Bernard Baruch was chairman of the American committee that presented the proposal to the United Nations Atomic Energy Commission, June 14, 1946. Since it was a broad policy proposal to the nations of the world, the American government did not elaborate the details of a treaty that would be necessary if the proposal was adopted and implemented. It is possible, therefore, that the Congress would not have agreed to a final treaty based on the government's plans, but there is no reason to suppose it would not have done so. No nation had ever possessed such a monopoly of power as the United States possessed in 1946, and no nation had ever made an offer to surrender a comparable power advantage.

Russia rejected the American offer and made a counterproposal. She suggested that the United States should destroy its atomic weapons, that each nation should agree not to manufacture or use such weapons, and that each nation should enact domestic legislation to enforce these provisions. As far as international control of atomic energy was concerned, Russia proposed that this should be placed under the supervision of the Security Council of the United Nations, where action could not be taken without the concurring votes of the five permanent members. These proposals were completely unacceptable to the United States, for they offered no guarantee that Russia or some other nation would not develop atomic potential secretly while other nations respected treaty obligations. A commission appointed by the United Nations to draw a detailed treaty plan on the basis of the American offer made no progress, and by 1948 virtually abandoned any attempt to do so.

President Truman announced in September, 1949, that an atomic explosion had occurred in Russia. Although Russia may not have had an atomic bomb at that time, the American monopoly of atomic power was essentially at an end. During the years that followed, great technological advance was made in the development of destructive weapons. Russia, Britain, and France produced atomic bombs, the United States and Russia developed the hydrogen bomb, and each nation either paced or followed the other in developing atomic-powered submarines, missiles equipped with atomic warheads that could be fired from under water as well as from the surface or from land, long-range, high-altitude airplanes, and probably acquired the ability to carry on bacteriological warfare. The world passed from the so-called air age into the space age with Russia and the United States being able to place vehicles in orbit around the earth and to return them to the earth at some designated place. It seemed possible to fill such vehicles with destructive materials. In short, both the United States and Russia soon possessed the power to destroy each other, and peace appeared to exist because there was a balance of terror.

The world watched these events with growing concern, and the United States made constant efforts to find a way to reach an agreement with the Soviet Union for the limitation and control of all weapons of war. Its basic policy was to make war impossible because no nation would have the means of carrying on a war, to create a "substantially disarmed" world, with each nation maintaining only sufficient military strength for internal security and for any obligations it might have for peace under the authority of the United Nations. It insisted, however, that disarmament had to be accompanied by international agreements which permitted international inspection and verification of national armaments, in brief the establishment of "an open world." Every program, every proposal, every approach made by the United States, and every feasible suggestion by other non-Communist nations toward this objective, was rejected by Russia. While Russia pretended to favor world disarmament, she denounced every practical proposal to this end which would establish conditions guaranteeing its effectiveness.

Many American scholars have devoted themselves to the study of Russia, her history, social and political structure, economic development, foreign policies, tortuous diplomacy, official and unofficial pronouncements, and what appears to be the stresses and conflicts within the Russian Communist orbit. Attempts have been made, therefore, to discover the basic factors in Russian policy, the reason for Russian attitudes toward the world, and the direction in which her policy is likely to move. Some of these students of Russia feel that her foreign policy has been based on a genuine fear of the non-Communist world and that this fear explains Russia's desire to control a cordon of satellite states, her violation of treaty agreements, and her unwillingness to accept Western proposals for arms limitation or control. Other students of Russia reject this explanation because in their opinion it neglects Russia's consistent devotion to the "Communist conspiracy" to overthrow by subversion, intimidation, or war, all "capitalist" governments and to dominate the world. These people believe that Russia felt certain that when the United States had a monopoly of atomic power this power would not be used for aggressive purposes. Russia felt safe, therefore, in rejecting American proposals for the control of atomic energy while she developed nuclear power herself. As soon as she developed this power, she could threaten the world with destruction unless her demands were met at any point of attempted Russian expansion, and could rely on propaganda among neutralist nations and pacific-minded people to make it appear that the United States would be responsible for war if Russian demands were not met. In this respect, the advantage of terror seemed to rest with the Communist nations. Whatever the value of the estimates of Russian motivation and policy, little progress was made toward the limitation of arms. The Soviet Union agreed, however, in 1963, to a ban on testing nuclear weapons in the atmosphere, outer space, and under water. The solidarity of the Communist world was weakened by an ideological rift between the Soviet Union and Communist China, but Communist subversive activities in the free world continued.

THE UNITED STATES AND THE NEWLY EMERGING NATIONS

The term "newly emerging nations" refers to two groups of states: former colonial areas that have recently acquired independence, and older "underdeveloped" states whose "rising expectations" have given them new interests and ambitions. Both groups present problems for American foreign policy. By November, 1962, fifty-nine new nations had been added to the original fifty-one members of the United Nations, the new nations being largely African and Asian.

The new states vary considerably in economic development, education, internal unity, and experience in self-government. Many of the African states have artificial boundaries as far as racial or geographic unity is concerned, possess no common language or cultural heritage, and are largely a collection of tribal societies. Yet, as members of the United Nations, each new state has one vote in the General Assembly, the same as the United States. The United States is confronted with the fact that since the beginning of the United Nations it has promoted the assumption that an action by the General Assembly, particularly by a two-thirds majority, provides some kind of vague and shadowy international legal sanction, as in the cases of the partition of Palestine and American action in Korea. It has promoted the assumption also that a two-thirds majority vote in the General Assembly represents the "moral judgment" of the world. When a two-thirds majority of the General Assembly was composed of states of western Europe and the Western Hemisphere, where the traditions, laws, and customs of Western civilization were strong, the United States may possibly have had some basis for thinking it was safe as far as its own national interests were concerned to make the assumption referred to. At any rate, this situation no longer exists. By 1962, the African members of the United Nations numbered thirty-two, the largest geographical group in the organization. When these nations combine with an Asian group in an Afro-Asian bloc, they form together about 50 percent of the General Assembly.

Both groups of emerging states present the problem of American responsibility for the fulfillment of their "rising expectations." On this subject the American people are divided, with tenacious opinions on both sides and with the government trying to find a middle ground. On the one side are those who believe the emerging states are poised between sustained economic growth and chaos, that their economic decline would be harmful to American prosperity and security and offensive to the American conscience. They hold that the United States has a moral obligation to meet the economic needs of these nations and that they have a *right* to American support. They propose, therefore, extensive economic aid from the public sector of the American economy in the form of gifts and in the form of loans extending over long periods of time—as much as a half century—at interest rates so low they convert the loans into partial grants. These views find support among a group of economic theorists, the bureaucracy that administers foreign aid, and the economic interests in the United States that profit indirectly from the aid program. These views appeal also to American people whose humanitarian instincts arouse in them sympathy for those who live in areas where overpopulation, poverty, ignorance, disease, maladministration of government, unequal distribution of wealth, and accompanying evils create human misery.

On the other side are those who believe that while the United States should provide foreign economic aid, such aid should be limited and conditioned by a large number of considerations. They feel that in extending foreign economic aid consideration should be given to the status of American economy, to the conduct of recipient states with regard to the struggle against Communism, to their capacity to absorb foreign aid efficiently, to their willingness to create domestic conditions of social and economic reform and political stability that will make aid significant, and to the co-operation in aid programs of other nations who are as able as the United States to provide assistance to underdeveloped areas. Those who hold these views see no advantage to the United States and no assistance to its prosperity or security in exhausting its resources for the benefit of nations that denounce American policies and ideals and support its enemies. They do not think foreign aid should be used as an indirect subsidy to American industry and agriculture, or that the humanitarian argument for aid is valid respecting states that will not meet their social problems.

The foreign aid program, both with respect to its size and its administration, met with increasing criticism in the Congress, where there seemed to be a growing sensitiveness to public opinion regarding the relationship of foreign aid to other American economic problems, particularly the tax burden and the mounting national debt. In 1962 Congress sharply reduced the aid authorization requested by the Administration even though the President had declared that any substantial reduction in the amount requested would pose "a threat to free-world security." The debate on the issue indicated a closer scrutiny by Congress of the foreign aid program in the future.

LATIN-AMERICAN PROBLEMS

Most Latin-American states could be included among the nations that desire increased American economic assistance in connection with their "rising expectations." A diversity of opinion exists, however, as to whether the United States has "neglected" Latin America. During the decade of the 1950's, about $8 billion of American capital flowed into Latin America through private investment, government loans, and grants. Far more private capital would have been available to the area if Latin-American governments had not either prohibited private foreign investment or had not, through policies of nationalization, taxation, and exchange regulations, made such investment hazardous and unprofitable. Ample funds could be secured for sound projects of economic development from the International Bank for Reconstruction and Development or the American Export-Import Bank. Latin America desires capital, however, for such things as public housing, schools, transportation, currency stabilization, or other needs that will not produce an immediate economic return on investment. In addition, some Latin-American nations frequently seek capital for development projects of doubtful economic suitability to the country but are desired because of extreme nationalistic impulses. Many Latin-American states are divided against themselves. They refuse to deal with the causes for their economic problems, such as inflation, inefficient management of government-owned industries, social welfare programs they cannot support, and population growth, while at the same time they refuse private capital, demand public grants and loans, and threaten to secure assistance from Communist sources.

In 1959 the United States agreed to participate in the establishment of an Inter-American Development Bank and to supply about one half of its capital. This bank, initially with a capital of $1 billion, was supposed to provide loans that could not be secured from the International Bank mentioned above, but still on a sound banking basis. In 1961 the United States government decided to make further efforts to assist Latin-American economic development and to improve inter-American relations through a program called the Alliance for Progress. In August of that year a meeting was held of the Inter-American Economic and Social Council of the Organization of American States, and a charter for the Alliance for Progress was adopted. The program under the charter envisioned a capital expenditure for Latin-American development during the next ten years of $100 billion, of which $80 billion would be provided by Latin America and $20 billion by the United States. The program was not greatly different in general principles from previous programs advocated by the United States except that it had greater proportions and called for a greater amount of organization and planning. It assumed that prior to increased American governmental aid, the Latin-American states would carry out various social and economic reforms of the kind mentioned earlier which they had been reluctant to implement. President Kennedy requested Congress in

January, 1962, to make available for this program $300,000,000 for the current year. Latin-American nations made rather slow progress in formulating their programs under the terms of the charter of the Alliance for Progress, and the continued expropriation of American private property in some Latin-American states, together with the reluctance of Latin America to co-operate fully with the United States concerning Cuba, tended to reduce the enthusiasm of Congress for greater economic aid to Latin America. The alliance program might be regarded as constructive and promising, but its success was not assured.

The United States was confronted also with two particular political questions that arose directly or indirectly from the revolution in Cuba led by Fidel Castro which overthrew in January, 1959, the government of Fulgencio Batista. Castro considered himself the champion of movements elsewhere in Latin America designed to overthrow "dictatorial regimes." His activities were extensive, but he centered his attention on the government of the Dominican Republic, which for a long time had been dominated by Rafael Trujillo. In this enterprise he was assisted by President Romulo Betancourt of Venezuela, who led a movement within the Organization of American States to condemn the Dominican government. An attempted assassination of President Betancourt in June, 1960, led to an investigation of the incident by the Organization of American States, and when it was decided that agents of the Dominican government had been involved in the matter, the inter-American body recommended that all American states break diplomatic relations with the Dominican Republic and suspend trade in arms with it. The United States felt that Cuba presented a far more serious problem for the independence of Latin America than the Dominican government, but followed the recommended policies nevertheless. The Dominican government was confronted with internal dissatisfactions as well as foreign problems, and when Trujillo was assassinated in May, 1961, the Dominican situation verged on chaos. Gradually, however, order was restored, a temporary government was established, and the United States recognized the new government in January, 1962. In the same month, the Organization of American States removed the sanctions against the Dominican Republic that had been recommended in August, 1960.

The revolutionary movement in Cuba, which began in 1956, appeared at first to be a democratic reform enterprise against a ruthless dictator. The United States remained neutral, gave no aid to the Castro forces, and cut off military assistance to the Batista government as soon as it appeared that American arms were being used in the civil war. In his rise to power, Castro promised many social and economic reforms, free elections, and compliance with Cuban treaty obligations. The United States immediately recognized his government and offered economic assistance. American policy seemed to be based on the theory that although Castro had people of known Communist connections in his government, he was not himself a Communist and could be weaned away from any Communist tendencies by American friendship, co-operation, and assistance. He soon began, however, a reign of terror in Cuba, mass executions of his opponents, confiscation without adequate compensation of American property, renunciation of his former promises of holding free elections, and the establishment of closer ties with the Soviet Union. The United States retaliated by cutting off trade with Cuba save in medical supplies and a few other items. At the meeting of American foreign ministers in San José, Costa Rica, in 1960, Secretary of State Christian A. Herter urged that some action be taken against Cuba, and warned the ministers that Cuba was becoming a Communist state and a threat to the whole hemisphere. Cuba denounced the Organization of American States, and asserted that she would secure military aid from Communist China and the Soviet Union against "intra-continental aggression." The ministers were unwilling, however, to denounce the regime of Castro as sharply as they denounced the government of the Dominican Republic.

During 1960 tensions between the United States and Cuba mounted. Castro consolidated his power in Cuba, purged the judiciary of any independence, curbed the press, turned the schools into anti-American propaganda agencies, established closer economic ties with Communist states, and strengthened his military establishment with Communist arms. The United States had at least four alternatives of policy. It could let the situation remain as it was, could make a strong appeal for collective action against Cuba by the Organization of American States under the terms of the Caracas resolution of 1954 concerning Communism, could itself openly intervene and justify its action under international law, or could promote intervention in Cuba by some of the numerous Cuban refugees in the United States. It selected the latter course, and trained, equipped, and controlled a refugee interventionist attempt in April, 1961.

This movement was based on considerable misjudgment concerning the situation in Cuba and, initially at least, on the assumption of American military support which was withdrawn. The interventionist forces were few in number (estimated to be 1,200 men), inadequately prepared, and incredibly mismanaged. The result was ignominious failure. Although no American troops took part, the enterprise to all intents and purposes was an American affair. The policy contradicted public statements of the United States concerning intervention in Cuba, was contrary to its avowed principles, and violated its treaty commitments. It was adopted without the knowledge of the American people or the authorization of Congress. It left Communism triumphant in Cuba and American Cuban policy bankrupt. The only bright spot on the horizon of Cuban affairs was the existence of some gradual disenchantment with "Fidelism" in Latin America, where ten governments before the end of 1961 had broken diplomatic relations with Cuba. This disenchantment did not extend, however, as far as the United States desired. At a meeting of the foreign ministers of the Organization of American States in Uruguay, in January, 1962, the United States hoped the Latin-American states would support drastic economic sanctions against Cuba, but was obliged to abandon this proposal when it became clear it would not receive general Latin-American support. Resolutions were adopted at the meeting recommending the suppression of trade in arms with Cuba and removing that country from membership in the Organization of American States. Brazil, Chile, Mexico, and Ecuador abstained from voting on both resolutions, and Argentina and Bolivia were additional abstainers on the resolution for dropping Cuba from the Organization of American States. On this latter resolution the nations that abstained from voting represented 70 percent of the population of Latin America.

As the year 1962 advanced the United States had increasing evidence of a military build-up in Cuba including air power and the construction of missile bases with Russian weapons and with the aid of Russian civilian and military personnel. The American government attempted, with limited success and by voluntary action on the part of the non-Communist nations, to strengthen the economic strangulation of Cuba, but held that the military preparation in Cuba was defensive only. The President, in September, 1962, and in response to public concern over Cuba, said that while no forceful action against Cuba was at that time required or justified, if Cuba should become aggressive, or "an offensive military base of significant capacity for the Soviet Union," the United States would undertake whatever action was necessary for its own security and the security of the Western Hemisphere. Later in the same month, Congress passed a joint resolution referring to the Monroe Doctrine and declaring that the United States would prevent Cuba from "extending by force or threat of force its aggressive or subversive activities" to the hemisphere, and from "the creation or use of an externally supplied military capacity endangering the security of the United States." This resolution was a statement of policy and not an enabling act authorizing the President to use the armed forces for the purposes indicated.

Early in October, Secretary of State Dean Rusk held an informal meeting with representatives of the Latin-American nations and found that although they were concerned with the situation in Cuba, they had taken the United States at its word regarding the defensive character of Cuban military preparation, were opposed to unilateral intervention in Cuba, which the President had also said was not justified, and relied for hemispheric security on the machinery of the Inter-American Treaty of Reciprocal Assistance (1947). Various congressmen, however, were dissatisfied with the policies of the Administration, were calling for a blockade of Cuba or other forceful action, and the issue was becoming of increasing importance in the political campaigns leading to congressional and state elections on November 6, 1962. Meanwhile the United States had been conducting aerial photo-

graphic reconnaissance over Cuba, and over ships leading to
Cuba, and became convinced after October 16 that Russia had
supplied Cuba with medium-range ballistic missiles and was
erecting missile launching bases. In view of this information, and
perhaps in consideration of all factors involved in the Cuban discussion, the President addressed the nation and the world on
October 22 and announced the establishment of a "quarantine
of all offensive military equipment under shipment to Cuba," and
declared it would be the policy of the United States to regard
"any nuclear missile launched from Cuba against any nation in the
Western Hemisphere as an attack by the Soviet Union on the
United States, requiring a full retaliatory response upon the *Soviet
Union* [italics supplied]."

The "quarantine" announced in the address was not put into
effect for two days, during which time acceptance of the action
was sought from members of the North Atlantic Alliance and
the Organization of American States, although these nations were
not consulted in advance nor had Congress been called into session
to sanction the action. Selected members of Congress were consulted before the decision was announced, but evidence is lacking
regarding any influence they may have exerted. Nor can it be
determined what the attitude of American allies would have been
if they had been approached earlier. In a proclamation implementing the decision, the President ordered the armed forces to
"interdict" the "delivery of offensive weapons and associated
material to Cuba," and authorized such forces to intercept vessels
proceeding toward Cuba, to visit and search them, and to use
whatever compulsion was necessary. Although this action was
called "an interdiction" and "a quarantine," it was in fact a blockade, which is legal in international law only as a war measure.
The President gave as his legal authority a resolution passed on
October 23, 1962, of the Organization of American States supporting the action, the joint resolution Congress had passed in
September, and the authority conferred upon him by the Constitution and statutes of the United States. As already noted, the
congressional resolution was a statement of policy, and the President did not specify what particular United States statute or constitutional provision he had in mind.

After about a week of anxiety during which a number of communications were exchanged between the Russian and American governments, an agreement was reached under which Russia promised to remove her missiles from Cuba, dismantle her missile bases, and permit inspection of these operations by agents of the United Nations. In return, the United States promised not to attack or invade Cuba if Russian offensive weapons were removed. Russia appeared to abide by her agreement regarding missiles, but difficulties arose over United Nations inspection and over the removal from Cuba of Russian-built military aircraft. The United States continued its surveillance of Cuba. The Cuban crisis, therefore, was eased but not all attendant problems were immediately settled.

American reaction to the Cuban crisis took on a number of aspects. Naturally there was universal relief that it had not erupted into a general nuclear war, and this tended to overshadow all other matters. Some people felt the crisis had been managed in a masterful way by the government, which had demonstrated iron firmness, and made use also of the advantage of having limited objectives, showing a willingness to compromise as soon as the paramount national interest had been accomplished, in this case the removal of Russian "offensive" weapons from Cuba. Others felt that the United States in promising not to attack or invade Cuba had surrendered its freedom of action toward Cuba and had given the Soviet Union a safe haven for future subversive activities in the Western Hemisphere. No prominent person in Congress or elsewhere in the United States seemed concerned over the constitutional or legal bases for the President's action, or its meaning with respect to future relations with American allies. Time would be required for the unfolding of such considerations.

NEITHER WAR NOR PEACE

The problems of the United States relating to the expansion of Communism in Southeast Asia continued without abatement as the United States entered the decade of the 1960's. The spearheads of Communist advance were against the Republic of Vietnam and the Kingdom of Laos, areas included within the protection of the Southeast Asia Treaty Organization. The situation in Laos was particularly important because of its location and its internal instability. Bordered on the north by Communist China and on the northeast by Communist North Vietnam, it could be easily penetrated by Communist guerrilla troops, and its strength to resist such penetration was weakened by the division of its people into political factions—pro-Communist, neutralists, and anti-Communists. From the beginning of its independence to 1960, the United States had given it about $500,000,000 in economic and military assistance in order to promote its stability. This effort was partly or largely rendered futile by the disunity within the country and the resulting civil war between the Communists and pro-Communist "neutrals" on one side and the anti-Communist forces on the other.

The United States acquiesced in a movement sponsored by the United Nations for the creation of a neutralist coalition government, and a cease fire in the civil war while this was arranged. Although a cease fire was proclaimed, it never was completely respected by the guerrilla Communist forces, and the attempt to form a coalition government failed. Many people in the United States, mindful of what had happened in other coalition governments with Communist membership, believed the coalition movement was only a face-saving way of abandoning Laos to the Communists. Only Thailand and the Philippines, however, of the Southeast Asia Treaty powers favored a strong policy in support of Laos. The United States announced it would take "a most serious view" of the situation if the Communists on the borders of Laos intervened in the area, and continued to give some military assistance to the non-Communist forces. The Soviet Union sent military supplies and possibly some trained personnel to the Communist elements. Thus the United States was confronted with a major dilemma. If Laos became Communist, there was a strong probability that Communism would continue its march, already under way, into the Republic of Vietnam, and would extend to neutralist Burma, to Thailand, and to Cambodia, and spread from there to all Southeast Asia. The United States could not rely on the United Nations or on the Southeast Asia alliance to support Laos because both Britain and France favored a weak

policy, and neutralist nations like India followed the same path.
If the United States upheld the anti-Communist forces in Laos,
it would do so alone. It was equally reluctant to abandon the
area or to repeat its experiences in Korea.

The period of indecision was brought to an end in 1962 when
a strong Laotian Communist army, assisted by some "neutralist"
forces and guerrilla bands from Communist North Vietnam, defeated the America-supported Royal Laotian Army and sent portions of it fleeing across the border into Thailand. Meanwhile the
United States had decided to support the establishment of a coalition government in Laos, a policy advocated by the Communists,
and brought pressure to bear on the Western-oriented leaders of
Laos to accept such a government, formed in June, 1962. At the
same time, the United States increased its military assistance to
South Vietnam for the purpose of resisting North Vietnamese
guerrilla attacks, and sent about five thousand American troops
to Thailand, at its request, to protect that country from Communist invasion from Laos. The United States appeared, therefore, to be fully committed to the defense of Thailand, partially
committed to the defense of South Vietnam, and reconciled to the
existence, in fact if not in name, of Communist control in Laos.

A small but persistent element among the American people continued to advocate a change in American policy regarding Communist China and Formosa. They argued that the Communist
government of mainland China was in fact the government, had
been recognized by many non-Communist states, some of whom,
like Britain, were strong American allies, and that since the
United States allegedly would be forced for practical reasons to
recognize the Communist government sometime, it should do so
at once. They said the United States would have difficulty in
effecting an international agreement for the limitation or control
of armaments without including Communist China. As far as
principles were concerned, they thought Communist China had as
much right to be recognized and admitted to the United Nations
as other Communist states. They appeared to believe also, as
many of their most important spokesmen had believed in 1947,
that Communist China and Russia were not natural allies, and
that if Communist China could be appeased and weaned away

from its Russian connection, she would abandon her expansionist tendencies in Asia. They proposed the acceptance of a "Two-Chinas" policy, the recognition of Communist China and her admission to the United Nations, and the continued recognition and protection of Formosa as a separate state and a member of the General Assembly but not of the Security Council. There were, of course, variations of argument among the advocates of this policy.

The opponents of change in policy, including virtually every member of the Congress, accepted as valid or as relevant none of the arguments for a change in policy and presented counterarguments. They held that Communist China had not fulfilled the obligations of states under international law, was still branded as an aggressor in the Korean War by the United Nations and could not be considered "a peace-loving state" within the terms of the Charter, was firmly wedded to Russia, was even more violent than Russia in her hate propaganda against the United States, and had declared she would not accept a "Two-Chinas" solution to the problem. They held further that to recognize Communist China would contribute to her prestige and weaken the opposition to Communism elsewhere in Asia and possibly in Africa. The more extreme opponents of recognition believed the United States should not only "veto" the admission of Communist China to the Security Council in place of the Republic of China (Formosa) but should leave the United Nations if the General Assembly admitted Communist China as a member of that body. The United States government did not threaten to take this drastic step and was not forced to meet the issue, since, up to and including the meeting of the Assembly in 1962, the United States was able to prevent the seating of Communist China.

Weary of the continuing crisis and longing for peace and security, a large number, perhaps a majority, of the American people were led to believe that the abrasive factors in world affairs, the tensions, conflicting interests, and dispositions of aggressors, could somehow be removed by "direct diplomacy," *summit* conferences between the heads of states. Public pressure was built up for such a conference between France, Great Britain, the United States, and Russia in 1960. The United States was reluctant to have a conference unless there was substantial evidence it would make a significant contribution toward the settlement of particular problems. It seemed difficult for the people at large to understand that diplomatic negotiations between Russia and the United States were in constant process in their respective capitals, and that a summit conference which failed to achieve results might be a disservice rather than a benefit to the non-Communist world. It was difficult also for the people to realize that while flexibility in foreign policy could mean acceptable adjustment, it could also be piecemeal surrender. Since it was impossible to prove that a summit conference would not be fruitful, it was relatively easy for critics of the Eisenhower Administration to secure what appeared to be public demand for such a conference.

An attempt was made by the United States at a meeting of foreign ministers in Geneva in the summer of 1959, and through discussions with Nikita Khrushchev during a visit he made to the United States in September of the same year, to reach firm understandings or bases of agreement that could be further developed and confirmed at a summit meeting. These efforts were largely fruitless but not wholly without promise, and President Eisenhower agreed to attend a conference that was scheduled to open in Paris on May 16, 1960. Among the most important issues to be considered were those of Berlin and the unification of Germany, and the control or limitation of armaments. For reasons that can only be speculative, the Russian government decided to let the conference assemble, with all the fanfare of publicity that attended it, and then to wreck the meeting with a violent denunciation of the United States, allegedly because of American high aerial reconnaissance over Russian territory.

In view of what appeared to be increasing cold war tensions, the great growth in the technology of nuclear weapons, and the possibility, therefore, of a sudden and devastating attack on the United States by the Soviet Union, the American government felt obliged to use all possible means of keeping itself informed about the military activities of the Soviet Union. Among other means to this end, it had been conducting high aerial photographic surveillance of Russia through the use of the U-2 type airplane. It was obvious that if these flights violated the air sovereignty of the Soviet Union, the pilot of such aircraft had the status of a spy the same as if he had entered Russia any other way. The Russian government knew about these flights, not only before the Paris conference, but also before the visit of Mr. Khrushchev to the United States in 1959 and his conciliatory conversations at that time with President Eisenhower, conversations which had led to the assumption that the Paris conference might be fruitful and that Russia would welcome a visit from the President later.

Before leaving Washington for the conference, the President had directed the discontinuance of the U-2 flights, and this was known to Premier Khrushchev before he made his public denunciation of the United States allegedly because of these flights. He was able to make this dramatic denunciation because Russia had been able to bring down one of the U-2 aircraft about two weeks before the conference was scheduled to meet. It seems beyond reasonable doubt, therefore, that the U-2 flights were not significant in the Russian decision to wreck the Paris conference. It is more probable that Russia had discovered she could not drive a wedge between the United States and its allies over the issues to be considered, that Russia would gain nothing from the conference, while she might influence public opinion in the United States against the Administration and in the world against the United States by making use of the U-2 affair for her own purposes. After President Kennedy assumed office in 1961, he held conversations with Premier Khrushchev in Vienna, but no thawing of Russian-American relations took place. They tended rather to become more critical with regard to the problems of Germany, arms control, and the Communist activities in Southeast Asia.

NEW FACTORS IN ECONOMIC FOREIGN POLICY

No item of American national policy has been under more continuous discussion than the tariff. The first breach in the policy of high protectionism following the First World War was the passage of the Reciprocal Tariff Act of June, 1934, called also the Trade Agreements Act. This measure authorized the President to negotiate trade agreements under which tariff duties, aside from articles on the free list, could be raised or lowered as much as 50 percent of the existing rates, those of the Smoot-Hawley Act of 1930. Although the Trade Agreements Act was supported by those who believed in freer trade as a general policy, it was presented to Congress primarily as a part of the recovery program from the Depression. The world's trade had declined 65 percent since 1929, and the American share had declined from 14 percent in 1929 to less than 10 percent in 1933. Opposition to the act came from people who believed that tariff protection had not been a significant cause of the Depression, who thought the act was an unconstitutional delegation of congressional authority over tariffs and taxation, and who held that industry and agriculture would be harmed by the act more than benefited.

In the years that followed, up to 1962, the Trade Agreements Act was extended under various forms and for varying periods of years, the extension of 1958 being for a four-year term, and during those years American tariffs were drastically reduced from the rates of 1930. Those who opposed the reciprocal trade policy changed their arguments against it very little when each extension of the Trade Agreements Act was considered, but the supporters of the policy adjusted their arguments to the context of the times. In 1945, for example, the policy was defended as a part of the whole postwar endeavor to expand world markets, stabilize currency, and promote economic growth. After 1951 the policy was supported as a measure for strengthening the non-Communist world. In the original act and in all extensions of it, the stated objective of the policy was to expand American foreign markets without abandoning *some* tariff protection. By 1962, however, a new factor in relation to world trade caused the American government to advocate an extension of the reciprocal trade policy that would decrease or eliminate what little remained of its protectionist features. This new factor was the establishment of the European Economic Community.

Although this community was an internal European development, it had been promoted directly or indirectly by a series of American measures having their origin in the Lend-Lease Act of 1941. This act authorized the President to extend aid to foreign nations under stated conditions and to accept whatever payment or repayment he deemed "satisfactory." In reporting to Congress about lend-lease agreements, President Roosevelt noted that final settlements would be deferred until after the war and would be related to programs designed to promote greater production and trade among nations under stable exchange rates and liberal principles of commerce. This policy was consistently followed in the planning for postwar economic arrangements and institutions, as noted in Chapter XI, and in the proposal of 1947 known as the Marshall Plan. In implementing the Marshall Plan under the Foreign Assistance Act of 1948, Congress declared it was the policy of the United States to assist Europe in bringing about "the progressive elimination of trade barriers" and the "economic co-operation of Europe," and that the continuance of American aid would depend upon the "continuity of co-operation among the countries participating in the program." In the Mutual Security Act of 1954, Congress declared that it should be so administered as to promote "greater political federation, military integration, and economic unification in Europe." Congress expressed similar ideas in other foreign aid and mutual defense measures.

From the time of the Marshall Plan, various European nations moved in the direction suggested by American policy, but their efforts were not always unified and often resulted in a complex of agreements and institutions too numerous to be considered here. Two accomplishments, however, were particularly notable. One was the establishment of the European Coal and Steel Community (into effect, June, 1952) between France, Belgium, the Netherlands, Luxembourg, Italy, and the Federal Republic of West Germany, and the other was the creation by the same nations of the European Economic Community under the treaty of Rome, which went into effect in January, 1958.

Under this "Common Market" treaty, the members of the community undertook, among other things, to remove by stages trade barriers between themselves and to create a uniform external tariff, to abolish restrictions on the movement within the community of capital and labor, to co-ordinate their monetary and fiscal policies, to establish a common agricultural policy, and to create an investment bank. It was anticipated in 1962 that Great Britain, Norway,

Sweden, Denmark, Ireland, Austria, and Switzerland would soon become members or associate members of the community. Enlarged in this way, the community would have a combined population of about 252,000,000 people and a gross national product —based on production in 1960—of $282 billion. It appeared probable, in addition, that the community could not fully implement all its economic plans without further political integration or federation of some kind.

This community development in Europe could not be assured of success in 1962, but it demonstrated remarkable progress toward its goals and, together with the prospect of its enlargement, created a new challenge for American economic foreign policy. If the community was successful, and if the United States remained aloof from it, the United States might find itself cut off economically and ultimately politically from nations with whom it had many important common interests. It seemed possible also that other non-Communist nations outside the European Community might make agreements with it to the disadvantage of American trade. For these and other reasons, support was given to the request of President Kennedy for an extension of the Trade Agreements Act giving the President more authority than under previous acts to reduce tariffs further or to abolish them on certain articles in order to enable the United States to accommodate its trade policies to those of the European Community.

One segment of American opinion relative to economic foreign policy held the view that although reciprocal tariff negotiations under the several trade acts since 1934 had benefited the United States and that such negotiations should be allowed to continue under specific limits as prescribed by Congress, need did not exist for the expanded authority requested by the President. The whole free world, it was thought, rather than the European Community in particular, should be the object of American economic policy, and the free world should provide a greater share in the common defense against the Communist bloc, and should achieve greater unity with respect to trade with Communist countries. This segment of opinion also believed that greater attention should be given to economic unity under the North Atlantic Alliance, to domestic economic policies, to the persistent deficit in American balance of payments, and to the continued foreign drain on the American supply of gold. These matters, it was said, were of greater importance than further tariff reduction. In this conflict of opinion it was clear that no one in the Administration, the Congress, or the nation had a trouble-free solution for American economic foreign problems. The President's request concerning trade agreements was in line, however, with established trends of American economic policy as noted already, and was approved by a large portion and perhaps a majority, of American industry. As a result, Congress passed the Trade Expansion Act in 1962 delegating to the President the authority to adjust tariffs substantially as he had requested. In an address on July 4, 1962, the President said that when Europe had formed a "more perfect union" the United States would be prepared to discuss with it the "ways and means of forming a concrete Atlantic Partnership."

THE NEW DIPLOMACY

After the Second World War, United States foreign policy underwent a great revolution and its diplomacy became involved in the whole realm of world politics. As one of the 110 members of the United Nations in 1962, the United States was virtually obliged to take a stand in one form or another on every problem that arose in that body. It had commitments under alliances with forty-two nations and special responsibilities in the Western Hemisphere. It could no longer restrict its diplomatic affairs to the "old diplomacy," carried on largely in secret by accredited diplomats who were most successful when they smoothed international frictions without the world in general knowing of their existence. The "new diplomacy" was open diplomacy enacted before a world forum, and included summit conferences, visits and good-will missions of heads of states and other high officials, the diplomacy of the dollar, which embraced all factors of economic foreign aid, and the diplomacy of education, involving news broadcasts and a variety of activities designed to influence the opinions of people. There was in addition the diplomacy of example, for no nation could escape being judged by what it was at home and by its conduct abroad.

There seemed to be no place in the world where economic and political stability and the absence of Communist activity or of revolutionary ferment permitted a tranquil scene. The United States had reason to look forward with some apprehension concerning its national security, and its people had reason to be alarmed over the burden of defense spending, the erosion of free enterprise, and the growing centralization of authority that maintained a precarious adherence to the basic necessities of constitutional government in a free society. It was true, nevertheless, that the American people enjoyed economic prosperity and individual freedom and opportunity as great as could be found in any place in the world and far greater than in most places. Whatever might be their fate, they were still the masters of their government, and if they had the will, they could see to it that their public affairs, both domestic and foreign, were conducted with justice, dignity, and honor, the touchstones of civilization.

BIBLIOGRAPHY

GENERAL REFERENCES

THE MOST COMPREHENSIVE general reference work on American diplomatic history is S. F. Bemis, ed., *The American Secretaries of State and Their Diplomacy* (10 vols., 1927–1929). This series, covering the first 150 years of American independence, could be supplemented by N. A. Graebner, *An Uncertain Tradition: American Secretaries of State in the Twentieth Century* (1961). Among the many standard general histories of American foreign relations are S. F. Bemis, *A Diplomatic History of the United States* (1955); T. A. Bailey, *A Diplomatic History of the American People* (1955); and R. W. Leopold, *The Growth of American Foreign Policy* (1962). The history of the Department of State is covered in William Barnes and J. H. Morgan, *The Foreign Service of the United States* (1961).

A scholarly edition of American treaties prior to 1863 is Hunter Miller, ed., *Treaties and Other International Acts of the United States of America, 1776–1863* (8 vols., 1931–1948). The United States government publishes a continuous series of volumes on *American Treaties, International Acts, Protocols, and Agreements Between the United States and Other Powers,* and current treaties may be found in the Treaty Series of the Department of State. A selection of treaties, diplomatic correspondence, and other important documents bearing on American foreign policy are in Ruhl J. Bartlett, *The Record of American Diplomacy* (1954); and Dorothy B. Goebel, *American Foreign Policy: A Documentary Survey, 1776–1960* (1961).

CHAPTER I

A series of volumes under the general title of *The Rise of Modern Europe,* edited by W. L. Langer, provide an excellent coverage of modern European history. The volume in this series by W. L. Dorn, *Competition for Empire, 1740–1763* (1940) is of special value for its account of the Seven Years' War. One of the great literary and historical classics of the United States is Francis Parkman, *France and England in North America* (1851–1892). An indispensable reference work on the British Empire and a fine example of modern scholarship is L. H. Gipson, *The British Empire Before the American Revolution,* a work still in progress, Volume 9 carrying the story to 1766 (1946–   ). Important European treaties can be found in Frances Davenport, ed., *European Treaties Bearing on the History of the United States and Its Dependencies* (3 vols., 1917–1934), a work continued in an additional volume edited by C. O. Paullin (1937). Two excellent works on British-French relations in the New World are Max Savelle, *The Diplomatic History of the Canadian Boundary, 1749–1763* (1940); and G. M. Wrong, *The Rise and Fall of New France* (2 vols., 1928). Another area of the European conflict for America is treated in A. P. Newton, *European Nations in the West Indies, 1493–1688* (1933). Of the many studies of the discovery of America, none is better than S. E. Morison, *Admiral of the Ocean Sea: A Life of Christopher Columbus* (1942).

CHAPTER II

The Diplomacy of the American Revolution (1935), by S. F. Bemis, is still the standard general work on that subject. A brief but excellent survey of American history during the Revolution is provided by Esmond Wright in *Fabric of Freedom: 1763–1800* (1961), and more extended coverages of the American side of the revolutionary struggle are the studies of John C. Miller, *Origins of the American Revolution* (1943); J. R. Alden, *The American Revolution: 1795–1783* (1954); and E. C. Burnett, *The Continental Congress* (1941). The efforts of Britain for reconciliation with her former Colonies is competently surveyed in Weldon A. Brown, *Empire or Independence* (1941). The internal affairs of Britain during the war are described in F. A. Mumby, *George III and the American Revolution* (1923); in H. Butterfield, *George III, Lord North, and the People, 1779–80* (1949); and in L. B. Namier, *England in the Age of the American Revolution* (1930). Among the best studies of the principal American diplomatic agents are Gerald Stourzh, *Benjamin*

Franklin and American Foreign Policy (1954); Carl Van Doren, *Benjamin Franklin* (1938); Gilbert Chinard, *Honest John Adams* (1933); and Frank Monaghan, *John Jay* (1935).

Among the most important collection of documents are Francis Wharton, ed., *The Revolutionary Diplomatic Correspondence of the United States* (6 vols., 1899); Worthington C. Ford, ed., *Journals of the Continental Congress, 1774–1789* (34 vols., 1904–1937); and Lawrence Kinnaird, ed., *Spain in the Mississippi Valley, 1765–1794* (3 vols., 1946–1949). No one interested in the Revolution or in the era that followed it should overlook the brilliant work of D. S. Freeman, *George Washington* (6 vols., 1948–1954). Since Freeman did not live to complete this biography, a final volume was prepared by his research associates, J. A. Carroll and M. W. Ashworth (1957).

CHAPTER III

A good introduction to the general history of the United States during the Confederation is Merrill Jensen, *The New Nation* (1950); and a companion volume continuing the story is John C. Miller, *The Federalist Era, 1789–1801* (1960). Standard accounts of American relations with Spain are in S. F. Bemis, *Pinckney's Treaty* (1926); and in A. P. Whitaker, *The Spanish-American Frontier: 1783–1795* (1927). Relations with Britain are treated from somewhat different standpoints in S. F. Bemis, *Jay's Treaty* (1923); Bradford Perkins, *The First Rapprochement: England and the United States, 1795–1805* (1955); A. L. Burt, *The United States, Great Britain and British North America* (1940). Discussions with Britain took place in a context of relations with France involving the interpretation of American responsibilities under the Franco-American treaties of 1778. This latter subject, together with the movement in the United States to free itself from the French alliance, are considered in Alexander DeConde, *Entangling Alliance: Politics and Diplomacy Under George Washington* (1958).

The Administration of John Adams is well handled in Stephen Kurtz, *The Presidency of John Adams* (1957). Anyone interested in the conflict of ideas of Jefferson and Hamilton over both foreign and domestic issues should consult Adrienne Koch, *Jefferson and Madison: The Great Collaboration* (1950); Volume 2 of *Jefferson and His Time* by Dumas Malone, entitled *Jefferson and the Rights of Man* (1951); and John C. Miller, *Alexander Hamilton: Portrait in Paradox* (1959). Foreign relations aspects of American constitutional development are brought out in Merrill Jensen, *The Articles of*

Confederation (1940), and in A. T. Prescott, *Drafting the Federal Constitution* (1941).

CHAPTER IV

One of the classics of American history, comparable with the works of Francis Parkman, is Henry Adams, *History of the United States of America During the Administrations of Jefferson and Madison* (9 vols., 1889–1891). The parts of this work dealing with American foreign policy should be compared, however, with Irving Brant, *James Madison: Secretary of State, 1800–1809* (1953) and the same author's *James Madison: The President, 1809–1812* (1956). A perceptive general history of the era is C. M. Wiltse, *The New Nation, 1800–1845* (1961). American diplomacy connected with the purchase of Louisiana is thoroughly discussed in A. P. Whitaker, *The Mississippi Question, 1795–1803* (1934); in E. W. Lyon, *Louisiana in French Diplomacy, 1759–1804* (1934); and in A. B. Darling, *Our Rising Empire, 1763–1803* (1940).

Valuable special studies on the struggle of the United States for maritime rights are J. F. Zimmerman, *Impressment of American Seamen* (1925); L. M. Sears, *Jefferson and the Embargo* (1927); and Claude G. Bowers, *Jefferson in Power: The Death Struggle of the Federalists* (1936). F. A. Updyke, *The Diplomacy of the War of 1812* (1915) is still the standard work on that subject, but other important studies are S. F. Bemis, *John Quincy Adams and the Foundations of American Foreign Policy* (1949); A. L. Burt, *The United States, Great Britain and British North America* (1940); Julius W. Pratt, *Expansionists of 1812* (1925); Bernard Mayo, *Henry Clay; Spokesman of the New West* (1937); and Bradford Perkins, *Prologue to War: England and the United States, 1805–1812* (1961).

The acquisition of the Floridas is competently treated in I. J. Cox, *The West Florida Controversy, 1789–1813* (1918); in C. C. Griffin, *The United States and the Disruption of the Spanish Empire, 1810–1822* (1937); and in P. C. Brooks, *Diplomacy of the Borderlands: The Adams-Onis Treaty of 1819* (1939). Basic works on the Monroe Doctrine are A. P. Whitaker, *The United States and the Independence of Latin America, 1800–1830* (1941); Dexter Perkins, *The Monroe Doctrine, 1823–1826* (1927); and C. K. Webster, ed., *Britain and the Independence of Latin America, 1812–1830* (2 vols., 1938).

CHAPTER V

The diplomacy of the northern boundary of the United States is thoroughly surveyed in A. B. Corey, *The Crisis of 1830–1842 in*

Canadian-American Relations (1941); in H. L. Keenleyside, *Canada and the United States* (1929); and in J. B. Brebner, *North Atlantic Triangle* (1945). Good accounts of the acquisition of Oregon are J. S. Reeves, *American Diplomacy Under Tyler and Polk* (1907); E. I. McCormac, *James K. Polk* (1922); Frederick Merk, *Albert Gallatin and the Oregon Problem* (1950); and F. W. Howay, W. M. Sage, and H. F. Angus, *British Columbia and the United States* (1942). Diplomatic relations with Texas and Mexico are treated in Dexter Perkins, *The Monroe Doctrine, 1826–1867* (1933); J. H. Smith, *The Annexation of Texas* (1911); John D. P. Fuller, *The Movement for the Acquisition of All Mexico, 1846–1848* (1936); P. N. Garber, *The Gadsden Treaty* (1923); and N. A. Graebner, *Empire on the Pacific* (1955). Central American and Cuban diplomacy is covered in Mary W. Williams, *Anglo-American Isthmian Diplomacy, 1815–1915* (1916); Gerstle Mack, *The Land Divided* (1944); and Basil Rauch, *American Interest in Cuba, 1848–1855* (1948).

A pioneer work on American commercial expansion into the Pacific is T. Dennett, *Americans in Eastern Asia* (1922). Other standard works are P. J. Treat, *Diplomatic Relations between the United States and Japan, 1853–1895* (2 vols., 1932); K. S. Latourette, *The History of the Early Relations between the United States and China, 1784–1844* (1917); H. W. Bradley, *The American Frontier in Hawaii: The Pioneers, 1789–1843* (1942); Sylvia Masterman, *The Origins of International Rivalry in Samoa, 1845–1884* (1934); and G. H. Ryden, *Foreign Policy of the United States in Relation to Samoa* (1933).

The most scholarly and comprehensive work covering the acquisition, government, and in most cases, relinquishment, of the American colonial empire, is Whitney T. Perkins, *Denial of Empire: The United States and Its Dependencies* (1962).

CHAPTER VI

The diplomacy of the Civil War era, from the viewpoint of the United States government and with emphasis on the influence of President Lincoln, is covered in J. G. Randall, *Lincoln the President* (4 vols., 1945–1955); and in Allan Nevins, *The War for the Union* (2 vols., 1960), a work, still in progress, that takes the story of the war to 1863. The influence of Secretary of State William H. Seward on wartime diplomacy is competently discussed in J. Monaghan, *Diplomat in Carpet Slippers* (1945). The foreign relations of the Confederacy are covered in F. L. and H. C. Owsley, *King Cotton*

Diplomacy (1958); and in J. M. Callahan, *Diplomatic History of the Southern Confederacy* (1901). Special studies of American relations with European states are Ephraim D. Adams, *Great Britain and the American Civil War* (2 vols., 1925); B. P. Thomas, *Russo-American Relations, 1815–1867* (1930); T. A. Bailey, *America Faces Russia: Russian-American Relations from Early Times to Our Day* (1950); and D. Jordan and E. J. Pratt, *Europe and the American Civil War* (1931).

The relations between the United States and Mexico and the problem of European intervention in Mexico are authoritatively considered in Dexter Perkins, *The Monroe Doctrine, 1826–1867* (1933). Other useful accounts are J. M. Callahan, *American Foreign Policy in Mexican Relations* (1932); J. F. Rippy, *The United States and Mexico* (1931); Ralph Roeder, *Juarez and His Mexico* (2 vols., 1947); and E. C. Corti, *Maximilian and Charlotte of Mexico* (2 vols., 1928). American relations with Canada are thoroughly treated in L. B. Shippee, *Canadian-American Relations, 1849–1874* (1939); and in William D'Arcy, *The Fenian Movement in the United States: 1858–1886* (1947). Postwar American expansionist activities are covered in the two volumes by C. C. Tansill, *Purchase of the Danish West Indies* (1932) and *The United States and Santo Domingo, 1798–1873* (1938); and in Victor Farrar, *The Annexation of Russian America to the United States* (1937). Postwar negotiation with Britain is well explored by Allan Nevins in *Hamilton Fish: The Inner History of the Grant Administration* (1936).

CHAPTER VII

The growth of American concern over the Monroe Doctrine and the events that led to its strengthening are covered in Dexter Perkins, *The Monroe Doctrine, 1867–1907* (1934); Allan Nevins, *Grover Cleveland: A Study in Courage* (1933); C. C. Tansill, *The Foreign Policy of Thomas F. Bayard* (1941); A. L. P. Dennis, *Adventures in Diplomacy, 1896–1906* (1928); C. L. Barrows, *William M. Evarts* (1941); and Alice Tyler, *The Foreign Policy of James G. Blaine* (1927). An authoritative work dealing with the ideas that led to American imperialistic ventures is Julius W. Pratt, *Expansionists of 1898* (1936). Other useful studies of American imperialism and the Spanish-American War are F. R. Dulles, *The Imperial Years* (1956); Harold and Margaret Sprout, *The Rise of American Naval Power* (1942); J. E. Wisan, *The Cuban Crisis as Reflected in the New York Press, 1895–1898* (1934); E. J. Benton, *International Law and Diplo-*

macy of the Spanish-American War (1907); Orestes Farrara, *The Last Spanish War* (1937); and E. R. May, *Imperial Democracy: The Emergence of America as a Great Power* (1961).

The standard work on the relation of the United States with the nations of the Caribbean nations is W. H. Callcott, *The Caribbean Policy of the United States, 1890–1920* (1942). Works dealing particularly with the Panama Canal problem are H. F. Pringle, *Theodore Roosevelt* (1927); E. T. Parks, *Colombia and the United States, 1765–1934* (1935); M. P. Duval, *Cadiz to Cathay* (1940); and N. J. Padelford, *The Panama Canal in Peace and War* (1942). Important studies of the Latin-American as well as the Far Eastern relations of the United States are H. K. Beale, *Theodore Roosevelt and the Rise of America to World Power* (1956); and T. Dennett, *John Hay: From Poetry to Politics* (1933). T. A. Bailey, *Theodore Roosevelt and the Japanese-American Crises* (1934); and A. W. Griswold, *The Far Eastern Policy of the United States* (1938) are standard works on Far Eastern affairs. Other important studies are Charles Vevier, *The United States and China, 1906–1913* (1955); E. H. Zabriskie, *American-Russian Rivalry in the Far East, 1895–1914* (1946); P. H. Clyde, ed., *United States Policy Toward China* (1940); and P. A. Varg, *Open Door Diplomat: The Life of W. W. Rockhill* (1952).

CHAPTER VIII

Woodrow Wilson's approach to foreign policy and some of his early problems regarding Latin America and the Far East are considered in Harley Notter, *Origins of the Foreign Policy of Woodrow Wilson* (1937); Ray S. Baker, *Woodrow Wilson: Life and Letters* (8 vols., 1927–1939); Tien-Yi Li, *Woodrow Wilson's China Policy, 1913–1917* (1952); Carl Kelsey, *The American Intervention in Haiti and the Dominican Republic* (1922); and A. S. Link, *Woodrow Wilson and the Progressive Era: 1910–1917* (1954). Excellent and well-balanced brief accounts of American diplomacy during the period of neutrality are in Charles Seymour, *American Neutrality, 1914–1917* (1935); and A. S. Link, *Wilson the Diplomatist: A Look at His Major Foreign Policies* (1957). More detailed treatment of the same period are in A. S. Link, *Wilson: The Struggle for Neutrality, 1914–1915* (1960); E. R. May, *The World War and American Isolation, 1914–1917* (1959); A. J. Mayer, *Political Origins of the New Diplomacy, 1917–1918* (1959); and S. R. Spencer, Jr., *Decision for War* (1953). Highly critical accounts of American policy are in C. C. Tansill, *America Goes to War* (1938); and H. C. Peterson, *Propa-*

ganda for War: The Campaign Against American Neutrality, 1914–1917 (1939).

A competent general work on wartime diplomacy is Charles Seymour, *American Diplomacy During the World War* (1934). Dealing with special aspects of this subject and the peace conference are T. A. Bailey, *Woodrow Wilson and the Lost Peace* (1944); G. F. Kennan, *Soviet-American Relations, 1917–1920* (2 vols., 1956–1958); R. J. Bartlett, *The League to Enforce Peace* (1944); Betty Unterberger, *America's Siberian Expedition, 1918–1920* (1956); D. H. Miller, *Drafting of the Covenant* (2 vols., 1928); and Seth Tillman, *Anglo-American Relations in the Paris Peace Conference of 1919* (1961). Far Eastern affairs are considered in R. H. Fifield, *Woodrow Wilson and the Far East: The Diplomacy of the Shantung Question* (1952).

Important works on the struggle in the United States over the Treaty of Versailles are D. F. Fleming, *The United States and the League of Nations, 1918–1920* (1932); T. A. Bailey, *Woodrow Wilson and the Great Betrayal* (1945); and J. A. Garraty, *Henry Cabot Lodge, a Biography* (1953).

CHAPTER IX

The best general coverage of American diplomacy during the Harding administration is M. J. Pusey, *Charles Evans Hughes* (2 vols., 1951). This should be compared with Dexter Perkins, *Charles Evans Hughes and American Democratic Statesmanship* (1956); and D. F. Fleming, *The United States and World Organization, 1920–1933* (1938). The Washington Conference on the limitation of armaments is thoroughly treated in J. C. Vinson, *The Parchment Peace: The United States Senate and the Washington Conference, 1921–1922,* (1955); Merze Tate, *The United States and Armaments* (1948); and H. H. and M. T. Sprout, *Toward a New Order of Sea Power* (1943). Economic foreign policies are considered in Herbert Feis, *The Diplomacy of the Dollar: The First Era, 1919–1932* (1950); Joseph M. Jones, *Tariff Retaliation: Repercussions of the Hawley-Smoot Bill* (1934); and R. L. Buell, *The Hull Trade Program and the American System* (1938). For the Coolidge era and the negotiation of the Pact of Paris, the most important works are L. E. Ellis, *Frank B. Kellogg and American Foreign Relations, 1925–1929* (1961); R. H. Ferrell, *Peace in Their Time: The Origins of the Kellogg-Briand Pact* (1952); and J. C. Vinson, *William E. Borah and the Outlawry of War* (1957).

A general coverage of the Hoover era is R. H. Ferrell, *American*

Diplomacy in the Great Depression (1957). Other important studies are W. S. Myers, *The Foreign Policies of Herbert Hoover* (1940); R. N. Current, *Secretary Stimson: A Study in Statecraft* (1954); Sara R. Smith, *The Manchurian Crisis, 1931–1932* (1948); Dorothy Borg, *American Policy and the Chinese Revolution, 1925–1928* (1947); and E. E. Morison, *Turmoil and Tradition: A Study of the Life and Times of Henry L. Stimson* (1960). American hemispheric affairs are treated in Alexander DeConde, *Herbert Hoover's Latin-American Policy* (1951); and E. W. McInnis, *The Unguarded Frontier: A History of American-Canadian Relations* (1942).

The Franklin D. Roosevelt Administration is covered in A. M. Schlesinger, Jr., *The Age of Roosevelt* (4 vols., 1957–1962), and a stout defense of the foreign policies of the era is in Cordell Hull, *Memoirs* (2 vols., 1948). Latin-American affairs are treated in E. O. Guerrant, *Roosevelt's Good Neighbor Policy* (1950); and in Bryce Wood, *The Making of the Good Neighbor Policy* (1961).

CHAPTER X

The most useful general reference work on American foreign policy since 1931 is a series of volumes published annually, with the exceptions noted, by the Council on Foreign Relations under the title *The United States in World Affairs.* (No volumes appeared between 1941 and 1945, and the years 1945–1947 were covered in a single volume.) Important and balanced studies of the years just prior to the Second World War are the two volumes by joint authors W. L. Langer and S. E. Gleason, *The Challenge to Isolation, 1937–1940* (1952) and *The Undeclared War, 1940–1941* (1953); D. F. Drummond, *The Passing of American Neutrality, 1937–1941* (1955); Herbert Feis, *The Road to Pearl Harbor* (1950); H. L. Trefousse, *Germany and American Neutrality, 1939–1941* (1951); and P. W. Schroeder, *The Axis Alliance and Japanese-American Relations, 1941* (1958). Highly critical views of American policy during the era are C. C. Tansill, *Back Door to War: The Roosevelt Foreign Policy, 1933–1941* (1952); and C. A. Beard, *President Roosevelt and the Coming of the War, 1941* (1948). A fine account of events in Japan leading to the war is R. J. C. Butow, *Tojo and the Coming of the War* (1961); and a Japanese view of the events leading to war is Shigenori Tōgō, *The Cause of Japan* (1956).

Among the important studies of American wartime diplomacy are the three volumes by Herbert Feis, *Churchill, Roosevelt, Stalin: The War They Waged and the Peace They Sought* (1957), *Between War and Peace: The Potsdam Conference* (1960), and *Japan Subdued: The Atomic Bomb and the End of the War in the Pacific* (1961). Other useful studies are R. H. Dawson, *The Decision to Aid Russia, 1941* (1959); W. L. Langer, *Our Vichy Gamble* (1947); J. L. Snell, *The Meaning of Yalta* (1956); R. E. Sherwood, *Roosevelt and Hopkins: An Intimate History* (1948); Roland Young, *Congressional Politics in the Second World War* (1956); and E. E. Morison, *Turmoil and Tradition: A Study of the Life and Times of Henry L. Stimson* (1960).

CHAPTER XI

The best general accounts of American wartime planning for peace are E. F. Penrose, *Economic Planning for the Peace* (1953); H. A. Notter, *Postwar Foreign Policy Preparation, 1939–1945* (1949); and L. W. Holborn, ed., *War and Peace Aims of the United Nations, September 1, 1939–December 31, 1942* (1943). Peace treaties with the Axis powers except Germany and Japan are included in Amelia Leiss and Raymond Dennett, eds., *European Peace Treaties After World War II* (1954). The foreign policies of the Truman Administration are strongly defended in Harry S. Truman, *Memoirs* (2 vols., 1956); but this account should be compared with Walter Millis, ed., *The Forrestal Diaries* (1951), and with H. B. Westerfield, *Foreign Policy and Party Politics: Pearl Harbor to Korea* (1955).

American policies concerning China are discussed in Herbert Feis, *The China Tangle* (1953); P. M. Linebarger, *et al., Far Eastern Governments and Politics: China and Japan* (1956); and H. M. Vinacke, *The United States and the Far East, 1945–1951* (1952). Latin-American relations are studied in J. L. Mecham, *The United States and Inter-American Security, 1889–1960* (1961); and A. P. Whitaker, *The Western Hemisphere Idea: Its Rise and Decline* (1954). Useful works on relations with Germany are L. D. Clay, *Decision in Germany* (1950); and Eugene Davidson, *The Death and Life of Germany* (1959). Among the best studies of American relations with the Middle East are F. E. Manuel, *The Realities of American-Palestine Relations* (1949); and J. C. Hurewitz, *The Struggle for Palestine* (1950).

The best general history of the Marshall Plan is H. B. Price, *The Marshall Plan and Its Meaning* (1955). An excellent study of the Berlin crisis is W. P. Davison, *The Berlin Blockade* (1958).

CHAPTER XII

Important studies of American policy toward Korea and of the Korean War are L. M. Goodrich, *Korea: A Study of U.S. Policy in the United Nations* (1956); Carl Berger, *The Korea Knot* (1957); S. L. A. Marshall, *The River and the Gauntlet* (1953); and W. H. Vatcher, *Panmunjon* (1958). Conflicting views of the MacArthur controversy are A. M. Schlesinger, Jr., and R. H. Rovere, *The General and the President* (1951); and Courtney Whitney, *MacArthur, His Rendezvous with History* (1956). A more balanced view is presented in J. W. Spanier, *The Truman-MacArthur Controversy and the Korean War* (1959). Other valuable works on the Korean War are A. S. Whiting, *China Crosses the Yalu: The Decision to Enter the Korean War* (1960); and R. T. Oliver, *Verdict in Korea* (1952). American relations in the Far East are studied in R. H. Fifield, *The Diplomacy of Southeast Asia: 1945–1958* (1958); A. D. Barnett, *Communist China and Asia: Challenge to American Policy* (1960); and R. A. Fearey, *The Occupation of Japan: Second Phase, 1948–1950* (1950). A Japanese view of the American occupation is Kazuo Kawai, *Japan's American Interlude* (1960).

Competent studies of Latin-American relations are R. M. Schneider, *Communism in Guatemala, 1944–1954* (1959); R. J. Alexander, *The Peron Era* (1951); Dexter Perkins, *The United States and the Caribbean* (1947); C. O. Porter and R. J. Alexander, *The Struggle for Democracy in Latin America* (1961); and J. L. Mecham, *The United States and Inter-American Security, 1889–1960* (1961).

American relations with Europe are surveyed in B. T. Moore, *NATO and the Future of Europe* (1958); Lord Ismay, *NATO: The First Five Years, 1949–1954* (1954); M. E. Bathurst and J. L. Simpson, *Germany and the North Atlantic Community* (1956); Gerald Freund, *Germany Between Two Worlds* (1961); and Eugène Hinterhoff, *Disengagement* (1959). An excellent study of a special topic of American foreign policy is Paul Peeters, *Massive Retaliation: The Policy and Its Critics* (1958).

CHAPTER XIII

Important studies in problems of contemporary American foreign policy are A. P. Whitaker, *Spain and the Defense of the West: Ally and Liability* (1961); Lionel Gelber, *America in Britain's Place: The Leadership of the West and Anglo-American Unity* (1961); H. L. Roberts, *Russia and America: Dangers and Prospects* (1956); W. S. Schlamm, *Germany and the East-West Crisis: The Decisive Challenge to American Policy* (1959); Don D. Humphrey, *The United States and the Common Market* (1962); H. F. Haviland, ed., *The United States and the Western Community* (1957); John C. Campbell, *Defense of the Middle East* (1960); J. P. Armstrong, *Southeast Asia and*

American Policy (1959); R. P. Newman, *Recognition of Communist China? A Study in Argument* (1961); and J. R. Wilkinson, *Politics and Trade Policy* (1960).

Problems of American security are studied in G. B. Turner and R. D. Challener, eds., *National Security in the Nuclear Age* (1960); E. S. Furniss, Jr., *American Military Policy: Strategic Aspects of World Political Geography* (1957); H. A. Kissinger, *Nuclear Weapons and Foreign Policy* (1957); S. P. Huntington, *The Common Defense: Strategic Programs in National Politics* (1961); Louis Henkin, ed., *Arms Control: Issues for the Public* (1961); D. A. Graber, *Crisis Diplomacy: A History of U.S. Intervention Policies and Practices* (1959); L. P. Bloomfield, ed., *Outer Space: Prospects for Man and Society* (1962); and Alice L. Hsieh, *Communist China's Strategy in the Nuclear Era* (1962).

INDEX

ABOUT THE AUTHOR

RUHL BARTLETT is Professor of Diplomatic History at The Fletcher School of Law and Diplomacy, Tufts University, Medford, Massachusetts. A native of West Virginia, he has received degrees from Ohio University, the University of Cincinnati, and Ohio State University. He has taught at the University of Iowa and Ohio State University.

In addition to his work in American foreign relations, Professor Bartlett has a special interest in Latin American affairs. He is the author of *John C. Frémont and the Republican Party, The League to Enforce Peace, The People and Politics of Latin America* (with Mary W. Williams and Russell E. Miller), and *The Record of American Diplomacy*.